MW00596204

The Company They Keep

The Company They Keep

How Partisan Divisions Came to the Supreme Court

NEAL DEVINS

LAWRENCE BAUM

OXFORD
UNIVERSITY PRESS

OXFORD
UNIVERSITY PRESS

Oxford University Press is a department of the University of Oxford. It furthers the University's objective of excellence in research, scholarship, and education by publishing worldwide. Oxford is a registered trademark of Oxford University Press in the UK and certain other countries.

Published in the United States of America by Oxford University Press
198 Madison Avenue, New York, NY 10016, United States of America.

Library of Congress Cataloging-in-Publication Data
Names: Devins, Neal, author. | Baum, Lawrence, author.
Title: The company they keep : how partisan divisions came to the Supreme Court /
Neal Devins, Lawrence Baum.
Description: Oxford [UK] ; New York, NY : Oxford University Press, 2019. |
Includes bibliographical references and index.
Identifiers: LCCN 2018022571 (print) | LCCN 2018022721 (ebook) |
ISBN 9780190278069 (Universal PDF) | ISBN 9780190278076 (E-pub) |
ISBN 9780190278052 (hardback)
Subjects: LCSH: United States. Supreme Court—Decision making. |
Judicial process—United States. | Political questions and judicial power—United States.
Classification: LCC KF8748 (ebook) | LCC KF8748.D48 2019 (print) |
DDC 347.73/26—dc23
LC record available at https://lccn.loc.gov/2018022571

1 3 5 7 9 8 6 4 2

Printed by LSC Communications, United States of America

To my son Adam who makes me proud and fills me with joy
–ND

To Carol, always
–LB

Contents

Preface

ON OCTOBER 6, 2018, the Senate voted 50 to 48 to confirm Brett Kavanaugh to fill the Supreme Court seat vacated by Justice Anthony Kennedy. No Republican voted against the nomination (Alaska Senator Lisa Murkowski opposed the nomination but voted "present"); one Democrat voted for the nominee (Joe Manchin of West Virginia). This party-line division was the sharpest of any in 150 years. Perhaps more telling, the Kavanaugh fight was an ugly partisan brawl from the start. Allegations of sexual assault and harassment added gasoline to that conflagration—so much so that Kavanaugh became a passionate battle cry for each party and brought forward tribal behavior that was as palpable as it was unsettling. For all concerned, Kavanaugh was a defining moment for the nation and the Court. The *Washington Post*, reflecting prevailing sentiment, put it this way: "Underscoring the uncharted territory of deepening distrust and polarization that now defines the American system," the Kavanaugh confirmation battle "further distanced the Senate Judiciary Committee from its nearly forgotten bipartisan traditions and raised new questions about the potential for the Supreme Court to maintain an independent authority outside the maelstrom of politics."[1]

Flash back to November 1987. A Democratically controlled Senate votes 97 to 0 to confirm Ronald Reagan Supreme Court nominee Anthony Kennedy to fill the seat vacated by Lewis Powell. At that time, Powell was the Court's swing Justice—a moderate who was more often in the majority than any other member of the Court, especially in the major cases and the 5 to 4 decisions. One month earlier, the Senate had rejected Robert Bork for the Powell seat. Bork was seen as out of the "mainstream," in particular because of his rejection of privacy rights that had been applied to contraception and abortion. Bork's nomination was turned down by a vote of 58 to 42 with six Republicans voting against the nominee.

Bork's defeat was a turning point of sorts. Bork had a sterling record and was not accused of financial or other misdeeds; the Bork fight, instead, turned on ideology. Nonetheless, the era of party-line voting was yet to begin. Democrats and Republicans regularly crossed party lines—typically to vote for an opposition party nominee (like Kennedy) and occasionally to vote against a same-party nominee (like Bork). Indeed, when the Senate turned down Nixon Supreme Court nominees Clement Haynsworth (1969) and Harrold Carswell (1970), there were many deviations from party-line voting. Haynsworth was accused of financial misdeeds, and the nomination was defeated by a vote of 55 to 45. Seventeen Republicans joined thirty-eight Democrats in opposing the nomination; nineteen Democrats joined twenty-six Republicans in supporting the nomination. Carswell was accused of supporting racial segregation and was defeated 45 to 51. Thirteen Republicans joined thirty-eight Democrats in opposing Carswell; seventeen Democrats joined twenty-eight Republicans in supporting him. In 1991, Clarence Thomas—tainted by sexual misconduct charges—was confirmed 52 to 48. Eleven Democrats joined forty-one Republicans to push Thomas through the Senate.

Today, there is no prospect of Democrats or Republicans crossing party lines to save an embattled nominee. Likewise, the days of lopsided bipartisan votes are behind us. Even before the acrimonious rancor of sexual harassment allegations, Democrats and Republicans had lined up on opposite sides on Kavanaugh. Party-line voting is the new norm. Elena Kagan was opposed by all but five Republicans; three Democrats voted for Neil Gorsuch. Indeed, it is increasingly hard to imagine either a Democratic- or Republican-controlled Senate confirming a Supreme Court nominee of the other party. In 2016, when Republicans controlled the Senate, Majority Leader Mitch McConnell and Judiciary Committee Chair Chuck Grassley stood together to block hearings and a vote on Obama Supreme Court pick Merrick Garland. With the Court split four Republicans to four Democrats, McConnell and Grassley were not willing to cede the Court to the opposition party. Along the same lines, Republicans did away with the filibuster for Supreme Court nominees so that Neil Gorsuch could be confirmed in 2017; Democrats had earlier eliminated the filibuster for lower-court judges so that President Obama's nominees could get through a Republican logjam.

Differences among the stunningly bitter nomination fight over Brett Kavanaugh, the unanimity that greeted Anthony Kennedy, and the mishmash of Democratic and Republican votes in the Nixon era reflect basic changes in America's political landscape, changes that are connected with the growing polarization of politics along party and ideological lines. Focusing on polarization, this book shows how it has produced changes in both the selection of Justices and the Justices' own thinking.

In the selection process, the public officials who choose Supreme Court Justices now see the Court in more ideological and partisan terms. Democratic and Republican senators—along with their interest group sponsors—each act as a unified bloc, supporting or opposing nominees based on the president's party with little deviation. More telling, a Republican president would no longer be willing to nominate a conservative moderate like Anthony Kennedy; indeed, there are very few Anthony Kennedys in the Republican Party. Republican nominees are more conservative than ever before, in large part because they have been groomed and vetted by groups like the Federalist Society. With Brett Kavanaugh's confirmation, all five Republican Justices have ties to the Federalist Society; all have spoken at the Society's annual meeting; and all but Chief Justice Roberts are active participants in Society events. Similar changes have occurred on the Democratic side, albeit to a lesser degree: a Democratic president in the current era would never appoint a Justice who was not on the liberal side of the ideological spectrum, in part because there are few conservative Democrats left among potential nominees to the Court. In contrast, before the 1991 nomination of Clarence Thomas, Republican appointees were not uniformly conservative and their Democratic counterparts were not uniformly liberal. This was primarily because ideology was not critical in making Supreme Court appointments.

Changes in the Justices' own thinking are also related to larger societal developments, including the rise of conservative media outlets and the advent of a media echo chamber—where individuals seek out news that backs pre-existing views and share that news with an increasingly ideological, increasingly homogeneous social network. Future and current Justices are increasingly part of those competing social networks, and the psychological motivations of the Justices in appealing to those networks help to explain the ideological divide between Republican- and Democrat-appointed Justices.

Today's Justices are not simply partisan Democrats and Republicans. They are also graduates of the Harvard and Yale Law Schools who interface with the affluent and well educated, especially other elites in the legal profession, academy, and media. This book argues that they are elites who seek to win favor with other elites. In the period from the 1950s to the 1980s, journalists and academic and lawyer groups were largely left-leaning, and some Republican-appointed Justices were drawn toward the views of those elite groups. Today, in contrast, prospective Republican nominees are part of a conservative-leaning elite network when nominated, and they can gain validation from that network after joining the Court. Similarly, Democratic-appointed Justices are part of a liberal-leaning network.

Because of these developments, the Court since 2010 (and for the first time) has had ideological blocs that coincide with party lines: all Republican appointees are more conservative than any Democratic appointees. The appointment of Brett Kavanaugh to succeed the Court's most moderate Republican will accentuate the Court's division along party lines. This does not mean that Justices are simply politicians in robes. Supreme Court Justices still care about norms of judicial independence, collegiality, and law-oriented decision making, and as such, the Supreme Court is still a court. The great majority of decisions do not divide the Justices along party lines. Kavanaugh's appointment, moreover, puts Chief Justice Roberts at the ideological center of the Court. Roberts is an institutionalist who cares a great deal about the Court's legitimacy and his personal legacy. He may moderate his conservatism to establish that the Court is a court of law and not politics. Nonetheless, Roberts and the Court's other Republicans will not abandon their conservative ideals; consequently, the clear linkage between ideology and party means that a Court with a Republican majority often reaches different outcomes than one with a Democratic majority on the very issues that divide the parties. President Trump's 2018 nomination of Brett Kavanaugh and the ensuing confirmation fight underscore the widespread recognition of this reality.

The nomination. For a 2018 Republican Supreme Court nominee, Brett Kavanaugh came from central casting: 1990 graduate of Yale Law, handpicked by Yale's Federalist Society faculty adviser to clerk for conservative appeals court judge Alex Kozinski, law clerk to Supreme Court Justice Anthony Kennedy, political appointee to the George W. Bush White House (including a stint identifying judicial nominees and working with Supreme Court nominees throughout the confirmation process), and judge on the federal court of appeals for the DC Circuit since 2006, with an established conservative track record, and active in the Federalist Society as a judge—including participation in fifty Society events for student and lawyer groups. Kavanaugh, moreover, had been through numerous FBI background checks and there were no hints of the sexual misconduct allegations that later dogged him; indeed, his record of hiring women law clerks was exemplary.

Thus, it was no surprise that Kavanaugh was added in 2017 to the short list of potential Supreme Court nominees assembled by the Federalist Society and Heritage Foundation. It was noteworthy that candidate Donald Trump had asked these groups to assemble such a list, promising that his judicial nominees would be "picked by the Federalist Society."[2] Trump recognized that the best path to convince conservative voters that he was committed to their agenda was to outsource the vetting process to the Federalist Society and then precommit to a list of potential nominees.

If Hillary Clinton had been elected president, she too would have received strong pressure from some quarters to nominate a strong liberal to the Court. And she certainly would have chosen someone far to the left of Kavanaugh or any Republican pick. At the same time, Democrats have historically downplayed ideology to pursue other objectives. Barack Obama emphasized racial and gender diversity with his picks of Sonya Sotomayor and Elena Kagan; he focused on confirmability when selecting Merrick Garland. Certainly there would have been no single progressive group that came even close to dominating the nomination process, nor would association with any such group be regarded as a litmus test.

The confirmation. The confirmation of Brett Kavanaugh defines the divide between Democrats and Republicans and the key role that the Court plays in that divide. After accusations of sexual misconduct threw the confirmation into chaos, Senate Republicans doubled down. Recognizing that a majority of Republican voters thought Kavanaugh should be confirmed even if the accusations were true, Senate Republicans thought their political fortunes turned on their sticking with Kavanaugh and energizing their base—even if another nominee could have been confirmed in the lame duck session following the November 2018 elections. For Senate Majority Leader Mitch McConnell: "What [Kavanaugh] has done for us is provide the kind of adrenaline shot we had not been able to figure out how to achieve in any other way."[3] The Republicans' strategy was to depict the battle over Kavanaugh as the product of an out-of-control Democratic Party—willing to bring down an honorable man to prevent Republicans from taking control of the Court. Witness, for example, Senator Lindsey Graham's attack on Judiciary Committee Democrats, condemning Democrats for withholding sexual assault allegations until the eleventh hour, calling the confirmation process "the most unethical sham since I've been in politics," and warning Democrats that if "this is the new norm, you better watch out for your nominees."[4]

Democrats were equally outraged. Judiciary Committee Chair Chuck Grassley initially resisted efforts to invite Kavanaugh accuser Dr. Christine Blasey Ford to testify; Grassley subsequently resisted calls for an FBI investigation to ferret out the truth of Ford's accusations and Kavanaugh's denials. When Ford did testify, Democrats used those hearings to highlight Republicans' efforts to railroad the confirmation process, including purported efforts to diminish Dr. Ford in particular and victims of sexual misconduct in general. For Senator Dick Durbin: "No one should face harassment, death threats and disparaging comments by cheap shot politicians, simply for telling the truth."[5] Likewise, when the FBI conducted its investigation, Democratic senators condemned Republicans for limiting the scope of the investigation; they called the investigation a "sham" and a "horrific cover-up."[6]

For his part, Kavanaugh stoked these partisan flames. Encouraged by White House counsel Donald McGahn "to show the senators how he really felt, to channel his outrage and indignation at the charges he had denied," Kavanaugh angrily lectured Democratic senators that they had "replaced advice and consent with search and destroy."[7] Characterizing the sexual assault charges as a "calculated and orchestrated political hit," Kavanaugh said that the behavior of several Democrats on the Judiciary Committee at his original hearing had been "an embarrassment," that the "consequences" of the "political hit" will extend well past the confirmation fight, and that "in the political system of the early 2000s, what goes around comes around."[8]

The extreme partisanship and bitter name calling of Senate Democrats, Republicans, and Kavanaugh himself set the Kavanaugh hearings apart from all others and reinforced public opinion that Democratic appointees are good for Democrats and Republican appointments good for Republicans. Even before Dr. Ford's charge of sexual assault, partisan battle lines were drawn—so much so that the last act of this drama seems the inevitable byproduct of earlier acts. At the very start, before Trump settled on Kavanaugh, the Judicial Crisis Network committed $10 million to advance conservative goals by backing Trump's nominee; Americans for Prosperity promised a seven-figure effort. Liberal groups also entered the fray. Demand Justice promised to spend $5 million to defeat Trump judicial nominees. The Women's March sent out a press release slamming Trump's nominee as "extremist" immediately after the nomination was announced but forgot to replace the placeholder "XX" in the text with Kavanaugh's name.

Senators on both sides of the aisle followed suit, wasting no time to celebrate or condemn the nomination. For the Democratic Senatorial Campaign Committee, "This is an all hands on deck moment, team." Democrat Elizabeth Warren joined protesters at the Supreme Court immediately after the nomination, and she said that Kavanaugh "would overturn Roe v Wade," that he was "hostile to health care for millions," and that he "thinks presidents like Trump are above the law."[9] Corey Booker went one step further, saying that people who did not oppose Kavanaugh are "complicit in the evil" and that "you are either contributing to the wrong, or you are fighting against it."[10] Republican Majority Leader Mitch McConnell, in turn, complimented the president for his "superb choice" and castigated Democrats for engaging in the "same old scare tactics," depicting the nominee as a threat to our system of government without regard to who was even nominated.[11]

Throughout the hearings, floor debates, and Senate vote, Republicans and Democrats followed a predictable, seemingly predetermined script. Democrats did everything in their power to undermine the nomination and attacked Republicans for ramming through the confirmation. Dr. Ford's allegations were fodder for these Democratic attacks. Republicans did not bend. Sexual misconduct allegations largely strengthened Republican resolve; Kavanaugh would be defended, not sacrificed to Democratic critics.

The fact that not a single Republican broke ranks on Kavanaugh (or Gorsuch, Alito, or Roberts) reflects the simple fact that today's Republican constituents care passionately about the courts and expect Republican presidents and senators to advance the social conservative agenda through the appointment and confirmation of judges. Along these lines, Republican Senate leaders have pursued these goals through whatever means necessary. Blocking the Garland nomination, said Mitch McConnell, was the "most consequential decision I ever made";[12] reinforced by Trump's pledge to appoint a conservative to that vacancy, it won over evangelicals who were critical to Trump's election.

Concluding thoughts. The Kavanaugh nomination is the culmination of these efforts and signals a sea change in Supreme Court decision making. The Republican majority that existed from the 2010 to 2017 Supreme Court terms (except for the fourteen month period following Justice Antonin Scalia's death) did not translate into Republican dominion over the Court. Notwithstanding the fact that the Court's five Republicans were more conservative than its four Democrats, a Republican Justice—typically Kennedy—broke ranks with other Republicans on major decisions about gay rights, abortion rights, affirmative action, and the Affordable Care Act. During this period of eight Court terms, Democratic-appointed Justices were in the majority more often than Republicans in three terms and were in the majority as often as Republicans in another term. With Kavanaugh replacing Kennedy, in contrast, Republicans will dominate 5 to 4 decisions for the foreseeable future.

This does not mean that Supreme Court Justices will replicate congressional party-line voting. Notwithstanding his partisan bravado, Brett Kavanaugh took great pains to emphasize that he understands that judges are supposed to be independent of politics, not party loyalists. In his opening statement to the Senate Judiciary Committee (before the sexual misconduct allegations), he said that a "good judge must be an umpire—a neutral and impartial arbiter who favors no litigant or policy. . . . I don't decide cases based on personal or policy preferences."[13] Following his explosive partisan testimony, he published an extraordinary column in the *Wall Street Journal* where he formally recognized that he "might have been too emotional at times" and that he "said a few things I should not have said."[14] He also promised to adhere to judicial norms and be "hardworking, even-keeled, open-minded, independent and dedicated to the Constitution." He echoed these themes at his swearing-in ceremony, promising to follow his rule that a "good judge must be an umpire, a neutral and impartial decider."[15]

Whether now-Justice Kavanaugh adheres to norms of impartiality, independence, and collegiality remains to be seen. Nonetheless, these words are not simply an empty promise. Supreme Court Justices take pride in sometimes casting votes that break against type and in forging unanimous opinions. Justices are also concerned with the debilitating impact of partisanship on the Court's legitimacy. Chief Justice Roberts, for example, repeatedly emphasizes that Justices are neither Democrats nor Republicans. His decisive vote upholding the Affordable Care Act in 2012 may well be tied to his unwillingness to overturn Obamacare along purely partisan lines. He also has brokered numerous compromises so that the Court may issue a narrow unanimous or near-unanimous opinion rather than dividing sharply by party. Along these lines, there is some reason to think that Roberts may take steps to preserve the Court's legitimacy in the wake of the Kavanaugh confirmation. At the same time, Roberts joined purely party-line votes that backed the gutting of the Voting Rights Act and campaign finance legislation; today's partisan divide is very real.

Over the course of this book, we will document and explain the widely noticed fact that the polarization of the parties has spilled over to Supreme Court appointments—so that Democratic presidents will appoint liberals and Republicans will appoint conservatives. But we will argue that a less noticed phenomenon—the orientation of Supreme Court Justices toward elite networks whose approval is important to them—has also helped to create party-line divisions on the Court. Consider, for example, Brett Kavanaugh. At the time of his confirmation, Kavanaugh was a movement conservative and member of the Federalist Society. He also had cultivated a reputation as highly collegial among the liberal elite, as evidenced by the support of many law faculty and law students at Harvard (where he taught) and Yale (where he graduated). To seek approval from both audiences, Kavanaugh—like Roberts—might have occasionally modified his conservatism. After his bruising confirmation fight, it is unclear whether Kavanaugh will still seek approval from center-left law school audiences or, instead, will be drawn exclusively to the strong conservatives who backed him in his darkest hour. Under either scenario, he will be a conservative; the question is whether he will calibrate his conservatism to pursue other objectives.

The consequence of all this: it took until 2010 for there to ever be a partisan divide on the Supreme Court; at the same time, today's partisan split is anything but a flash in the pan. It now defines the Court and will likely play a key role in Court decision making for the foreseeable future. And while the Justices may sometimes moderate their decision making to preserve the Court's legitimacy and enhance their reputations for collegiality and independence, the Justices will not subordinate their legal policy preferences or break ranks from the liberal and conservative elite communities that they are part of to achieve those other goals. More than ever before, the future of Court decision making is therefore tied to presidential and Senate elections.

Acknowledgments

THIS BOOK HAS been ten years in the making, and there are a great number of people to thank and a bit of a story to tell.

In 2009, the *Georgetown Law Journal* was kind enough to ask one of us (Neal Devins) to write a book review of Barry Friedman's *The Will of the People*. Friedman argued that the Supreme Court was greatly influenced by the views of the American people and its decisions largely followed public opinion. Devins disagreed with Friedman, and that disagreement was moored to Larry Baum's 2006 book *Judges and Their Audiences*. Among other things, Baum argued that judges cared a great deal about their reputations within their social networks. Devins agreed with this common-sense proposition and—like Baum—thought that Supreme Court Justices were largely influenced by elite social networks.

Devins approached Baum with the idea of writing something more than a book review—a full-blown article explaining why the Supreme Court was more influenced by elite opinion than mass public opinion. Baum agreed, and the *Georgetown Law Journal* agreed to publish a 2010 article by Baum and Devins on this topic. Clayton Northouse, a second-year law student at Georgetown, was instrumental in making this happen and later served as the principal editor of the published article, "Why the Supreme Court Cares about Elites, Not the American People." We owe a great debt to Clayton and also to the current editors of the *Georgetown Law Journal*, who happily acquiesced to our request to make some use of that article in this book project.

The *Georgetown* article propelled this book. The article advanced a model of Supreme Court decision making that was at odds with leading political science and law professor models. The article was also well received by journalists, as well as academics; it was even featured in news analyses by Robert Barnes in the *Washington Post* and Adam Liptak in the *New York Times*. Within a year of publication, however, we felt compelled to revisit the article. In explaining the dominance of elite opinion, the article linked the leftward ideological movement of several Justices appointed by Republican presidents to the dominance of center-left views among academics, the media, and individuals with graduate degrees. By the start of the 2011 Supreme Court term, there was no doubt that all Republican nominees to the Court were more conservative than their Democratic counterparts. In other words, when Democrat Elena Kagan filled the seat vacated by liberal Republican John Paul Stevens in August 2010, the Supreme Court had become a Court that was divided along party lines.

The question remained: Could our theory about elite influences explain this partisan divide? The first step was to put the current divide into historical context. In November 2011, we published a piece in *Slate* that documented the current divide and suggested the divide was unique in the Court's history. Dahlia Lithwick at *Slate* encouraged us to pursue the piece and was also our editor at *Slate*. Dahlia's enthusiasm helped convince us to pursue a full-blown academic article on this question.

From 2012 to 2016, we worked on that article, refining our thinking on the subject. We concluded that the partisan divide was a byproduct of elite polarization, the related emergence of the conservative legal movement, and other societal changes (most notably party polarization in Congress and the rise of Fox and other right-leaning media outlets). That paper went through several rounds of revisions and benefited from our presenting it at workshops at several law schools, including Berkeley, Cornell, Vanderbilt, William & Mary, and George Mason. Thanks to all those who attended those workshops and thanks in particular to Josh Chavetz, Jesse Choper, Eric Clayes, Mike Dorf, Paul Edelman, Peter Schuck, Tara Grove, and John Yoo. Thanks too to Adam Liptak, who used an early draft of that article as a pivot to a May 2014 feature piece he published in the *New York Times* on the polarized Court. That piece and the related attention we received from it were a very helpful shot in the arm.

The published version of that paper came out in the *Supreme Court Review* in 2017. Titled "Split Definitive: How Party Polarization Turned the Supreme Court into a Partisan Court," the article advanced many of the central claims of this book. In particular, the article highlighted how today's partisan divide is unique, that the Court virtually never divided along partisan lines on prominent cases until 2011, and that elite polarization underlies today's partisan divide. David Strauss and Geoff Stone, two of the editors of the *Supreme Court Review*, were very helpful in refining our thinking about the project. We are indebted to them and also appreciative of the *Supreme Court Review* (and its publisher the University of Chicago Press) for allowing us to make use of that article in this book project.

In the winter of 2015, while still working on the "Split Definitive" paper, we thought that the topic warranted a book-length treatment that would integrate, update, and substantially expand the two article projects. We wanted the book both to advance a model of Supreme Court decision making and to show how that model explained the leftward drift of many Justices appointed before 1991 and the hardening of ideological positions since then. We approached Dave McBride at Oxford University Press and were delighted to receive an enthusiastic response. Dave quickly championed the project and worked with outside reviewers and Oxford's delegate process. It has been smooth sailing with Oxford throughout the process. We are grateful to Dave for his advice and support. We are also appreciative of his willingness to let us separately publish the "Split Definitive" paper; we believe that the book is much stronger because we pursued that paper and, through it, refined our thinking about the book.

In writing the book, we were buoyed by continuing attention to our work by academics and journalists, including positive mentions of our work by columnists E. J. Dionne in the *Washington Post* and Linda Greenhouse in the *New York Times*. We also appreciate the support of *Slate*'s legal affairs editor Jeremy Stahl. In March 2016, we published a piece on the Merrick Garland nomination, "Ideological Imbalance"; in January 2017, we published a piece on the Federalist Society's role in judicial selections, "Federalist Court." Those two pieces were useful to us in thinking about differences between Democratic and Republican appointments to the Court.

There are many others to thank. We are grateful to Helen Nicholson, Danielle Michaely, and Leslie Johnson for all their help in turning our manuscript into a book. The book was improved by comments from Mark Tushnet, Sandy Levinson, and Northwestern law faculty (especially Shari Diamond, Steve Calabresi, John McGinnis, and Jim Pflander), who participated in a workshop on chapter 4. Throughout the project, Paul Hellyer at the William and Mary Law Library helped us over several research humps and offered useful analysis too. Our research assistants were also amazing; thanks especially to Barb Marmet, Peter Kyle, Suzanne Cordoner, Caitlin Cater, Amber Shepherd, Zach Singerman, and Imani Price.

The Company They Keep

1

Summary of Book and Argument

ON SEPTEMBER 12, 2005, Chief Justice nominee John Roberts told the Senate Judiciary Committee that "nobody ever went to a ball game to see the umpire. . . . I will remember that it's my job to call balls and strikes and not to pitch or bat."[1] Notwithstanding Roberts's paean to judicial neutrality, then-senator Barack Obama voted against the Republican nominee. Although noting that he had "absolutely no doubt" that Roberts was "qualified" to sit on the Court, Obama said that what mattered was the "5 percent of cases that are truly difficult," cases not resolved by adherence to legal rules but decided by "one's core concerns, one's broader perspectives of how the world works, and the depth and breadth of one's empathy."[2] But with all fifty-five Republicans backing Roberts, objections by Obama and other Democratic senators did not make a difference.

Today, some version of the dance between Roberts and Senate Democrats and Republicans is so predictable that it now seems a given that there will be proclamations of neutrality by Supreme Court nominees and party-line voting by senators. Indeed, Senate Republicans blocked a vote on Obama Supreme Court pick Merrick Garland in 2016 so that (in the words of the Majority Leader and Chair of the Judiciary Committee) "the American people" could "make their voice heard in the selection of Scalia's successor as they participate in the process to select their next president."[3] And following Donald Trump's victory and subsequent nomination of Neil Gorsuch, Senate Republicans undid a Democratic logjam by repudiating filibuster rules intended to require supermajority support for Supreme Court nominees. The final vote on Gorsuch was 54 to 45, with every Republican supporting the nominee and all but three Democrats voting no. Yet in the midst of this battle, Gorsuch in his own confirmation hearing said that "we sometimes hear judges cynically described as politicians in robes, seeking to enforce their own politics rather than striving to apply the law impartially," but he strongly rejected that view. Speaking of the judges on his court, he said that "the answers we reach are always the ones we believe the law requires."[4]

Early in his tenure, from late in the Court's 2016 term through the 2017 term, Gorsuch voted with his Republican colleagues considerably more often than he did with the Court's Democrats and almost always backed conservative positions in major cases.[5] His position on the Court's ideological scale in the long term remains to be seen. But it is certainly true that Gorsuch is more conservative than Merrick Garland. As a result, his appointment to the Court did not disturb the most striking feature of the Supreme Court in recent years: an ideological spectrum on which Justices who were appointed by Democratic presidents are all to the left of all their colleagues who were appointed by Republican presidents.[6] Nor is Brett Kavanaugh likely to disrupt that pattern; indeed, he is far more likely to reinforce it by taking positions that put him distinctly to the right of his Republican predecessor Anthony Kennedy.

This book tells the story of how party polarization turned the Supreme Court into a Court in which ideological divisions follow party lines. In so doing, this book explains how the Supreme Court is shaped by the political and social environment in which the Justices work. We argue that this environment has a powerful effect on the Justices, but one that does not operate in the ways that most scholars and observers of the Court have assumed. We make and support three related points about the Court.

First, the partisan and ideological polarization of the current era, polarization that has had its greatest effects in elite segments of American society, has changed the Court in important ways. One effect has been to bring to the Court only Justices whose ideological views reflect the dominant views in the appointing president's party. Another effect of political polarization has been to give the Justices stronger ties with ideologically oriented subsets of elites that reinforce their own views. Because of these effects, beginning with the 1991 appointment of Clarence Thomas, the ideological distance between Democratic and Republican appointees has grown substantially. This growth culminated in 2010: since then, for the first time in its history, the Court has had liberal and conservative blocs that fall perfectly along party lines.

Before the mid-1980s, ideology played a less pronounced role in Supreme Court appointments. Republican presidents sometimes appointed liberals and Democrats sometimes appointed conservatives. Moreover, during the Burger and early Rehnquist Courts, some Republican appointees became more liberal—a shift that moved them closer to the dominant views of legal and media elites. Since 1991, however, all Republican appointees have been committed conservatives and all Democrats have been liberals. Politically polarized elite social networks have reinforced the conservatism and liberalism of Republican and Democrat appointees.

Second, the Justices do not respond primarily to pressures from the other branches of government or the weight of mass public opinion. Rather, the primary influence on them is the elite world in which the Justices live both before and after they join the Supreme Court. The Justices take cues primarily from the people who are closest to them and whose approval they care most about, and those people are part of political, social, and professional elites.

Finally, the Supreme Court is a *court*, and the Justices respond to expectations among legal elites that they will act as legal decision makers. Those expectations help to explain the frequency of unanimous or near-unanimous decisions and decisions that cut across ideological lines even in an era of high polarization. Indeed, the differences between the Court and Congress are highlighted by the differences in the ways that members of the two institutions respond to partisan and ideological polarization.

Partisan Polarization and Supreme Court Decision Making

Our inquiry in this book focuses on political parties, ideology, and the relationship between the two. Of course, the identities of the two major parties have been clear and stable for more than 150 years. Ideology is both less stable and less clear.[7] The definitions of conservative and liberal positions on legal and policy issues stem from a general logic only in part, and they sometimes change over time. When we speak of Justices or the positions they take as conservative and liberal or right and left, we are referring to the common understanding of ideology among political elites at the time in question. And because Justices and other individuals may be more liberal on some issues than others, our descriptions of their overall positions on the ideological continuum simplify what may be more complicated combinations of stances on particular issues.

In our inquiries, however, we frequently focus on subsets of the issues that the Court addresses. We give particular emphasis to civil rights and civil liberties, which encompasses issues of discrimination and equality, as well as individual rights such as freedom of expression and the procedural rights of criminal defendants. This field has been the single most important concern for the Justices and for their audiences outside the Court for the past half century. We generally refer to this field simply as "civil liberties."

Since 2010, when Democratic nominee Elena Kagan replaced liberal Republican John Paul Stevens, all of the Supreme Court's Republican-nominated Justices have been to the right of Democratic-nominated Justices. Before 2010, the Court never had clear ideological blocs that coincided with party lines. Table 1.1 illustrates that change by showing the proportions of liberal votes cast by each Justice during three "natural courts," periods when the Court's membership remained stable.[8] In the first two periods, the Justices nominated by Democratic presidents were more liberal than the Republican nominees as a whole, but the ideological ordering of Justices did not follow party lines fully. In the last period, in contrast, there was a clear division between Republican and Democratic nominees—one that continued after the death of Justice Antonin Scalia and the appointments of Justices Neil Gorsuch and Brett Kavanaugh. Other measures of the Justices' ideological positions show similar patterns.[9]

The Court's ideological and partisan divisions are most visible on controversial civil rights and liberties issues that often divide the Justices sharply. But those divisions exist on economic issues as well, especially those that pit the interests of businesses against those of employees and consumers. As in

Table 1.1. Percentages of Liberal Votes Cast by Justices, Selected Natural Courts

Terms								
1981–1985			1994–2004			2010–2014		
Justice	Pty	% Lib	Justice	Pty	% Lib	Justice	Pty	% Lib
Marshall	D	70.8	Stevens	R	66.5	Sotomayor	D	64.6
Brennan	R	69.3	Ginsburg	D	61.7	Ginsburg	D	63.7
Blackmun	R	55.6	Souter	R	61.3	Kagan	D	63.3
Stevens	R	54.6	Breyer	D	57.1	Breyer	D	57.7
White	D	42.4	O'Connor	R	41.3	Kennedy	R	46.2
Powell	R	37.6	Kennedy	R	41.0	Roberts	R	44.6
O'Connor	R	37.4	Rehnquist	R	33.5	Scalia	R	42.9
Burger	R	34.4	Scalia	R	31.5	Alito	R	37.7
Rehnquist	R	29.5	Thomas	R	29.6	Thomas	R	37.2

the political world generally, there is a strong correlation between Justices' positions relative to each other across a range of issues.[10]

Similar trends are shown in a different way in Figure I.1. The figure depicts the standard deviation of percentages of conservative votes by Democratic and Republican appointees per Court term over time, with terms aggregated primarily on the basis of continuity of the Court's membership. The lower the standard deviation is, the greater the similarity in voting among Justices of the same party. The high standard deviation for Democratic Justices in the 1986–1993 period was an anomaly, because the only Democratic appointees who served during that period were the very liberal Thurgood Marshall and the moderate conservative Byron White.[11] Still, the movement in both parties toward homogeneous voting patterns is striking: Republican and Democratic Justices constitute distinct blocs in a way that they did not in past periods.

The partisan divide that emerged in 2010 is now generally recognized. Senate Republicans' refusal to consider Merrick Garland, the repudiation of the filibuster to confirm Neil Gorsuch, and the rise of party-line voting on Supreme Court nominees are all testaments to the widely shared belief that Republican nominees will back conservative causes and Democratic nominees will champion liberal pursuits. What is not generally known is that this pattern is unique in this Court's history: as we have noted, never before were there competing ideological blocs that coincided with party lines.[12] In the era from the beginning of the Warren Court through the early Roberts Court, there were always liberal Republicans until the retirement of Justice

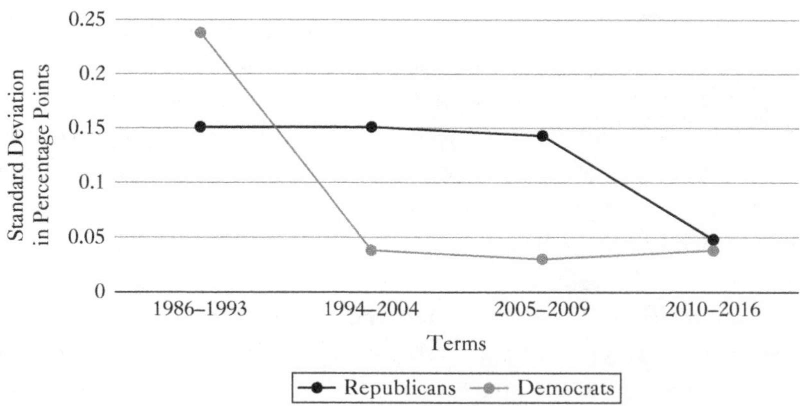

FIGURE I.1. Standard deviations of conservative voting percentages among Justices of the same party, averaged across terms.

John Paul Stevens in 2010; before the retirement of Justice Byron White in 1993, there were always moderate or conservative Democrats.

Moreover, unlike today's partisan divide, Republicans and Democrats often came together on issues that had divided the nation. Examples abound. In the 1940s, Republicans Owen Roberts and Harlan Fiske Stone embraced an extraordinarily broad reading of Congress's commerce clause power alongside their Democratic colleagues.[13] Republican Chief Justice Earl Warren famously orchestrated the Court's unanimous 1954 ruling in *Brown v. Board of Education*.[14] In the 1966 *Miranda v. Arizona* decision, the majority consisted of two Republicans and three Democrats, while the dissenters included two Republicans and two Democrats.[15] *Roe v. Wade* was decided seven to two; five of the Court's six Republicans were in the majority, as were two of the three Democrats.[16] More recently, Republican Justices played a critical role in decisions upholding affirmative action,[17] reaffirming abortion rights,[18] and establishing the rights of enemy combatants.[19] Between 1790 and early 2010, of 397 decisions that were designated as important by the *Guide to the U.S. Supreme Court* and that had at least two dissenting votes, only two had all the Justices from one party on one side and all the Justices from the other party on the opposite side.[20]

Major decisions that do not follow party lines perfectly have not disappeared since 2010, primarily (but not entirely) because of the continuing presence of moderate conservative Anthony Kennedy on the Court through the 2017 term. Kennedy joined the Democrats on the Court to create majorities in the Court's 2013 and 2015 decisions favoring same-sex marriage[21] and its 2016 decisions rejecting state efforts to limit abortion access and upholding affirmative action in university admissions.[22] But in contrast with the Court's history up to 2010, there have been several important decisions since then on which the Justices divided along party lines.[23]

Another feature of today's partisan divide that is not widely recognized is highlighted by Figure 1.1: Republican and Democratic appointees as groups have each become more homogeneous in their ideological positions. Republican appointees as a group have become increasingly conservative over time, as liberal and moderate Republicans are replaced by conservatives. For Democrats, moderate liberal Democrats replaced strong liberals and moderate conservatives. More important, the average ideological position of Democratic Justices has remained relatively stable, while the average ideological position of Republicans has become distinctly more conservative.

This difference between the parties is reflected in the proportions of conservative and liberal votes cast by the Court's Republicans and Democrats over time. But because the mix of cases that the Court hears changes over time, those proportions can be misleading. Political scientist Michael Bailey's ideological scores for the civil liberties field are computed in a way that minimizes that problem.[24] Although the scores run only through 2011 (they are calculated for calendar years rather than Court terms), they provide a good sense of trends from the Warren Court to the Roberts Court. Those trends are shown in Figure 1.2. The time period was divided into segments based primarily on the timing of important changes in the Court's membership, with 2010 and 2011 indicating the impact of the retirements of Republicans David Souter in 2009 and John Paul Stevens in 2010. More positive scores indicate greater conservatism.

There certainly has been fluctuation in the position of Democratic Justices as a group. They became distinctly more liberal as Roosevelt and Truman appointees with relatively conservative positions on civil liberties issues left the Court, and they moved in the other direction when Byron White was one of only two Democratic appointees on the Court after 1975 (and the only Democratic appointee in 1992 and 1993). Since White's retirement, however, the Court's Democrats have been stable in their positions on the ideological scale. In contrast, the Court's Republicans as a group have become increasingly

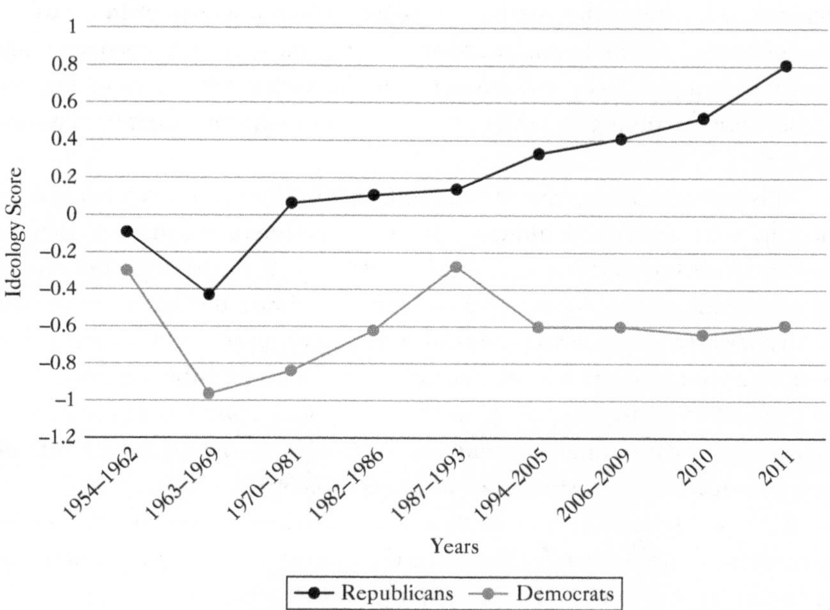

FIGURE 1.2. Mean Bailey ideology scores for Democratic and Republican appointees, 1954–2011.

conservative since the 1960s, as very liberal Republican appointees (Earl Warren and William Brennan) left the Court and, more recently, moderate liberals Souter and Stevens retired.

Both the Bailey measure shown in Figure 1.2 and the raw proportions of conservative and liberal votes cast by the Justices make it clear that the Court, like Congress and the country as a whole, has undergone partisan sorting: Republican and Democratic Justices are now separated much more in ideological terms than they were in past eras. This phenomenon is consequential, and it requires explanation.

The Supreme Court and Elites

Scholars who study the Supreme Court typically take one of two positions on the impact of the Court's environment on the Justices. The first is that the Justices are largely impervious to influence from outside the Court. In the "attitudinal model" described in *The Supreme Court and the Attitudinal Model Revisited*, Jeffrey Segal and Harold Spaeth argue that Justices simply vote their policy preferences, with external influence on the Court pretty much limited to the appointments process that staffs the Court.[25] In *The Choices Justices Make*, in contrast, Lee Epstein and Jack Knight embrace the external strategic actor model, arguing that the Justices take potential reactions from the other branches of government and the general public into account when reaching decisions and crafting opinions that further their legal policy preferences, because those reactions affect the Justices' success in achieving their legal policy goals.[26]

This strategic perspective on the Court has been widely accepted, and especially as it relates to the influence of public opinion on the Justices. There is an important line of thinking in legal scholarship about the impact of public opinion, reflected in major books by Barry Friedman and Jeffrey Rosen. In *The Will of the People*, Friedman took a historical approach in claiming that Supreme Court constitutional interpretation followed public opinion.[27] In *The Most Democratic Branch: How the Courts Serve America*, Rosen made a similar argument in broader terms, arguing for the normative desirability of public influence on constitutional interpretation by the Court.[28]

There is a related body of work of political scientists who argue that the general public has a powerful impact on the Court.[29] A growing body of scholarship holds that Justices respond to public opinion because of their interest in maintaining the Court's legitimacy and thus its institutional power. One important book, Tom Clark's *The Limits of Judicial Independence*, makes the same general argument as the Friedman and Rosen books from the perspective of a political scientist.[30] Clark analyzes the relationships among public opinion, "court-curbing" proposals in Congress, and the Court's decisions, concluding that public opinion operates through Congress to constrain the Court.

We agree with the view that Supreme Court Justices are subject to significant influence from the world around them. Justices are members of society and their decision making, over time, will reflect changes in the world that the Justices inhabit. Supreme Court Justices, as Chief Justice Rehnquist put it, "go home at night and read the newspapers or watch the evening news on television; they talk to their family and friends about current events." Inevitably, as Rehnquist suggested, those experiences affect the Justices' thinking.[31] Consider the Court's shift on homosexual sodomy prosecutions: In 1986, the Court upheld 5 to 4 Georgia's power to criminalize homosexual sodomy. The Court's swing Justice Lewis Powell voted with the majority. The reason, as revealed in a conversation with one of his law clerks, was that Justice Powell did not believe that he had "ever met a homosexual" and simply could not find in the Constitution a right to engage in sexual practices that he could not comprehend.[32] Justice Powell's replacement, Justice Anthony Kennedy, approached the gay rights issue from a much different position, and cast the fifth vote to overturn the Georgia decision in 2003. Unlike Justice Powell, Justice Kennedy's world was supportive of gay rights: the Court itself was a gay-friendly workplace and Justice Kennedy (who cited the European Court of Human Rights in his decision) often hobnobbed with foreign judges and, in one reporter's view, saw himself as a participant in "a worldwide constitutional conversation."[33]

But as insightful as the existing research on the Court and its environment is, we part company with that research in our perspective about which elements of that environment influence the Justices most strongly and about the motivational sources of that influence. In doing so, this book offers a new vantage point on the relationship between the Supreme Court, popular culture, social norms, and the political environment.

On the elements of the environment that influence the Justices, we recognize that elected government—principally through the appointments process—directly influences Supreme Court decision making. But we disagree with legal scholars and commentators who argue that the Court has largely followed broader cultural trends, related social movements, and public opinion. Rather, we argue that the Justices are more responsive to relevant segments of the social and political elite than to the public as a whole.

Correspondingly, by emphasizing the importance of elite social networks to the Justices, we offer an alternative to the motivational assumption that underlies widely accepted political science models. These models see Justices as single-minded maximizers of their legal policy preferences. The external strategic actor and attitudinal models treat "judges as people whose choices are based on a very narrow set of goals. If this assumption is accurate, judges' interest in shaping legal policy must be far stronger than other goals that might affect their decisions."[34] By calling attention to the significant role of the elite social networks that the Justices are a part of, we reject the assumption that Supreme Court Justices act solely on the basis of their legal policy preferences.

Our theory is rooted in social psychology. Unlike political science models that emphasize the single-minded pursuit of legal policy preferences, the social psychology model recognizes other goals that the Justices might pursue. Indeed, scholars have given attention to a wide array of goals that may be relevant to judges, including power, reputation, and harmonious relations with other Justices.[35] For our purposes, it is most important to think about the motivational basis for the goals that the Justices seek to advance. The Justices, after all, get nothing concrete from advancing favored policies; rather, they get symbolic benefits. But they get symbolic benefits from other things as well, so it is not self-evident that the Justices would devote themselves to the pursuit of favored policies.

Notwithstanding important differences in the social psychology and political science models, the two models converge in important respects. In particular, the social psychology model talks about the importance of personal beliefs and recognizes that individuals will not act in ways that are inconsistent with matters central to their cognitive networks.[36] For this reason, Justices—especially those with strong ideological predispositions—will typically cast votes that match their preferred legal policy positions.

The social psychology model veers more sharply from accounts of Supreme Court decision making that emphasize the role of public opinion. By giving emphasis to the basic psychological motivation to be liked and respected by other people, the social psychology model directs attention to the social networks Supreme Court Justices interface with and, consequently, gives priority to the views of elites, not mass public opinion.[37] This focus on elites has two bases.

First, it is likely that Supreme Court Justices will care greatly about the esteem in which they are held. The very process by which we select Supreme Court Justices tends to favor those with a strong interest in the esteem of others. Accepting a judgeship entails accepting relatively significant constraints on personal activities and behaviors. Moreover, the lawyers who are viewed as viable candidates for federal appellate judgeships typically give up considerable future income when they take seats on the bench. One of the things that Justices gain in compensation (in addition to an increase in personal power) is the esteem that attaches to a position on the highest court in the country. Not everyone would find this tradeoff attractive; it would be most attractive to those who care about the esteem in which they are held.

Second, Supreme Court Justices are elites and are far more likely to care about their reputation among the elite audiences they come from and interact with than their reputation among the general public. The great majority of Justices "grew up in privileged circumstances and do not rub shoulders with hoi polloi."[38] Because the Justices are "sheltered, cosseted," and "overwhelmingly upper-middle or upper-class and extremely well educated, usually at the nation's more elite universities,"[39] the views of social and economic leaders are likely to matter more to the Court than to popularly elected lawmakers (who must appeal to popular sentiment in order to win elections). Among the current Justices, even the two (Clarence Thomas and Sonia Sotomayor) who grew up in less affluent households attended Yale Law School and were part of elite social networks at a young age.

Correspondingly, once they join the Court, all Justices spend a high proportion of their time with members of the elite. Although Justices differ somewhat in the segments of the elite with whom they associate, for the Court as a whole relevant segments include federal and foreign judges, Supreme Court practitioners, law schools and lawyer groups, high-ranking government officials, and media elites. For example, in the public appearances that have become increasingly common for the Justices, Roberts Court Justices frequently speak at Harvard, Yale, and other elite law schools.[40] Moreover, there is a growing trend of Justices speaking to like-minded elite audiences; conservative Justices are often featured speakers before the Federalist Society and liberal Justices are headliners for the American Constitution Society.[41]

Because they care about their reputations among elites, moreover, Supreme Court Justices also embrace the norms of judicial decision making—norms that ensure that the Supreme Court operates as a court. These norms include maintaining collegiality and acting on the basis of law. These norms help explain why a high proportion of the Court's decisions are unanimous and why the Court's voting alignments in individual cases are often unpredictable—with conservative and liberal Justices joining together in unexpected ways. These norms are also relevant in understanding why Justices, far more than members of Congress, make use of general principles that transcend the stakes for policy in particular decisions. To a meaningful degree Justices make use of similar principles of constitutional and statutory interpretation across a broad range of cases, even if that means supporting liberal outcomes in some cases and conservative outcomes in others. None of this is to say that the Justices never divide along ideological lines or that they decide cases solely on a legal basis; it is to say simply that the Justices' personal reputations among elite audiences are tied to their adherence to collegiality and law-based decision making and, as such, the Supreme Court remains a court.

Sketch of the Book

In sum, we seek to offer a new vantage point on the Supreme Court and its members. By emphasizing the import of both Justices' legal policy preferences and the elite audiences they come from and interface with, we embrace a social psychology model that differs from the dominant ways that people think about the Court within its environment: that the Justices act essentially without regard to that environment or that they respond strategically to the other branches of government or the public primarily because they seek to protect the policies they make or their institutional legitimacy. Rather, we argue, the Justices are attentive to elite audiences that shape their choices in important ways.

The book is organized as follows: After this introductory chapter, chapter 2 describes and defends our social psychology model and our emphasis on elite audiences. In part, we contrast the decision making of the Justices to that of elected officials. To a considerable degree, the Justices are subject to the same influences as other public officials from their political and social environments. But there are two important differences: more than elected officials in the other branches of government, the Justices respond to elite groups rather than the general public; and they are influenced by a legal environment that limits and modifies the influence of the political and social environments. Contrary to the widespread assumption that the Supreme Court largely stays in line with mass public opinion, we discuss why the Justices are more responsive to elites than to the mass public. The key elite audiences for Justices are the legal profession, academia, news media, political groups, and personal social circles.

In addition to highlighting the profound role that elites play in defining Court decision making, we also make use of social psychology to talk about the import of legal elite norms like collegiality and law-based decision making.

In particular, we will explain why it is that the Justices have incentives both to join together in consensual decisions and to sometimes vote against their perceived ideological preferences.

Chapter 3 describes the period before 1985. We begin by laying out the multiple meanings of political polarization. Of those meanings, we have two primary concerns: partisan sorting of people by ideology, so that liberals cluster in the Democratic Party and conservatives in the Republican Party, and positive and negative affect toward ideological groups. Through most of the twentieth century, partisan sorting and affective polarization were relatively limited.

Limited polarization had two effects on the Court. First, ideological divisions on the Court did not follow party lines, because presidents frequently nominated Justices who did not adhere to their party's dominant ideological tendency. Second, the Justices responded to elite groups that were not sharply split along ideological lines. In the early twentieth century, elites were generally conservative, embraced laissez-faire economics, and were often hostile to government regulation. The so-called *Lochner* Court generally matched prevailing elite preferences. During the New Deal era, elites came to favor economic regulation, but there was no consensus among elites with respect to civil rights and liberties. Franklin Roosevelt's eight Supreme Court nominees reflected both elite consensus on economic matters and elite divisions on rights and liberties.[42] During the mid- to late-twentieth century, these elite groups leaned to the left, especially on civil rights and liberties issues, and their influence helped to move moderately conservative Justices to the left. Most notably, several Republican Justices became increasingly liberal during their tenure on the Court.

Chapter 4 considers the Court in a polarized world. The late twentieth century was a time of polarization among American political, social, and legal elites: both partisan sorting and affective polarization increased substantially. This polarization affected the Supreme Court in two ways. First, presidents increasingly chose nominees who did adhere strongly to their parties' dominant ideological tendency. This was the primary reason that by 2010, party and ideological lines on the Court matched perfectly. Second, with the rise of conservative legal networks, the social and political environments of the Justices were divided along ideological lines to a much greater extent than in the past. As a result, liberal and conservative Justices both lived in worlds that reinforced their ideological positions.

The polarization of the late twentieth century has been maintained and even strengthened since it first developed. However, polarization in both the senses we emphasize has had more limited effects on the Court than on other political institutions such as Congress, because of the Justices' efforts to adhere to expectations that they act as interpreters of the law. These expectations are reflected in the Court's frequent unanimity and in decisions that divide Justices along nonideological lines. Today's Court is more apt to divide along partisan lines on the most significant cases it hears—so that norms favoring judicial independence and collegiality are most apparent in low-salience cases.

Chapter 5 provides a brief conclusion—summarizing and extending our arguments. This chapter draws out the implications of the prior chapters for our understanding of the Supreme Court. We disagree with those who see the Court as essentially independent of the political world and society, but we also disagree with those who see the Court as responsive chiefly to the other branches of government and the general public. The Court is distinctive in the Justices' orientation toward elite audiences, and those audiences influence the Court in subtle but significant ways. Both the leaning of relevant elite groups toward the left in a prior era and the strong elite polarization of the current era have affected the Justices' thinking and thus the Court's direction.

The Court's future depends to a considerable degree on whether there is an easing of the current political polarization. If polarization persists, we can anticipate that today's ideological divide will grow and that Justices will increasingly turn to forums outside the Court (media and other public appearances, books) to strengthen their ties with the social networks they are a part of. Correspondingly, presidential elections will play an ever-increasing role in defining the Court's direction; Republicans will appoint committed conservatives and Democrats will appoint reliable liberals. Even with strong polarization, we expect that the Court will continue to issue a substantial number of unanimous opinions and otherwise adhere to legal elite norms. But at the same time, the Court will continue to reflect the polarization that has developed in the larger elite world.

2

The Supreme Court and Elites

AS WE DISCUSSED in chapter 1, our emphasis on the impact of political and social elites on Supreme Court Justices is a departure from the ways that scholars generally depict the Court. In this chapter we put our own perspective on the Justices in the context of the perspective that has dominated scholarship on the Supreme Court.

We begin by laying out the dominant perspective, embodied in what we call "political science models" of the Court. We then present our own perspective, which we identify with social psychology. We then apply those perspectives to the relationship between the Justices and the world outside the Court, first in broad terms and then by considering the impact of public opinion and the opinion of elites on the Court.

Models of the Justices

Justices as Seekers of Good Legal Policy

Among scholars who are interested in explaining the behavior of Supreme Court Justices, the dominant view within both law and political science is that the Justices are driven by the goal of making what they perceive to be good legal policy. Because the models that follow from this assumption are more explicit and receive closer examination in political science, we will refer to them as "political science models".

Scholars who share the dominant view have given relatively little attention to the validity of their shared assumption; instead, they focus on disagreements among them about what it means to seek good legal policy. The disagreements are about two issues: the relative weight of legal and policy considerations for the Justices and the extent to which Justices act strategically to achieve their goals.

At least at a conceptual level, we can distinguish between judges who seek to interpret the law as accurately as possible and judges who seek to make the law as consistent as possible with their conceptions of good public policy. Some traditional legal scholarship depicted judges as law oriented, but there were always scholars who departed from the conception that Justices acted only on legal considerations. In the first half of the twentieth century the legal realism movement gave a stronger foothold to the idea that judges are motivated in part by policy considerations.[1] In particular, legal realists argued that legal principles were the product of contentious political choices and, relatedly, that judges often concealed the actual reasons for their judgments through value-laden descriptions of both facts and law. For their part, the political scientists who undertook quantitative analyses of judicial behavior beginning in the 1940s underlined the role of policy considerations for judges. Focusing on the Supreme Court, they argued that disagreements among the Justices were primarily a product of ideological differences.[2]

Today the view that Supreme Court Justices act only on the goal of making good law has disappeared from scholarship, although it appears from time to time in statements by Justices (or, frequently, by nominees to the Court) about how they make decisions. Chief Justice Roberts attracted wide attention for the analogy that he made at his confirmation hearing between Supreme Court Justices and umpires calling balls and strikes, but other nominees have also described their task as one of simply interpreting the law.[3] Nonetheless, there is general agreement that policy considerations are important in decision making on the Court. The disagreement is about how much of a role legal considerations play.

This disagreement correlates with disciplinary lines. Legal scholars typically take the view that law matters to the Justices and that their choices reflect their efforts to get the law right, as well as their efforts to make good policy. Mark Tushnet, a leading legal scholar who has taken a highly realistic view of the clash of liberal and conservative viewpoints on the Court, nonetheless concluded that in "95 percent of the cases . . . the best explanation for the decisions is what the justices think rules and precedent require."[4] From a different perspective, Joshua Fischman and Tonja Jacobi have analyzed patterns in Justices' voting and identified what they see as a legal-oriented dimension to that voting.[5]

In contrast, political scientists tend to view policy considerations as dominant in the Court, and some treat the law as essentially irrelevant to explanation of the Justices' choices as decision makers. That is the position of what has been called the "attitudinal model," championed by Jeffrey Segal and Harold Spaeth in their highly influential books on the Court.[6] Other important work in political science shares that position.[7]

But not all scholars share the tendencies of their discipline. Some legal scholars today view the Court as acting overwhelmingly on the basis of its Justices' policy preferences. Richard Posner, highly regarded as both a scholar and federal court of appeals judge, argues that at least in decisions interpreting the Constitution, the Justices act almost solely on policy considerations.[8]

For their part, some political scientists treat the Justices as both law oriented and policy oriented. This viewpoint is especially common among scholars who subscribe to historical institutionalism, such as Howard Gillman, Keith Whittington, and Mark Graber.[9] Historical institutionalists see the Justices as working within a legal framework that guides their decisions even as they act on their policy preferences.[10] Some political scientists who work from other theoretical perspectives also depict legal considerations as important to the Justices' choices.[11]

The second disagreement, about strategy, is most easily understood from the perspective of Justices who seek only to make good policy. What does it mean to make good policy? One possibility is that such Justices simply cast votes on case outcomes and write or join opinions that reflect their policy preferences as closely as possible.

Alternatively, policy-oriented Justices might act strategically in the sense that they consider the short- and long-term effects of the positions they take.[12] In some cases they would support outcomes and legal doctrines that depart from their preferences in the interest of shaping the Court's collective decisions or the overall state of public policy. To take the most familiar example, compromising with colleagues on opinion language may help to secure the right outcome in a case from a Justice's perspective. Justice William Brennan, for example, was credited with being the primary architect of Warren Court liberalism precisely because he was willing to craft compromise opinions acceptable to five Justices.[13] Another form of strategy is acting to protect the Court's institutional position, which might involve avoiding decisions that potentially jeopardize public support for the Court or that trigger attacks on the Court by Congress and the president.

Strategy has always played at least an implicit role in scholarship on the Court's history, which often depicts the Justices collectively as taking the Court's institutional standing into account when that standing appears to be threatened. The impact of interactions among the Justices on the Court's collective decisions also receives extensive attention, though those interactions are not always interpreted as a product of strategic considerations.

Strategic perspectives on the Justices have been made more explicit and have been put in formal terms by political scientists, as well as some economists and legal scholars, beginning with the pioneering book by political scientist Walter Murphy in the 1960s and continuing since the 1990s with a flood of research.[14] Quantitative scholarship on Supreme Court decision making now routinely takes into account possible influence on the Justices from their colleagues and, outside the Court, from the public and the other branches.

For instance, one influential study analyzed patterns of behavior in the decision-making process to identify strategic behavior by the Justices that is aimed at shaping the Court's decisions and opinions.[15] In another study, Lee Epstein and Jack Knight reviewed the private papers of several Justices to provide evidence that the Court took potential backlash into account; Tom Clark analyzed the relationships among public opinion, "court-curbing" proposals in Congress, and the Court's decisions to identify the impact of the public on the Justices' choices.[16] In political science, a conception of Justices who act strategically to advance their policy goals has become the closest thing to an orthodox point of view.[17]

Yet not all scholars accept this conception. The most visible dissenters are Segal and Spaeth, whose attitudinal model of the Court depicts Justices as essentially autonomous, especially in relation to the world outside the Court. As Segal and Spaeth see it, Justices have little reason to worry about potential reactions to their decisions, so they can simply take the positions that accord with their policy preferences.[18]

The debates over these two issues are important for our understanding of Supreme Court decision making and judicial behavior in general. But the assumption about Justices' motivations that participants in these debates share paints the Justices as people with narrow concerns and perspectives. Among other things, they act without regard to anything that looks like self-interest in its conventional meaning.[19] In this way the political science models obscure the possible relevance of motivations that might lead to a quite different understanding of decision making in the Court. We turn now to those possibilities.

Justices as People Who Act on Multiple Goals

From the perspective of social psychology, the political science models seem simplistic. For one thing, those models give little attention to cognition;

rather, they assume that the path from goals to actions that maximize the achievement of those goals is unproblematic. For instance, if Justices need to make complex calculations to identify the most effective strategy to advance their policy goals, they will make those calculations and act on the results.[20] In contrast, social psychologists have emphasized attributes of cognition that limit people's ability to adopt the best course of action.[21] As one team of scholars has demonstrated in a series of studies, those attributes are found in judges as they are in other people.[22] Psychologists have also showed that motivation and cognition are intertwined, and some scholars have made use of Ziva Kunda's theory of motivated reasoning as a means to understand the mental processes that occur in judicial decision making.[23] For example, Christopher Schroeder explained the Rehnquist Court's revival of federalism limits on Congress as the byproduct of motivated reasoning, that is, that the policy desires of the Justices operated subconsciously, impacting the ways they accessed information to back up desired conclusions.[24]

Even if we limit ourselves to motivation and focus on judges' goals, psychological research has pointed to an array of basic needs or motivations that shape people's behavior and that plausibly could affect decision making in the Supreme Court.[25] Writing specifically about political leaders, David Winter has posited that they act on the basis of three motives: achievement, power, and affiliation.[26] As the labels suggest, the achievement motive centers on achieving excellence, success, and noteworthy accomplishments; the affiliation motive centers on "establishing, maintaining, or restoring friendly relations among persons or groups"; and the power motive centers on "having impact, control or influence" on others. [27] Those needs could translate into a range of specific goals, much wider than the legal and policy goals on which political science models focus.

This does not necessarily mean that those models are leaving something important out, because goals that are important to people's lives as a whole are not necessarily relevant to judicial decision making. This may be especially true of Supreme Court Justices. The relative simplicity of political science models of the Court rests on an assumption (sometimes explicit, more often implicit) that institutional attributes of the Court make some goals that are relevant to other positions largely irrelevant to Supreme Court Justices.[28]

For some goals, that assumption seems well founded. One example is career goals. The life terms of Supreme Court Justices virtually eliminate concerns about remaining on the Court, and in the current era Justices seem to have little interest in seeking other offices (with promotion to Chief Justice as a possible exception). Thus, career-related goals that may have considerable impact on decision making elsewhere in government, including other courts, are largely irrelevant to the Court.[29]

In contrast, scholars with a psychological perspective have shown that some other goals that lie outside the political science models are potentially relevant to decision making in the courts. Some students of judicial behavior who draw from psychological theory have probed motivations of judges other than efforts to make good law and good policy. For instance, a few studies have analyzed self-esteem as a goal shaping judges' choices.[30] Others, including one study of the Supreme Court, have examined the relationship between a range of motives for serving as judges and judges' behavior as decision makers.[31] For their part, scholars with other theoretical orientations, especially the perspective of economics, have also posited a wide range of possible motives for judges, including Supreme Court Justices.[32] For instance, Judge Richard Posner suggested that judges might seek the "satisfactions that people seek in a job" such as harmonious relations with judicial colleagues, "money income, leisure, power, prestige, reputation, self-respect, [and] the intrinsic pleasure (challenge, stimulation) of the work."[33] Although this research dates back a long time, it has had only a limited influence on the mainstream of scholarship on judicial behavior in law and political science. In that mainstream, scholars' focus continues to be on judges' interest in making good law, good public policy, or a combination of the two.

Our view is that perspectives based on social psychology can enhance our understanding of judicial behavior in powerful ways. That contribution is underlined by the research we have described already and by broader examinations of judicial decision making in psychological terms.[34] In particular, psychological perspectives open up inquiry into a broader range of motivations for judges than do the political science models. They allow us to consider the impact of basic human needs in ways that the political science models do not. They also incorporate the self-interest that economic models emphasize and that is largely absent from models of judges as seekers of good legal policy.

More specific to our concerns in this book, a perspective based on social psychology provides a way to think about how the Supreme Court's social and political environment shapes decision making on the Court. As we see it, political science models have done well in identifying some possible linkages between the Court and its environment, but they have largely left aside the most important of those linkages—one that emerges clearly from a psychological perspective. We develop that point in the next section.

Justices and the World outside the Court: A First Look

Political Science Models

In political science models, the key linkage between the Supreme Court and the outside world is the appointment process. This linkage is especially strong in the attitudinal model, in which Justices are influenced little by their environment once they join the Court. As a result of this autonomy, the process of choosing Justices is the primary way that the other branches of government and, indirectly, the voters shape what the Court does. It follows that direct pressure from the president or Congress and the state of public opinion have no meaningful effect on the Justices' choices in decision making.

As already suggested, strategic models are quite different. These models emphasize the strategic choices that Justices make in order to advance their interests in the content of legal policy and in the Court's standing. In particular, these models hold that Justices are open to direct influence from outside the Court to advance their goals. Even a strategic model might posit that the Justices seldom have any reason to modify what they are doing with the outside world in mind. Thus, the attitudinal model could be understood as a special type of strategic model. But the strategic models that scholars have propounded incorporate an explicit or implicit assumption that strategic considerations have considerable impact on the Justices' choices.

That assumption is reflected in depictions of the Supreme Court's relationships with the other branches of the federal government and with the general public. On the other branches, as noted earlier, scholars have long pointed to episodes in which it appeared that the Court (or at least some of its members) had retreated under pressure from the other branches. The shift in position of two pivotal members of the Court on New Deal legislation and the movement of pivotal Justices away from civil liberties doctrines that aroused congressional wrath in the late 1950s are frequently cited as examples. Such episodes have been incorporated into strategic models. These episodes are often treated as exceptional, and David Glick has argued that such retreats occur only under conditions that rarely exist, namely, a perception by the Justices that the other branches have a strong interest in the outcome of a case and their recognition of a credible threat that those branches will directly challenge the Court if it rules in the "wrong" way.[35]

Several scholars with a strategic perspective have posited a more regular and routine process in which Justices adjust their votes and opinions to the preferences of the president and Congress. As those scholars see it, Justices work to avoid reversals of their statutory decisions and action to undercut constitutional decisions by adjusting those decisions where necessary to minimize the likelihood of those negative responses. Those strategic calculations typically are conceptualized in ideological terms. If the Court is considerably more liberal than Congress and the president, for instance, Justices will move the Court's statutory decisions sufficiently in a conservative direction to avoid triggering the enactment of new statutes to override the Court's decisions.[36] Correspondingly, as William Eskridge argues in his study of the Court/Congress interface on statutory interpretation questions, the Justices are far more interested in whether the current Congress will back their statutory interpretations than in whether their interpretations are faithful to the desires of lawmakers who enacted the statute.[37]

The empirical evidence on the existence of this ideological adjustment in the statutory and constitutional arenas is mixed.[38] We have some skepticism about whether Justices routinely take into account the ideological positions of policymakers in the other branches: even if Justices are strategic, such modifications would not necessarily constitute good strategy. For one thing, legislation to overturn decisions is very difficult to predict; for another, the Court is not necessarily better off if it avoids a decision that would trigger an overturning rather than making such a decision.[39] But the empirical evidence that has been presented thus far indicates that this possibility should not be dismissed.

Like the other branches, the general public has been widely viewed as a significant influence on the Justices. Of course, the public cannot overturn the Court's decisions. Even so, commentators and Justices themselves have argued that Justices need to worry about loss of public support for the Court as an institution, what is often called legitimacy. For this reason, they say, Justices take public opinion into account. We are skeptical of this claim as well; in the next section of this chapter, we consider the logic of that argument and the evidence on its validity.

In their focus on the other branches of government and the general public, political science models depict the influence of the Court's environment on decision making by Justices as operating in a way that is impersonal and utilitarian. When Justices take the outside world into account, they respond not to individuals with whom they have direct relationships but to other institutions or to the mass public. They respond to that environment only as a means to the end of advancing their conceptions of good law or good policy. Such simplified models certainly have value. But there is also value in thinking about Justices who care about what others think of them for its own sake, Justices who are like the people that social psychologists depict.

Social Psychology Models

Models of behavior in social psychology would not rule out the kinds of influence on Justices that political science models emphasize. But their conceptions of the relationship between people and their environments have a quite different emphasis, one that focuses on the fundamental importance to people of how they are regarded by others. Self-esteem rests heavily on the esteem in which one is held by other people.[40]

There is no reason to think that Supreme Court Justices lack this motivation, nothing about their backgrounds or professional experiences that would render irrelevant what other people think of them. Indeed, as we discussed in chapter 1, there is reason to think that on average, an interest in the esteem of other people is especially strong for the Justices. That is because a strong interest in the esteem that judges on higher courts receive helps to make those judgeships attractive despite the disadvantages of holding judicial positions.

All of this would be irrelevant to explanation of judicial decision making if interest in the esteem of other people did not affect people's behavior. But because that interest is so important to people, it has a powerful impact on their behavior. We routinely engage in "self-presentation" or "impression management" to maximize the esteem of people who are important to us. As one social psychologist put it, self-presentation is an "essential component of social interaction," and it is a component that affects behavior not just in social roles but in professional roles as well.[41]

For this reason, judges' interest in how other people view them could affect their choices as decision makers. Indeed, some scholars have analyzed judges' interest in how other people view them as a potentially important element in decision making.[42] It might be argued that Supreme Court Justices are an exception, because membership on the Court guarantees that Justices garner a high level of respect and admiration from people who are aware of their position. Even so, the reputations of Justices differ considerably, and there is no doubt that Justices' votes and opinions have an impact on how they are viewed by people who pay attention to the Court's work. Indeed, the Justices' work is scrutinized to a degree that is unusual and almost certainly unique among courts in the United States. Thus, it is reasonable to assume that Supreme Court Justices are like other judges—and other people—in acting on an interest in the esteem of other people.[43]

If Justices do act on their interest in esteem, whose esteem do they care about? Of course, a wide variety of specific individuals and groups of people might be important to particular Justices. There surely is considerable variation among the Justices in the kinds of people they care about. But we think that several generalizations can be made.

At the broadest level, the scholarship on social identity underlines the importance of people's identifications with groups of which they are part.[44] Like others, Supreme Court Justices want most to be liked and respected by people with whom they identify directly.

One implication is that the audiences that strategic models depict as highly relevant to the Court are not automatically important to Justices at a personal level. Perhaps Justices do take the general public and the other branches of government into account to advance their policy goals or to protect the Court as an institution. But they do not necessarily care about the esteem of either the public or people in the other branches for its own sake, because those groups are generally peripheral to their social identities.

It is undoubtedly true that some Justices seek respect from the general public because they enjoy that popularity. This might be especially true of Justices who actually ran for public office, both because an interest in public approval motivated their decisions to seek elective offices and because experience as candidates (especially as successful candidates) may create a habit of looking to the public for approval.[45] But we are in an era in which it is rare for Justices to have experience as political candidates: since the appointment of Potter Stewart in 1958, Sandra Day O'Connor is the only appointee who has actually run for office. In part for that reason, the general public is unlikely to be a significant reference group for most Justices.

It seems even less likely that the other branches as institutions serve as reference groups for members of the Supreme Court. Some Justices have personal ties with people who serve in those branches, although that is less common today than it was when Justices often had extensive experience in Congress or in the executive branch. But such ties are very different from a generalized identification with one of the branches that could serve as a basis for influence.

Of the audiences that *are* important to the Justices, the most obvious are the circles of family, friends, and acquaintances who are highly salient to them at a personal level. People in these circles are not necessarily interested in the Justices' choices as decision makers, and at least some of them may give unquestioning acceptance to those choices. But to the extent that they hold and voice preferences about the issues that the Court addresses, these people are in an especially good position to help shape the Justices' thinking. Thus, while it is uncertain whether family and friends affected the positions that some Justices have taken on abortion, it is plausible that some influence occurs.[46]

Justices can be expected to care about their reputations among their colleagues in the legal profession. Many of their friends and acquaintances are in that profession; they are likely to identify with the profession as a peer group; and lawyers constitute the most knowledgeable audience for the Supreme Court's work. That is especially true of what might be called the elite segments of the bar: judges, law professors, and respected and high-status practitioners. Indeed, the Justices are very much part of a network of super-elite lawyers that includes former Supreme Court clerks, the Office of the Solicitor General, and the Supreme Court bar, that is, private sector lawyers who regularly practice before the Supreme Court. Eight of the fourteen Justices who have served on the Roberts Court were members of this super-elite network; two others were law professors.

Justices' interest in the esteem of people in the legal profession also gives weight to the media that can shape that esteem. Law reviews (and now legal blogs) review the Court's work and offer judgments about its quality. General news media that cover the Court get attention from lawyers, as well as other people interested in law and government.

Justices' reference groups may include sets of people, both within and outside the legal profession, who share views about politics and policy. If it is now rare for Supreme Court appointees to be career politicians, it remains true that the great majority of them have some experience in government and politics. That activity can create personal links with specific individuals. More broadly, people with substantial interest in politics and policy typically develop identifications with political parties and with liberal or conservative ideological groupings. Justices are not exceptions to that pattern.

In an era of political polarization, identifications with certain political groups and positive or negative affect toward other groups have tended to strengthen. There is no reason to think that Supreme Court Justices are an exception to that tendency either. As a result, we could expect political groups to become a more important audience to most Justices. As we discussed in chapter 1, we think that this development has had a powerful effect on the Court.

Our discussion of social psychology models reflects our belief that their lessons are compelling. Presidential appointments of Supreme Court Justices have the most pervasive impact on the Court's policies. But once Justices are sitting on the Court, we think that the strongest source of influence on them from outside the Court is their interest in the esteem of other people. In turn, this means that they are oriented toward individuals and groups who are part of the social and political elites of the country. In the two sections that follow, we begin our inquiry into the lessons of the social psychology models by examining the impact of public opinion and elite opinion on the Justices.

The Impact of Public Opinion

In thinking about the influence of the mass public on the Justices, we begin by considering why Justices might be subject to that influence. We then turn to evidence on the extent of that influence.

The Majoritarian Supreme Court?

Why would Supreme Court Justices take the general public into account when they make decisions? From the perspective of social psychology models, one reason is that Justices might seek popularity that extends beyond the world of political and social elites. We have already suggested why we think that the general public is much less salient to the Justices in this respect than elite groups, especially in the current era when few Justices have experience in elective politics. Still, the possibility that some Justices seek recognition and approval from the public as a whole cannot be dismissed. For instance, Barry Friedman has said, "The fact that the justices are only human may say a lot for why responsiveness to public opinion occurs. The justices are no less vain than the rest of us, and it is human nature to like to be liked or even applauded and admired."[47]

But this is not the primary source of influence that scholars posit for the general public. Rather, as Friedman puts it, "The most telling reason why the justices might care about public opinion, though, is simply that they do not have much of a choice. At least, that is, if they care about preserving the Court's institutional power, about having their decisions enforced, about not being disciplined by politics."[48] To use a term that is commonly employed by scholars, the public's perception of the Court's legitimacy is thought to be critical to its security and power.[49] Without public support for the Court's position in the political system, it is thought, the Court will not be able to secure compliance with its decisions and enforcement of those decisions. Nor will it be able to fend off attacks on its institutional powers.

Based on this premise, scholars frequently posit that Justices take the public into account in their decisions to maintain the Court's legitimacy. Two possible results of that consideration have been emphasized.[50] The first is avoidance of decisions that run contrary to public sentiment, especially on issues of high salience to that public. Two major historical studies of the Court, for instance, take that position.[51] The second result, suggested by scholars with a strategic perspective, is analogous to the primary theme of strategic analyses of the relationship between the Court and the other branches. In this account, Justices adjust the ideological content of their decisional outputs in response to trends in the ideological positions of the public.[52]

These two accounts see public opinion as significant but indirect; that is, the Court is subject to direct influence by political actors and in turn political actors take public opinion into account. There is, of course, little question that the Court is subject to the tugs and pulls of the political process. Through the inherently political process of presidential nomination and Senate confirmation, as Robert Dahl famously observed, "the Supreme Court is inevitably a part of the dominant national alliance."[53] As such, "the policy views dominant on the Court are never for long out of line with the policy views dominant among the lawmaking majorities of the United States."[54] Further, the Justices are well aware of the Court's relationship to elected government and broader social currents. Court decision making and the writings of Supreme Court Justices explicitly recognize the profound role of elected government, the media, ever-changing social norms, and the American people in shaping Court decision making.

At the same time, the Court is not necessarily responding to public opinion when it responds to changing social norms, the appointments process, and backlash and other implementation concerns. There is certainly a linkage between public opinion and both social norms and the actions of elected officials (whether those actions are tied to appointment politics or elected government resistance to judicial edicts), but the Court may well be responding most directly to the views of political and other elites—albeit views that are partially shaped by the mass public.

Consider, for example, the influence of changing social norms. These norms are the confluence of a range of factors—media and elite opinion, popular culture, mass public opinion, elections and action by elected government officials, social movements, and interest group initiatives. It would be wrong to conflate public opinion and social norms or to treat as dominant any of the varied range of factors that contribute to changing social norms.

One example of the Court's updating of doctrine in light of changing social conditions, discussed in chapter 1, is its treatment of issues involving sexual orientation. Another example is the nexus between the 1960s women's movement and the Court's increasing receptiveness to constitutional attacks on gender classifications. Before 1971, the Court had never invalidated a gender classification under the equal protection clause. By 1976, the Court had deemed gender a problematic classification. That change was very much in line with what one scholar at the time called "the single most outstanding phenomenon of our century," that is, profound changes in gender roles, including a sharp increase in the proportion of women working outside the home.[55]

To the extent the Justices respond to pressure, it is from the other branches rather than the general public. For example, elected government directly shapes Supreme Court decision making in cases where the Court takes the risk of elected government backlash into account. In the Watergate tapes case (*United States v. Nixon*), the Justices thought that President Richard Nixon might disobey a divided Court ruling—so, to speak unanimously, they compromised with each other and issued a narrow, indeterminate ruling.[56] Likewise, Chief Justice Earl Warren, recognizing potential Southern resistance to *Brown v. Board of Education*, felt strongly that the Court should issue a unanimous holding—even if it meant that the decision would be watered down to accommodate the competing preferences of different Justices.[57] Equally telling, the Court refused to hear a 1955 challenge to Virginia's prohibition of interracial marriage rather than risk "thwarting or seriously handicapping" its decision in *Brown* and, with it, its institutional prestige.[58]

The most vivid examples of the Justices taking backlash into account are decisions in which the Court distances itself from earlier, unpopular decisions.[59] In some cases, the Court's composition has changed—so it may be that appointments and confirmation politics explain the change of position.[60] In other cases, the Court is clearly responding to attacks on its earlier rulings by elected government officials.[61]

The Logic of High Impact

The idea that Justices take public opinion into account to maintain the Court's institutional standing is not unreasonable, yet there are reasons to doubt the strength of this influence. We can start with the limits of public knowledge and interest in the Court. Of course, these limits are not unique to the Court; on the whole, as decades of survey research make clear, Americans have little knowledge of politics in general.[62] This lack of knowledge is not the result of limited intelligence, limited education, or irrationality. Instead, most people are "rationally ignorant" about politics because their incentives to learn more are weak.[63]

Compared to elected government, moreover, "the Justices' newsworthy activities are infrequent."[64] There are no election campaigns, no press releases, no televised oral arguments or announcements of decisions; indeed, the Justices typically oppose the broadcasting of oral arguments to limit public discourse about the Court.[65] Only a handful of decisions each year are salient to the general public, and most of those decisions are released over the course of one or two weeks at the end of each Court term.

The nexus between presidential appointments and Supreme Court decision making on issues that matter to voters is also indirect; a single appointment does not necessarily affect the direction of the Court, and it is unclear whether or when the Court will tackle issues that matter to voters. Presidential elections, moreover, rarely take place against the backdrop of an open Supreme Court seat—let alone a Supreme Court seat where the election outcome might affect the direction of the Court. Indeed, although the political imbroglio following the death of Antonin Scalia propelled the Court to electoral significance in 2016,[66] the hospitalization of William Rehnquist one week before the 2004 elections did not register with the public. Even though there was a sharp conservative-liberal split on the Court, only 1 percent of voters rated the Court as the most important factor in their decision and fewer than 0.5 percent of voters ranked the Court as President Bush's top priority for his second term.[67]

Evidence on public knowledge of the Supreme Court is mixed. On the one hand, surveys regularly suggest that knowledge about the Court is exceedingly thin—that far more people can name two of the Seven Dwarfs than two of the Justices, to take one example.[68] Only 3 percent of Americans knew that William Rehnquist was Chief Justice of the United States; 7 percent of Americans can identify John Roberts as Chief Justice.[69] More generally, Americans are ignorant about the Constitution—fewer than one in four can name more than one First Amendment provision.[70] On the other hand, there is evidence that indicates widespread understanding of some basic attributes of the Court.[71]

For assessment of the linkage between public opinion and the Court's decisions, awareness of decisions is more important than basic knowledge about the Justices' names or the Court's institutional attributes. It is clear that the great majority of Supreme Court decisions are essentially unknown to the general public.[72] These decisions get little coverage in the news media,[73] and the public receives little information about them through other channels. As a result, a great deal of the Court's work is essentially invisible to the public. This is especially true of the mass public; polling data suggest that elites are far more aware of the Court and its handiwork.[74]

This point should be underlined. Decisions in fields such as antitrust and patent law can have powerful effects on the economic system, but there is little reason to think that there is much awareness of those decisions among the general public. Even the unusually visible and salient Microsoft antitrust trial in 1998 and 1999 received attention from only a small proportion of the public.[75]

Another example, more directly relevant and more striking, concerns the Rehnquist Court's revival of state powers under the Constitution. Between 1992 and 2006, the Court invalidated eleven federal statutes on federalism grounds.[76] In doing so, it shifted the balance between the federal government and the states substantially. These decisions were the subject of considerable commentary in law reviews, and they received attention in the elite news media.[77] Still, those decisions appeared to have low political salience. Of 229 Gallup Poll questions that explicitly referred to the Supreme Court during the period in which the decisions were handed down, there was not a single question about these decisions—or, for that matter, about any other decisions in which the Court invalidated federal statutes.[78] The choice not to ask such questions reflected the reality that few voters knew much about these decisions.

Even when people are aware of decisions, they do not necessarily have strong views about the desirability of those decisions. They may be ambivalent, or the issues in question may not be salient to them. When either condition exists, Justices would not seem to have reason to fear adverse public reactions to their rulings.[79]

Although there is little public awareness of most Supreme Court decisions as individual decisions, people may gain an impression of the Court's decisions in broad fields of policy through information that they garner from the news media. In part because of well-publicized criticisms of the Court by political leaders and news media, it is likely that a large share of the public recognized the liberalism of the Warren Court of the 1960s on civil liberties issues, especially issues of criminal procedure. This recognition is suggested by surveys taken in the 1960s that showed a strong relationship between attitudes toward the Supreme Court and both political ideology and attitudes related to ideology.[80]

In contrast, public impressions of the Court's ideological position in more recent periods do not seem to be nearly as clear. Indeed, patterns in public evaluations of the Court suggest that there is only limited awareness of the Court's rightward shift.[81] Rather, perceptions of the Court's ideological position are heavily influenced by the most visible decisions, which are not necessarily representative of the Court's policies as a whole.[82] At least prior to the Court's turn to a stronger conservatism in 2018, the most visible decisions in recent years have been more liberal than the Court's full output.[83]

But what about the most visible decisions? Certainly there are some decisions that do receive considerable coverage in the news media, so that many or even most people become aware of those decisions. Examples include *Brown v. Board of Education, Miranda v. Arizona, Roe v. Wade*, the Court's 1989 and 1990 decisions protecting flag burning, *Bush v. Gore*, the Court's 2012 response to the constitutional challenges of President Obama's health care plan, and the Court's 2013 and 2015 decisions on same-sex marriage.[84] Not only is knowledge of these decisions widespread, but also many people have strong views about whether they are desirable. It seems reasonable to think that unhappiness with such rulings will erode public support for the Court, but that is not inevitable.

It is true that public support for the Court as measured by survey items has declined since the 1980s,[85] but that decline appears to result primarily from a general growth in negative attitudes toward government. As Chief Justice John Roberts said in 2012, "I think we're low because people's view of government is low."[86] Fundamental support for the Court remains considerably higher than comparable support for Congress and the president. In one 2017 survey, for instance, respondents were asked which branch of the federal government they trusted most. The proportion choosing the Supreme Court was higher than the proportions for the other two branches combined.[87] A 2018 survey showed that confidence in the Court was far higher than for Congress and the president, and a 2018 survey of young adults showed that trust in the Court was also quite high compared with the other branches. More generally, there is widespread political support for judicial independence and a related acknowledgment of the power of the Court to interpret the Constitution to invalidate elected government action.[88] Political polarization, in other words, has fueled a general decline in support for all governmental actors; it has not eroded the Court's advantage over the other branches in public approval.

Political scientists have done considerable research on public support for the Court and—most important for our concerns—the impact of the Court's decisions on that support.[89] This research has examined both "specific support," primarily evaluation of the Court's decisional outputs, and "diffuse support," deeper views about the Court as an institution that encompass the concept of legitimacy. The findings of this body of scholarship are not entirely consistent, and there is sharp disagreement about whether disapproval of specific decisions can have a short-term effect on people's diffuse support for the

Court. But it seems clear that the Court's public standing is resilient and that the effects of its decisions on its overall legitimacy are limited in both strength and permanency. In part, this is because any negative effects of some people's disapproval of major decisions are counterbalanced to a degree by positive effects for those who approve of the same decisions. As a result, the Court's legitimacy tends to remain stable even after major and controversial decisions.[90]

These strengths of the Court's position are reflected in public reactions to *Bush v. Gore*. In the short run, approval of "the job the Supreme Court is doing"—a measure of specific support—declined considerably among Democrats and liberals.[91] Similarly, fully half of the Gore voters who were surveyed immediately after the decision chose the response option that the decision had made them "lose confidence in the U.S. Supreme Court."[92] But comparison of a 2001 survey about attitudes toward the Court with earlier surveys strongly suggests that the decision did no damage to the Court's overall level of legitimacy.[93]

This does not mean that the Court's decisions cannot have some impact on perceptions of its legitimacy. At least under unusual circumstances, trends in the Court's decisions may foster negative views of the Court as an institution. Thus, there is evidence that as of the 1990s, African Americans who came of age after the Warren Court era gave limited diffuse support to the Court relative to African Americans who were born between 1933 and 1953 and to whites. This low support may have reflected the relatively unfavorable policies of the Court toward the African American community in the period since the end of the Warren Court.[94] But that trend appears to be an exception to the rule. And even if decisional trends have had other effects on diffuse support for the Court, it is striking that the Court continues to elicit much greater support than do the other branches of government.

Thus, Justices do not seem to have much need to take public opinion into account when they reach their decisions. Most of their work receives little attention from the public at large, and little of it creates much excitement among the public. The Supreme Court's growing conservatism on economic issues in the post–Warren Court era is consequential, but it has gone largely unnoticed outside of some elite circles. Even widely observed and unpopular decisions are unlikely to do much harm to the Court's standing. Thus, it appears, Justices who simply followed their own preferences—legal, policy, or a combination of the two—would do no harm to the Court as an institution.

The Justices still might act on a concern with legitimacy if they exaggerate the fragility of that legitimacy or if they are highly risk averse. In the current era, Justices do refer to the Court's legitimacy in their opinions with some frequency, sometimes indicating that it is a consideration that they are taking into account.[95] On the other hand, there is no reason to think that Justices would often act on even an exaggerated sense of vulnerability. Justices who take positions that differ sharply from their preferences in important cases in the interest of protecting the Court's legitimacy pay an immediate price for an uncertain benefit in the future. Justices who regularly depart from their preferences to help keep the Court's overall ideological position in line with public opinion pay an even bigger price for the same uncertain benefit. In the absence of empirical evidence to the contrary, it is extremely doubtful that Justices are often willing to pay that price. We now turn to evidence about Justices' responses to public opinion.

The General Public: Empirical Evidence

Influence of the general public on Supreme Court decisions could be manifested in multiple forms. As discussed earlier, scholars have given particular attention to two of those forms. The first is refraining from decisions that conflict with public sentiment, especially on issues on which strong sentiment exists. The second is covariation between the ideological content of the Court's decisions and what has been called the "public mood"—the overall ideological position of the general public.[96] There is a long-standing body of empirical research on the first form and a more recent body of research on the second.

In his two books on public opinion and Supreme Court decision making, Thomas Marshall addressed the first form broadly and systematically by examining public opinion surveys on issues that the Supreme Court addressed at around the same time as the surveys. The decisions covered the period from 1934 to 2005. On the whole, of course, these issues are ones that are expected to be salient to the public. On these issues, Marshall found that the Court and the majority of the public were on the same side around 60 percent of the time. The Court was about as likely to agree with the public when there was a "landslide" margin in surveys as when the margin was closer.[97] Some Justices took positions in agreement with the public more often than others, though none were strictly majoritarian.[98]

Marshall's findings can be interpreted in multiple ways, but the overall rate of agreement is not as high as we would expect if the Court was regularly responsive to public sentiment. A 60 percent agreement rate is not a great deal higher than the result of a flip of the coin. Further, the agreement that does exist does not necessarily reflect direct public influence on the Justices. For one thing, the appointment process could link the public and the Court: the outcomes of presidential elections reflect public attitudes, and appointments to the Court staff the Court with Justices who share the president's views.[99] For another, specific events and broader social developments shape the issue positions of Justices and the public in similar ways. As Benjamin Cardozo put it, "The great tides and currents which engulf the rest of men, do not turn aside in their course, and pass the judges by."[100] And when surveys are taken after a relevant Court decision rather than before, alignment between Court and public might be fostered by the Court's impact on public opinion.[101] Thus, agreement between Supreme Court decisions and public opinion may result from the indirect influence of the public through the outcomes of presidential elections, from the influence of the Court on the public, or from social forces that do not involve influence of either Court or public on the other.

Other studies, especially those that take a historical perspective, focus more narrowly on individual decisions and sets of decisions that are highly salient to the public. These decisions have the greatest potential to threaten the Court's legitimacy if they are at variance with public opinion. As a result, some scholars argue, the Justices rein themselves in as a means to avoid that threat. Jeffrey Rosen, summarizing the historical evidence, expressed both ideas: "It should be obvious by now that the Supreme Court has followed the public's views about constitutional questions throughout its history and, on the rare occasions that it has been even modestly out of line with popular majorities, it has gotten into trouble."[102]

It is difficult to assess the argument that the Court has refrained from adopting decisions and lines of doctrine on major issues that are unpopular with the public, in part because episodes in the Court's history are susceptible to multiple interpretations. And we have no direct evidence on public opinion for most of the Court's history. But it seems clear that the Court has not always adhered closely to public views, even at times when deviation from those views carried potential costs to the public.

One relatively recent example is the work of the Court under Chief Justice Earl Warren, especially in the 1960s. The Warren Court adopted a series of expansions of constitutional protections for civil liberties in fields such as freedom of expression, racial equality, and criminal procedure. Some major lines of Warren Court policy appeared to enjoy at least substantial support from the public, though seldom strong majority support. But on other issues, the Court's positions appeared to be at considerable variance with the state of public opinion. This was true of most of the Court's expansions of the rights of criminal defendants, its decisions limiting religious observances in public schools, and its limits on the regulation of sexually oriented material. The school prayer decisions, to take one example, were highly unpopular.[103] In criminal justice, the Court ignored both opinion polls showing opposition to earlier Warren Court criminal procedure decisions and the calls by twenty-seven states in *Miranda* for the Court to slow down its criminal procedure revolution.[104] By 1968, public opposition to the Court's decisions was sufficiently strong that presidential candidates Richard Nixon and George Wallace made their own opposition to those decisions a significant element of their campaigns.[105]

The disjunction between public opinion and some Warren Court decision making underscores the critical difference between the direct influence of political elites through the nomination and confirmation process and the indirect influence of the public through elections. The national political establishment may be to the left or the right of median voter preferences; consequently, the fact that the Justices often reflect prevailing president-Congress preferences at the time of their nomination does not necessarily mean that Court decisions track either public opinion or the preferences of elected officials. As one scholar put it, the Warren Court "virtually rewrote the corpus of our constitutional law" in ways that did not always match public opinion;[106] from 1962 to 1967, President Kennedy's and President Johnson's Court appointees played a key role in that development.

Even so, Jeffrey Rosen and Barry Friedman argue that the Warren Court was basically acting in accord with public opinion. Both point to issues on which the Warren Court's constitutional jurisprudence arguably was in tune with public opinion.[107] Even when the Court took highly unpopular positions, as it did in its decisions on internal security in the mid-1950s and in its school prayer decisions, Friedman suggests that the Justices may have thought they were in accord with the general public but simply misunderstood public opinion.[108] These readings of the evidence are a useful caution against reading the Warren Court's record as one that was wildly at variance with public sentiment. But they do not overcome the reality that the Justices on the majority side in a number of significant decisions took positions that were highly unpopular among the general public.

There are more recent examples of decisions on salient issues that were highly unpopular. One is flag burning; in the months after the Court's 1989 decision providing First Amendment protection for flag burning as a form of protest, about three-quarters of the public disagreed with the Court.[109] Another is eminent domain, on which a survey after the Court's 2005 decision approving a city's use of its power to take homes for a development project found 81 percent disagreement.[110] A third is corporate speech; 80 percent of Americans disagreed (and 65 percent strongly disagreed) with the Court's 2010 ruling allowing corporations to spend unlimited sums advancing their political agendas.[111] The breadth of public opposition to these decisions was matched by its depth, which was reflected in strong attacks on the Court and efforts to blunt the effects of its rulings.[112]

Of particular interest are occasions in which the Court rules on an issue, the Justices are confronted with evidence that their decision was unpopular among the public, and they then rule again on the same general issue. Adherence to the unpopular position indicates that the Justices who were on the "wrong" side in the original decision (or at least enough Justices to preserve a majority) were willing to stay on that side despite the evidence of public disapproval. In contrast, shifting over to the popular position might be explained by acquiescence to public views.

We can start with instances in which the Court did shift to the position held by a majority of the public. It is not difficult to find instances in which such shifts appeared to occur, although relevant public opinion data are not available in all of them. Examples include the Court's abandoning its opposition to New Deal economic policies beginning in 1937,[113] its shift away from civil liberties protections for people accused of subversive activities in the late 1950s,[114] its approval of a new set of death penalty laws in 1976 after rejecting existing laws in 1972,[115] and its softening of support for the procedural rights of criminal defendants in the 1970s.[116]

These examples illustrate the reality that movement toward a popular position does not necessarily indicate direct public influence on the Court. The Court's abandoning its opposition to New Deal legislation, a product of shifts in position by two pivotal Justices, appears to be a tactical withdrawal in the face of strong criticism from the president and Congress along with other elites, although public opinion may also have played a role.[117] The shift of the late 1950s was influenced both by the near enactment of legislation stripping power from the Court and by criticisms of the Court by bar groups and distinguished judges.[118] The death penalty decisions of 1976 may well have reflected acquiescence by the Court's pivotal Justices to strong public support for the death penalty, but other factors may have been important as well or instead.[119]

Further, when the Court as a body moves closer to the views of the general public, that movement is often a byproduct of changes in the Court's membership rather than changes in the positions of individual Justices in response to public opinion. One example is the Court's growing conservatism on issues of criminal procedure as the Warren Court became the Burger and Rehnquist Courts. Other examples include the Court's expansion of the states' power to regulate abortion and rulings that facilitated the termination of busing as a remedy for school segregation.[120] In such instances, the Court was not responding to the public but to its own members' views about issues of legal policy.

Even more striking are the instances in which the Court stands fast despite public disapproval. Before personnel changes contributed to the Court's reversing course on busing and the regulation of second-trimester abortions, the Court maintained its position in the face of blistering attacks by lawmakers—whose condemnations matched public opinion polls.[121] Despite incontrovertible evidence that the Court's 1989 decision striking down a state prohibition of flag burning was highly unpopular, the five Justices in the majority ignored that disapproval, as well as strong pressure from the other branches, to strike down a similar federal law a year later.[122] School prayer is an even more dramatic illustration of the same phenomenon. Not only did the Court reinforce its unpopular 1962 decision against school prayer a year later, but also it has struck down other forms of religious observance in public schools since then, even as its membership has become more conservative and public disapproval has continued.[123]

In 2008, the Court was presented with an unusual opportunity to reconsider an unpopular ruling in the same case. The Court had invalidated the death penalty for sexual assault of a child, a ruling that ran contrary to the majority view of the public. After it became clear that the Justices had not been aware of a relevant federal statute, they were asked to grant a rehearing in the case, but no member of the five-Justice majority in the original decision voted to do so.[124]

In 2012 and 2014, the Supreme Court reaffirmed and extended another unpopular ruling, *Citizens United v. FEC*. Even though 72 percent of Americans backed congressional efforts to impose limits on corporate and union contributions,[125] the Court in 2012 summarily reversed a Montana Supreme Court ruling upholding a state law limiting corporate contributions, a decision grounded in Montana's unusual history of corporate corruption.[126] In 2014, the Court rejected aggregate limits to the total amount that an individual might give to all candidates and parties.[127] In both these cases, the five Justices who made up the *Citizens United* majority bucked public opinion in favor of a position that had strong support among Republican Party elites.[128]

The evidence that we have discussed is not definitive. Ideally, we would like to know the proportion of the time that Justices adopt particular positions to adhere to public sentiment and the proportion in which they choose to take positions despite unfavorable public attitudes. There is no way to ascertain those proportions. But the frequency with which the Court takes unpopular positions and the occasions on which it adheres to those positions despite clear evidence of their unpopularity are striking. In light of the evidence that the Justices have little to fear from public disapproval, there is good reason to be skeptical about the belief that the Justices generally rein themselves in to avoid running afoul of public opinion.

As some of our examples indicate, there are times when the Justices do seem to depart from their preferences to avoid coming into conflict with the general public. Moreover, a case can be made that public opinion sets outer limits on the Court's decisions, effectively putting certain possible decisions off the table. Thus, to take two examples, *Roe v. Wade* and *Obergefell v. Hodges* were highly controversial when they were handed down,[129] but thirty years earlier each would have been unthinkable because there was little public support for legalization of abortion or same-sex marriage. But it was not just public attitudes that might have made those decisions unthinkable: elites, including the Justices themselves, would also have dismissed the arguments for those legal positions.[130]

The second form of possible influence for public opinion is a process in which Justices adjust the overall ideological content of their decisions in response to shifts in the ideological content of public opinion. As the public becomes more liberal or more conservative, the Justices (or at least the Court's pivotal Justices) might move in the same direction. Using James Stimson's measure of "public mood," the overall ideological position of the public on issues,[131] several studies have analyzed the statistical impact of changes over time in the public mood on the mix of liberal and conservative decisions by the Court or the mix of liberal and conservative votes by individual Justices. These studies control for other influences on the Court's ideological tendencies, such as measures of the Justices' own ideological preferences.[132]

Taking various analytic approaches, these studies differ considerably in their findings. But nearly all find some evidence that individual Justices or the Court as a whole move along the ideological scale in tandem with the general public, even with controls for other factors that affect decisions.[133] This evidence rests on methodological choices that are subject to disagreement. Moreover, the evidence can often be interpreted in multiple ways, including how one assesses the magnitude of the statistical relationship between the public mood and decisional outputs.

A key question is the extent to which this covariation actually results from public influence on the Justices. As we have discussed, one possible source of this covariation is change in the Court's membership that stems from the outcomes of presidential elections. Studies of covariation take that source into account either by controlling for the ideological composition of the Court or by focusing on individual Justices. More difficult to take into account is the possibility that Justices and members of the public are moved in the same direction by the same events and developments. One study that sought to measure and control for developments that affect the public mood had mixed findings.[134]

The body of evidence about the impact of public opinion on Supreme Court decisions is far from definitive—it is incomplete and susceptible to differing interpretations. But read in conjunction with the logic of the Justices' responses to public opinion, this evidence strongly suggests that the public does not exert a powerful influence on the Justices. Even so, this does not mean that the Justices are essentially autonomous and unaffected by the world outside the Court. In addition to the influence that the public does exert, the Justices are affected more fundamentally by the social and political elites in their environment. We turn next to those elites.

The Impact of Elites

For scholars who posit that the general public exerts an influence on the Supreme Court, the primary motivation for accepting that influence is instrumental—the desire to maintain the Court's institutional power and standing. We have argued that the Justices' interest in the esteem of individuals and groups that are important to them creates the potential for a more powerful influence on them. In turn, because those important audiences come primarily from elite segments of society, it is elites that have the greater impact on the Justices.

The idea that judges are oriented primarily toward elite audiences (beyond the other branches of government) diverges from the standard perspectives on judicial behavior that are incorporated into political science models. But this idea is not novel. Those scholars who have pointed to judges' interest in their reputations give primary attention to elite groups.[135] Thomas Miceli and Metin Cosgel, for instance, identify the relevant audience as other judges and people in the legal profession.[136]

Moreover, this idea makes considerable sense. As we have noted, the people whose esteem is most important to the Justices come predominately from social and political elites. Justices' personal circles are composed primarily of people in those elites. They interact chiefly with elites, and they are assessed by elite segments of the news media, as well as the legal community. If Justices' interest in how they are regarded by other people influences what they do as members of the Supreme Court, that influence comes overwhelmingly from elite segments of American society. Thus, it is the opinions of social and political elites and especially the most relevant segments of those elites that have the greatest impact on the Justices.

Our own analysis of the impact of elites on the Court begins in this section. We examine segments of the political and social elites that are in the best positions to influence decision making in the Court and then consider evidence of that influence.

Elite Audiences

As we suggested earlier, people in the legal profession—especially people in the most elite segments of that profession—are a highly salient audience for Supreme Court Justices. The Justices typically have personal ties with other legal elites, their training and professional experience make lawyers relevant to them, and they are likely to see lawyers as the people who are best qualified to assess their work. For their part, other judges and legal academics evaluate the Justices' votes and opinions more intensely than anyone else.[137] Put differently, Justices have particular reason to care about the esteem with which they are held by other legal elites, and those elites are especially likely to base their esteem on assessment of the Justices' work as decision makers.

Legal elites may be even more important to Justices in the current era than in past eras, because the Justices who have been appointed to the Court in the past half century typically come from careers in law rather than politics. In a development that has received considerable attention, presidents since 1969 have turned primarily to sitting judges for their nominees to the Court.[138] Since the appointments of Lewis Powell and William Rehnquist in 1971, the only appointee who was not serving on an appellate court was Elena Kagan (appointed in 2010).[139] Just as important, the prior careers of the Justices appointed since 1969 have been dominated by work in the legal system rather than political positions.[140] Indeed, Kagan and Rehnquist were high-ranking Justice Department lawyers at the time of their appointment; Powell was managing partner of a large law firm and a former president of the American Bar Association. This trend is also underlined by the fact that Sandra Day

O'Connor, selected in 1981, was the most recent appointee who had ever run for public office.

Moreover, the links between the Justices and other segments of the legal elite in the current era are striking. All but two Justices who have sat on the Court since 1987 attended Harvard, Yale, or Stanford Law School;[141] six of the eleven Justices who have served on the Court since 2010 clerked for a Supreme Court Justice;[142] four were law professors at elite law schools;[143] and five had argued cases in the Court.[144] Justices draw their clerks from the same kinds of elite law schools that they attended,[145] and their law clerks frequently become law professors or Supreme Court advocates themselves.[146] A 2015 study, for example, found that all but one of the top eight Supreme Court advocates in the private bar had clerked on the Court or served in the solicitor general's office.[147] Supreme Court Justices also cultivate their reputations with elite lawyer audiences through regular appearances at law schools and bar groups. As we will discuss later, the Justices' close ties with the elite segment of the legal profession give that audience special influence with them.

One indicator of the salience of the legal profession to the Justices is the public and semipublic appearances they make. It is striking that the Justices collectively take the time and effort to make substantial numbers of appearances, making use of opportunities to interact with relevant audiences and to enjoy—and potentially enhance—their reputations. The volume of such appearances and other means to reach out to their audiences may be unusually high in the current era,[148] but they were common in earlier eras as well.[149]

More specifically, the Justices' appearances show that they give particular attention to legal audiences. Table 2.1 provides summary information on reported appearances between 2014 and 2018.[150] The sheer number of appearances is noteworthy, especially because not all appearances are reported. Among the reported appearances, at least half were before legal groups—law schools, the bar, and the bench.

A longer-range count of appearances outside of DC for which the Justices received more than minimal reimbursements, only a portion of all their appearances, provides a similar picture.[151] During the years 1988–2017, at least 53 percent of those appearances were sponsored by law schools or bar and bench groups. Another 23 percent were listed under colleges and universities, and it appears that many of these appearances were specifically at law schools.

Although we focus here on legal audiences, it is worth noting that the great majority of the Justices' appearances put them in contact with social

Table 2.1. Reported Public Appearances by Supreme Court Justices, 2014–2018

Justice	Total Appearances	Law Schools	Other College/ University	Bar/Bench	Other
Alito	64	21	6	18	19
Breyer	113	17	10	24	62
Ginsburg	127	23	17	37	50
Gorsuch	12	2	3	4	3
Kagan	53	22	4	18	9
Kennedy	25	6	2	12	5
Roberts	31	5	4	18	4
Scalia	40	10	5	12	13
Sotomayor	128	27	38	28	35
Thomas	30	11	4	10	5
TOTAL	623	144 (23.1%)	93 (14.9%)	181 (29.1%)	205 (32.9%)

elites. The Justices frequently appear before groups that are not part of academia or the legal profession, but the people who organize and attend most of those events are those with a particular interest in the Supreme Court or in the cultural topics that frequently are involved—from opera to legal history.[152]

Undoubtedly, the frequency of the Justices' interactions with legal audiences of various sorts results in part from their sense of duty as Justices. But that frequency also reflects the Justices' interest in legal audiences. In themselves, such appearances reinforce the relevance of those audiences to the Justices. Further, for at least some Justices, their clerks and "the larger law school culture around which the Justices sometimes travel" convey evidence to them "of the current attitudes of young intellectuals, of law professors, and of the intellectual classes in general."[153]

The importance of legal academics should be underlined. Beyond their direct interactions with law faculty and students, Justices are linked with them by their clerks and by some of the attorneys who appear before the Court. Many members of both groups serve as editors of the nation's leading law reviews, and many of the clerks later become academics who write journal articles and books about legal issues in the Court and about the Court itself.[154] More generally, legal academics function as the most knowledgeable reviewers of the

Justices' work, and their expertise gives their judgments weight with people whose opinions the Justices care about and with the Justices themselves.

The salience of elite legal audiences to the Justices can affect their decision making in multiple ways. The most distinctive effects relate to norms that are widely shared within the legal profession. In turn, among these norms, the most consequential is the emphasis on legal bases for decisions. As we discuss in the second part of this section, legal audiences are a key source of differences in the decision-making process between the Supreme Court and the other branches of government.

A second relevant segment of the elite is political and ideological groups. For most of the Court's history, it was common for Justices to have substantial experience in electoral politics and nonjudicial office. This experience brought other participants in politics into their social circles, and it undoubtedly enhanced the relevance of political parties and other political groups to the Justices.

The changes in Justices' career experiences that we have described might seem to make political and ideological groups less relevant to them, but we think this is not the case. For one thing, although Earl Warren was the last career politician appointed to the Court, even today most Justices have spent some time working in the "political" branches of government before they joined the judiciary. For Clarence Thomas, Samuel Alito, Brett Kavanaugh, Elena Kagan, and Sonia Sotomayor, among others, that service lasted for several years.[155]

More important, Justices today are like their predecessors in that most if not all of them have affective ties to political groups such as the parties, to ideological groups, to groups with a position on particular issues, or to some combination of those categories. In an era of political polarization, when those affective ties have tended to strengthen among people who are interested in politics and policy, undoubtedly that is true of Supreme Court Justices as well.

A more specific development in the current era is the creation of formal groups within the legal profession that have strong ideological orientations. Unlike earlier eras, partisanship and ideology are linked today in ways that facilitate the interface of political actors with ideological law-oriented groups. The Federalist Society was established in 1982 as a counterbalance to what its founders saw as a liberal bias in the legal academy, and the Society has grown to become a major center of activity, a reference group, and a participant in legal and policy debates on behalf of conservatives.[156] In 2001, the American Constitution Society (ACS) was established as a liberal counterpart to the

Federalist Society.[157] Although it does not rival the Federalist Society in influence, it has become a significant organization.

Lawyers who developed affective ties with political and ideological groups prior to their judicial service are likely to maintain their identifications with those groups during their service on the Supreme Court. Indeed, it is common for Justices to continue interactions with groups on one side of the political and ideological divide. Those interactions are not unique to the current era. One example from an earlier era is the lunches that included liberals on the Supreme Court and the federal court of appeals for the District of Columbia circuit along with other Washingtonians in the 1960s and 1970s.[158] But those interactions have become more visible with the establishment of the Federalist Society and the ACS. We will discuss the Justices' participation in activities of the two groups in some detail in chapter 4, but two examples may be useful. When the Federalist Society celebrated its twenty-fifth anniversary at its 2007 annual convention, Chief Justice John Roberts and Justices Antonin Scalia, Clarence Thomas, and Samuel Alito all appeared at the convention.[159] For their part, Justices Stephen Breyer, Ruth Bader Ginsburg, and Sonia Sotomayor have been keynote speakers at the national convention of the ACS.

These linkages between the Justices and groups with political and ideological orientations might make Justices more sensitive to the political implications of cases, such as their potential impact on the fortunes of the political parties. But probably the most pervasive effect of the linkages is to reinforce the impact of the Justices' ideological leanings. If Justices care about the esteem of like-minded people, their incentives to follow a consistent conservative or liberal path are thereby enhanced.

The news media that report on the Supreme Court's work and make judgments about that work are heterogeneous in their attributes, increasingly so with the development of new types of media that make use of the internet. Of particular importance to the Justices are the media with wide audiences among elite groups that are salient to the Justices. Like other people, Justices may care about depictions of their work in the news media in themselves, but even more significant is the potential influence of media depictions on the opinions of people who are part of the Justices' reference groups.

The salience of the news media to at least some Justices is indicated by their willingness to interact with reporters and their sensitivity to portrayals of them in the media. Some Justices grant on-the-record or off-the-record interviews to reporters, and some develop acquaintanceships with reporters. One scholar, for instance, reported that several reporters referred to "a close personal relationship" with Justice Harry Blackmun.[160] The files of some Justices include news stories about cases, and some Justices are alert to critical coverage.[161] Justices Potter Stewart and Antonin Scalia even wrote letters to the editor to complain about news stories.[162]

The Justices' interest in favorable media coverage might affect their decisions in specific cases, especially if decisions on related issues had received heavy criticism from reporters and editorial writers. Some observers of the Court have perceived that the news media had a more pervasive impact on a subset of Justices. Conservative commentators who were disappointed with the decisional records of several Republican appointees to the Court from the 1950s to the early 1990s argued that the unexpected moderation or liberalism of those appointees reflected the influence of elites—especially elite news media—that were predominantly liberal.[163]

The validity of this argument can be debated, but it certainly should not be dismissed out of hand. If Justices care about their reputations, it is plausible that they would be swayed toward the positions taken by a relatively homogeneous press that covers the Court, especially if other segments of the elite were reinforcing those media. In chapter 3, we will look at the evidence on whether the media and the larger elite audience of which they are a part had such an effect in the era prior to the current era of high polarization within the elite. In chapter 4, we will consider the ramifications of the growth of partisan media outlets and the related rise of personalized media—where individuals gravitate toward news outlets that reinforce pre-existing biases.

We should emphasize that any influence of social and political elites on the Justices does not necessarily stem from deliberate choices by the Justices. To the extent that Justices act in ways that might draw favorable reactions from relevant elites, they are likely to do so unconsciously. For that matter, elite opinion may influence Justices' choices by shaping their preferences. In other words, Justices may come to share the attitudes that predominate among relevant elites, so that they need not depart from the positions they favor to appeal to elite audiences. The existence of multiple mechanisms of influence enhances the potential for elite opinion to influence the Justices' behavior.

The Justices' elite audiences might affect multiple aspects of that behavior, of which we will consider two. The first is the ideological content of the policies that the Court adopts, especially on the major issues that are most visible and consequential. We will examine the relationship between elite opinion and the Court's decisions on controversial issues of civil liberties. The second is related to norms that are accepted by legal elites on how the Justices make their choices as decision makers—specifically norms of consensual decision making and adherence to legal analysis.

Elite Opinion and Supreme Court Decisions

If Justices do respond to elite opinion, they must be aware of that opinion. Direct interactions between Justices and other elites help to create that awareness, as does the Justices' exposure to news media. There is also an institutional mode of communication, amicus briefs, and that mode merits consideration because of its potential importance. Aside from their other functions, amicus briefs provide information about the views of elite groups.[164] Among those elites, academics may hold a special place: in a survey of seventy Supreme Court law clerks, 88 percent said they would be inclined to give "closer attention" to amicus briefs filed by academics—especially the prominent academics who teach at the nation's leading law schools (the very schools most law clerks come from).[165]

One important piece of information for the Court is the overall stance of political elites. In this respect, amicus briefs filed in the 2004, 2006, and 2008 enemy combatant cases are noteworthy.[166] While elite groups consistently opposed Bush administration claims about both presidential war making and the rights of enemy combatants, elite opposition to the administration intensified throughout this period. In 2004 filings, several prominent academics supported administration claims regarding executive branch control of the Guantanamo Bay detention facility; still, more than two out of three amicus briefs opposed the administration. In 2006 and 2008, no academics filed briefs supporting the administration. Further, bar groups, retired federal court judges, and several hundred members of the European Union and United Kingdom parliaments filed briefs opposing the Bush administration.[167] Elite opposition to the administration was also manifest in academic commentary and newspapers editorials: all major newspapers (except the *Wall Street Journal*) formally opposed the administration, as did the vast majority of academic commentary on these cases.[168]

Amicus briefs can provide more specific information about elite positions. During most of the Court's history amicus briefs were relatively rare, even in major cases: none were submitted in *Lochner v. New York*, and few were submitted in *Brown v. Board of Education* and *Roe v. Wade*.[169] Over the last several decades, amicus briefs have become far more common. Few cases lack any amicus briefs. And even in the Court's 2016 term, with a dearth of "big" cases, there was an average of ten amicus briefs per case.[170] As a result, Justices can now learn a good deal from the lineups of groups on the two sides.

For Justices who have affective ties to political groups on one side of the ideological spectrum, amicus briefs convey a picture of where conservatives and liberals stand on the specific issues that arise in a particular case or the broader issues that exist in fields such as criminal procedure and freedom of expression. That information is especially helpful when it is not obvious which sides liberals and conservatives could be expected to take.[171] Not surprisingly, as Republicans and Democrats have become more polarized, there has been a dramatic upswing in amicus briefs signed only by Republican members of Congress or only by Democratic members.[172] Moreover, the Supreme Court bar regularly coordinates the filing of varied amicus briefs to signal to the Justices where political and academic elites stand on the issues before the Court.[173] These briefs are especially important to Supreme Court clerks who will later work with these very lawyers in filing amicus briefs before the Court.[174]

Similarly, when specific elites take unexpected positions as amici, those positions can affect Justices' perceptions of the issues in a case. One example is the amicus briefs in cases arising from challenges to affirmative action in university admissions. In *Grutter v. Bollinger* (2004), which involved admissions to the University of Michigan Law School, 83 of the 102 amicus briefs backed the university's affirmative action program.[175] That tilt in itself was striking, especially because the briefs that supported Grutter's challenge to the university program generally did not represent significant elite groups. But especially noteworthy were the briefs supporting affirmative action from the business community and from retired military officers—groups that would generally be regarded as conservative. There was a similar pattern in the lineup of amici in *Fisher v. University of Texas* (2016), in which supporters of the university included a substantial list of major corporations, thirty-six former military officers who had held leadership positions, and even a set of leading college basketball coaches.

Gay rights is another example. Justice Scalia famously lamented the Court's recognition of a right to same-sex sodomy in *Lawrence v. Texas* as "the product of a Court, which is the product of a law-profession culture, that has largely signed on to the so-called homosexual agenda."[176] Scalia may have been thinking about a coordinated campaign by attorneys for same-sex couples, attorneys who worked with several members of the Supreme Court bar to file high-profile amicus briefs on behalf of academics and professional associations. Paul Smith, who argued for Lawrence, said that "sophisticated parties and counsel often convene meetings of potential amici in an attempt to form coalitions and to influence the nature of the presentations that will be made."[177] The team that coordinated the challenge to sodomy laws dubbed the person in charge of these filings as their "*Amicus* Queen"; in related litigation involving a successful challenge to the Defense of Marriage Act, the coordinator was called the "amicus whisperer."[178] These coordinated efforts paid off: amicus briefs made it clear that Supreme Court lawyers, academics, and other professionals supported the cause of gay rights.

There is some evidence that the lineup of groups that submit amicus briefs influences the Court's decisions. The numbers of amicus briefs on the two sides appear to affect the likelihood that the Court will rule in one direction or the other, and the kinds of interest groups that support the two sides may have an impact as well.[179] The Justices' use of briefs in their opinions sometimes suggests the existence of influence; Justice Sandra Day O'Connor's citation of briefs from the business and military communities in her opinion for the Court in *Grutter* is one example.[180] Undoubtedly, some Justices have negative reactions to the segments of political and social elites that are associated with certain amicus briefs. In any event, amici serve the function of informing Justices about the distribution of opinion among social and political elites on the issues that they address in their decisions.

Our discussion of amicus groups highlights the difficulty of pinpointing how much elites affect a Justice's decision making. After all, the Justices' own inclinations and the views of the elites that serve as reference groups undoubtedly coincide in many instances, in part because people are drawn to groups with which they share values. That coincidence of views does not mean that such groups do not shape the Justices' positions in cases,[181] but it creates complications for efforts to ascertain that influence.

However, the difficulty of identifying this kind of influence is reduced somewhat when Justices change positions on an issue from one case to another, because something other than stable personal preferences must account for that change. Elite audiences are one potential source of such changes.

Two examples involve the possible influence of academics and especially the news media. The first example concerns the media alone. In *Gannett v. DePasquale*, the Court reached a complicated decision in which it held that the Sixth Amendment did not guarantee public access to pretrial proceedings in criminal cases.[182] One year later, after a storm of criticism in the news media,[183] the Court held in *Richmond Newspapers v. Virginia* that the First Amendment did protect public access to trials.[184]

The two decisions can be reconciled, since they focused on different phases of criminal proceedings and were based primarily on different constitutional rights. But Justice Potter Stewart's opinion for the Court in *Gannett* suggested that the Sixth Amendment right did not apply to trials either, and his opinion also turned aside a First Amendment argument. Thus, the three Justices who were in the majority in both decisions (Stewart, Warren Burger, and John Paul Stevens) did seem to shift positions, and those shifts may reflect the media criticism. Indeed, Burger and Stevens were among the four Justices who commented publicly about the *Gannett* decision after it was issued, both of them apparently seeking to dampen criticism of the Court.[185]

The other example involved a direct shift in the positions of three Justices. In *Minersville School District v. Gobitis* (1940), the Court ruled by an 8–1 vote that public school students could be required to salute the flag. These students, all Jehovah's Witnesses, had refused to salute the flag on religious grounds.[186] Three years later, in *West Virginia State Board of Education v. Barnette* (1943), the Court explicitly overturned *Gobitis.*[187] The earlier decision was heavily criticized by law journals, the press, and religious organizations. Thirty-one of thirty-nine law review pieces that discussed the decision were critical of it.[188] Newspapers and magazines accused the Court of violating constitutional rights and buckling to popular hysteria.[189] This criticism may have influenced the three Justices—Hugo Black, William O. Douglas, and Frank Murphy—who shifted their positions in the *Barnette* case. According to Justice Felix Frankfurter, Douglas reported that Black had changed his view of the issue because "he has been reading the papers."[190]

These illustrations suggest the potential for elite groups—the Justices' personal circles, the mass media, or others—to pull Justices away from certain issue positions. They are especially striking because shifts in Justices' positions within a relatively short period are unusual. Of course, such illustrations have the same limitations as anecdotal evidence of the impact of mass public opinion on the Justices. For one thing, the influence of elite groups cannot easily be isolated from other forces that shape the Justices' positions. For example, the Court in *Barnette* may also have been moved by reports of hundreds of violent attacks against Jehovah's Witnesses, as well as signals sent by Congress and the executive branch.[191] Further, illustrative evidence does not tell us the frequency with which an influence operates. However, it seems highly plausible that the prospective and actual reactions of salient elite audiences to Justices' positions shape what the Justices do.

The opinions of social and political elites may be especially relevant to the Court's decisions in civil liberties. The Warren Court adopted innovative positions expanding liberties on a range of issues, especially during the 1960s. Although the Courts that followed the Warren Court have more mixed records on civil liberties, many of their most visible decisions also expanded liberties, including the 1972 decision that invalidated the existing death penalty laws,[192] *Roe v. Wade* and later decisions that limited state regulation of abortion,[193] and the decisions that prohibited discrimination based on sexual orientation.[194]

All of these decisions were controversial, and some seemed to run sharply against the views of most of the general public. As we have discussed, the series of libertarian innovations during the Warren Court is especially difficult to reconcile with a conception of public opinion as a powerful influence on the Justices. More than anything else, those innovations reflect the Justices' own values. But the Court's support for civil liberties in the face of public disapproval may also be fostered by the attitudes of the elite audiences that are most relevant to the Justices. Indeed, there is good reason to conclude that the education and socialization of elites tend to make them more favorable than other people to protection of individual rights.[195]

Ideally, we would compare the attitudes of mass and elite segments of the public toward the Court's libertarian decisions. Unfortunately, surveys that single out elite groups and that include questions about Supreme Court decisions are rare or nonexistent. But one landmark study of attitudes toward civil liberties came close. That study, by Herbert McClosky and Alida Brill, directly surveyed "community leaders and activists" such as lawyers alongside the general public and found much greater support for a range of rights among the leaders and activists.[196] Although the survey questions were not keyed to Supreme Court decisions, individual items that tapped the subject matter of the Court's past decisions expanding rights typically found the community leaders considerably more favorable than the general public.[197] A much larger number of questions were related less directly to Court decisions but captured attitudes relevant to acceptance of those decisions, and those questions produced similar patterns.

The attitudes of elites toward civil liberties issues during the Warren Court era and for some years afterward were reflected in the Court's decisions expanding the scope of constitutional rights. As Mark Graber has pointed out, this was largely because most of the Justices appointed to the Court in that era shared this "elite consensus."[198] But the substantial consensus in views among elites who were most relevant to the Justices reinforced their support for expansive conceptions of individual rights.

Opinion is far from homogeneous among social and political elites. Indeed, since the time of the McClosky-Brill study (published in 1983), political polarization has widened the gap in opinion between people in elite groups who are Republican and conservative and those who are Democratic and liberal. Still, for the reasons discussed by McClosky and Brill, among others, there is good reason to expect a continuing (though perhaps reduced) gap between elites and nonelite groups in support for civil liberties values that have been advanced by major Supreme Court decisions.

We can probe mass and elite attitudes further by examining the relationship between education and approval of Supreme Court decisions in surveys of public opinion. Highly educated people are not synonymous with social and political elites, but there is substantial overlap between the two groups. Thus, we can learn a good deal by comparing survey respondents who have high levels of education—specifically, postgraduate education—with other respondents.

Analyses of survey findings in one book show that highly educated people generally have more favorable attitudes toward the Court's expansions of rights and toward the rights themselves than do other respondents. This was particularly true of the period before 1990 when the most educated Republicans and Democrats converged on the very social issues that now divide the parties. During this prepolarization period, highly educated people—as compared to the mass public—backed Court rulings on school desegregation, school prayer, abortion, gender roles, and flag burning.[199]

To provide additional evidence about the relationship between education and support for pro–civil liberties rulings, we identified surveys on the subjects of such rulings that were more or less contemporaneous with the relevant Court decisions and that directly compared people who had postgraduate education with other respondents. The results are shown in Table 2.2.[200]

The table shows that even in the current period of high elite polarization, there is a tendency—albeit one with clear exceptions—for pro–civil liberties decisions by the Court to align more closely with the opinions of highly educated people than with the views of other people. Justice Scalia alluded to this pattern in several dissenting opinions, including one in which he complained that the "Court has no business imposing upon all Americans the resolution favored by the elite class from which the Members of this institution are selected."[201] Whether or not Justice Scalia's complaint was justified, he pointed accurately to the Court's tendency to support elite values on social issues. That tendency is especially striking for issues on which the Court majority continued to diverge sharply from mass public opinion even after that

Table 2.2. Attitudes of Respondents with Postgraduate Education, Compared with Attitudes of Other Respondents, on Selected Civil Liberties Issues in the Supreme Court

			% With Positions Consistent with Supreme Court Decision	
Issue	Year of Survey	Decision	Postgraduate	Lower Levels of Education
School prayer	1964	*Engel v. Vitale, Abington v. Schempp*	41.4	14.9
Flag burning	1990	*Texas v. Johnson*	44.1	14.3
Regulation of internet speech	1999	*Reno v. ACLU*	76.3	66.9
Homosexual relations	2003	*Lawrence v. Texas*	75.6	51.6
Affirmative action in school admissions	2003	*Grutter v. Bollinger*	43.0	25.4
Juvenile death penalty	2005	*Roper v. Simmons*	64.8	60.2
Rights of enemy combatants	2008	*Boumediene v. Bush*	50.0	32.7
Second Amendment	2008	*District of Columbia v. Heller*	60.1	75.0
Campaign finance	2010	*Citizens United v. FEC*	21.2	19.2
Same-sex marriage	2013	*Obergefell v. Hodges*	70.9	52.5

opinion was clearly manifested, as was true of the Court's limits on religious observances in public schools and flag burning.[202]

The Court's support for policies that are favored by elite segments of society might simply reflect the Justices' own values, but that is not necessarily the case. As Barry Friedman points out, "If a justice is in tune with his peer group, and his peers have elite views not shared by most of the country, the justice will seem to be going his own way."[203]

The implications of the patterns of opinion that we have described should not be overstated. For one thing, we have focused on only a single type of decision, albeit the most important part of the Court's work over the last seventy years: its expansions of civil liberties on social issues. Although there is reason to think that other major lines of policy in the Court such as the protection of property rights in the pre–New Deal era hewed to elite views rather than mass opinion, we do not have direct evidence on that question.[204] Further, many of the decisions in question closely divided the Justices; if a majority of Justices in those cases were closer to elite opinion than to mass opinion, that was not true of their colleagues. In the current era of political polarization, the divisions between competing camps of social and political elites are especially clear. Even so, the relationship between the Court's rulings and elite opinion that we have identified is noteworthy.

Elite Norms: Collegiality and Legal Orientation

Accounts of Supreme Court decision making tend to emphasize the impact of the Justices' core ideological beliefs and the ideological positions of those who influence the Justices. Indeed, a great deal about what the Justices do can be understood from that perspective. At the same time, the world of legal elites in which the Justices reside works against decision making based purely on ideology.

This influence, like other facets of decision making, can be understood in terms of basic human motivations. We have already emphasized one of those motivations, the desire to control how you are perceived by others (impression management). Also relevant is the desire to influence others and, inter alia, control or shape your world (power).[205] Different Justices will value these needs differently, but these basic motivations help explain both the Justices' interest in collegial—often unanimous—decision making and the Justices' interest in being seen as principled in the sense of acting on the basis of legal considerations. Because legal elites that are important to the Justices give weight to collegiality and to legally oriented decision making, the Justices have strong incentives to do so as well.

Judges on an appellate court have no choice but to "interact on a regular basis," and opinion writing is often the "product of an intensive and iterative process among the judges."[206] Studies of federal court of appeals decision making, for example, highlight both the infrequency of dissent and the costs associated with the filing of dissenting opinions. These studies also invoke "theories of cognitive dissonance, in which judges seek to reduce the psychic discomforts of standing alone" and "norms of reciprocity," "such that a judge's dissent from an opinion may cost him votes in his future opinions."[207]

Thus, even a judge who joined an appellate court from outside the legal system would have strong incentives to act in a collegial way. Judges who failed to follow collegial norms would lose both the respect of people with whom they interact intensively and their capacity to influence fellow judges to achieve the results they favor. But judges do come from within the legal system, having undergone legal training and having spent most of their careers in legal positions.[208] And among legal elites, collegiality and cooperation in appellate decision making are strongly emphasized as norms.[209]

With nearly all Supreme Court Justices in the current era having previously served on federal courts of appeals,[210] the Justices are accustomed to collegial norms that disfavor dissent. Even more important are attributes of the Court itself. Supreme Court Justices are members of a small interdependent group. The Justices are "locked into intricate webs of interdependence where the impulse to speak in a personal voice must always be balanced against the need to act collectively in order to be effective."[211] Four Justices must agree to hear a case, a majority of Justices must agree to stay a case pending appeal, and, of course, Court decisions require the approval of a majority of Justices. More than that, Justices meet as a single group at all important phases of the decision-making process—deciding which cases to hear, hearing oral arguments, and casting votes in conference. Over the past quarter century, all but three Justices have pooled their law clerks to make recommendations on which cases to hear.[212] Supreme Court Justices also embrace a range of practices that reinforce the idea that they are a collegial interdependent group—clerks or other staff do not attend Court conferences, conferences begin with a handshake, the Chief Justice always votes first in a conference, and the junior Associate Justice always votes last.[213] A persuasive body of scholarship "takes seriously the fact that judicial decisions on collegial courts are the product of group choices and, in that regard, takes into account the small group environment of collegial court decision-making."[214] That fact must be given weight in any effort to understand Supreme Court decision making.

Thus, the character of the Supreme Court favors cooperation and an effort to reach consensus. The Justices—as Chief Justice Rehnquist observed—"feel impelled to a greater or lesser degree to try to reach some consensus that can be embodied in an opinion that will command the support of at least a majority of the members of the Court."[215] This observation has been confirmed by scholarly work demonstrating a general movement toward consensus.[216]

It is true that the pull toward consensus has weakened considerably over the Court's history. Before 1941, there was a very strong norm of consensus, and over 90 percent of cases were decided unanimously.[217] Research has shown that during the Waite (1874–1888) and Taft (1921–1930) Courts, Justices would frequently dissent in conference and then withdraw their dissents (so, for example, 40 percent of Waite Court conference votes had at least one dissent as compared to 11 percent of published opinions).[218] As late as the 1934–1936 terms, which featured heated disagreements over review of New Deal policies, the Court achieved unanimity in several major cases through changes in position by Justices who dissented in conference.[219]

Once the strong presumption against dissent and separate opinions weakened, consensus in decisions declined considerably.[220] Even so, levels of agreement remained higher than we would expect in light of the Court's use of its discretionary jurisdiction to select primarily "hard" cases. In the period from 1941 to 2013, 39.5 percent of the Court's decisions were still unanimous (as compared to 16.6 percent of cases decided by one vote).[221] That remains true even in an era of political polarization, one in which the Court is perceived to be divided sharply into ideological blocs. In the Court's decisions with full opinions in the 2010–2016 terms, 49 percent were unanimous. And 37 percent of the time, all the Justices signed the Court's majority opinion.[222]

Anecdotal accounts of the Roberts Court, moreover, emphasize the Justices' desire to avoid fractured opinions. Chief Justice Roberts spoke of his desire to compromise to avoid dissent.[223] A 2011 study of early Roberts Court decisions found that the "vast majority of disputes in constitutional cases ... occurred in a respectful, collegial manner."[224] Following the death of Antonin Scalia, the Court had eight members for more than a year; during that time, the Justices worked toward compromise and avoided hearing arguments in cases that might divide them.[225] Even in Neil Gorsuch's first full term, the rate of unanimous decisions was 39 percent and the Justices compromised to reach a degree of bipartisan consensus in the cases that had raised the term's two most contentious issues—partisan gerrymandering and the clash between gay rights and religious liberty.[226]

In pointing to the norm of collegiality and the degree of consensus that the Court reaches in its decisions, we do not want to exaggerate these attributes. Only a large minority of decisions are unanimous, and in a portion of those unanimous decisions some Justices refuse to join the Court's opinion. Moreover, the Court is never free from interpersonal conflict, and in some periods the level of conflict has been high. The Court of the current era appears to be fairly harmonious, but opinions that express disagreement with colleagues in sharp terms are far from rare. Relatedly, the number of 5–4 decisions where the Justices divide along partisan lines is higher now than ever before.[227] Still, both consensus and collegiality are at considerably higher levels in the Court than they are in the other branches of government.

The norm of law-oriented decision making also operates as a significant constraint on both ideologically driven decision making and the formation of ideologically identifiable majority coalitions in individual cases. As noted earlier, Supreme Court Justices—like everyone else—engage in impression management, that is, the "process of controlling how one is perceived by other people."[228] In particular, people try to "project images of themselves that are consistent with the norms in a particular social setting and with the roles they occupy."[229] In this regard, as Wendy Martinek observed in her study of judges as members of small groups, "there is perhaps no other norm that has as strong a prima facie claim on judges than the norm that the decision making of judges should be governed by a consideration of the relevant legal factors."[230]

This norm is embedded in legal education and practice, and it is embraced by legal audiences; for example, a 2016 study showed that in comparison with members of the public, lawyers and state court judges were far more likely to put aside personal views related to ideology when answering legal questions.[231] By showing that legal training and experience inform professional judgment, this study highlighted the norm in favor of reliance on legal factors, and relatedly the norm disfavoring ideologically based decision making. This norm of law-oriented decision making, moreover, helps explain the institutional design of the Supreme Court—life tenure for federal court judges and the fact that Supreme Court Justices do not have staffs who accompany them to conference and bring "no cohorts" with them when they join the Court.[232] This norm stands in sharp tension with political science models championed by strategic theorists and attitudinalists; it instead speaks to the need to resist political influence and to stand up for principle—even when that principle cuts against preferred outcomes (or the preferred outcomes of political allies).

Examples of positions taken by Justices that appear to reflect the pull of law on their choices are legion. Justice John Paul Stevens claimed he personally supported medical marijuana reform when backing expansive federal power to outlaw medical marijuana,[233] Justice Antonin Scalia spoke of his personal dislike of decisions he joined embracing a broad view of criminal procedure protections,[234] and Justice Clarence Thomas provided the critical fifth vote to invalidate North Carolina voting districts based on an understanding of the color-blind Constitution that cut against

Republican Party interests.[235] In the 2017 term, Justice Neil Gorsuch joined the Court's four liberals in ruling that a provision of a federal criminal statute was "void for vagueness" under the Fifth Amendment.[236] Of course, the norm of law-oriented decision making does not prevent the Justices from acting largely on the basis of their policy preferences, nor does it prevent them from voting in ways that create identifiable ideological blocs. But it does operate as a countervailing force. Justices want to believe that they are acting on a legal basis, and they seek the esteem of legal audiences that want judges to act on a legal basis. They also want to be seen by their colleagues as acting in a principled way rather than simply voting their policy preferences into the law and as willing to act in ways that strengthen the Court as a whole.[237]

Leaving aside unanimous decisions, the Justices frequently divide in ways that deviate from the usual ideological lines.[238] Although these deviations stem in part from multiple dimensions to the Justices' policy preferences, they also reflect the impact of considerations other than policy, including the pull of legal considerations on the Justices.[239] The behavior of "swing Justices" who stand in the ideological center of the Court can be understood in part from the same perspective.[240] These Justices, such as Anthony Kennedy, can play a critical role in the most politically salient issues before the Court. Although "swing" status is primarily a product of policy preferences that put a Justice between colleagues on both sides, Justices may cultivate that position because they put a high value on the exercise of individual power or a reputation for independence from ideological considerations.

The incentives that Justices have to seek consensus and to act in part on a legal basis help to make the Court different from Congress. Consensus and principled decision making carry some weight in Congress as well, but considerably less than they do in the courts. As we will discuss in chapter 4, that difference has been accentuated in an era of political polarization.

Looking Ahead

In this chapter we have argued that social and political elites are an important audience for Supreme Court Justices—indeed, the most influential segment of the Court's environment. In the next two chapters we consider their influence from a different, historical perspective. In chapter 3 we look at the Court prior to 1985, with an emphasis on the era from the New Deal through the Burger Court of the 1970s and 1980s. In that era, we argue, the relative homogeneity of opinion in the elites most relevant to the Court and the absence of sharp polarization between the political parties had a subtle but powerful impact on the Court's ideological direction. In chapter 4 we turn to the era since the 1990s, an era marked by strong ideological and partisan polarization among elites. We argue that this polarization has changed the Court, making it a different institution in some important respects.

3

Elites, Ideology, and the Rise of the Modern Court

WE HAVE ARGUED that Supreme Court Justices are part of an elite world—chosen by other political elites, coming primarily from social and economic elites, and most attentive to elites during their tenure on the Court. It follows that the attributes of the elite world at any given time are reflected in the Court. By the same token, changes in that elite world are likely to change the Court.

One cluster of important attributes is captured by the term *polarization*, a term that has become a standard label for the state of American politics today. We believe that polarization goes far toward explaining the current state of the Supreme Court and its likely future. In this chapter and the next, we will examine how the growth in polarization over the past several decades has affected the Court. We examine the period up to 1985 in this chapter; at that time, ideology was less relevant to judicial appointments and there was not a well-established conservative legal network. The Justices did not sort along party lines during that period; more telling, during the Warren and Burger Courts, several Republican Justices became more liberal over their tenure and thereby came to reflect dominant left-center elite norms to a greater degree. In the next chapter, we consider the ramifications of growing polarization since 1985, including the rise of ideology in judicial appointments and the related rise of the conservative legal network. Far more than in earlier Courts, Democratic and Republican Justices today are members of social networks whose ideological orientations correspond with the Justices' party affiliations, and the Justices remain steadfast in their ideological commitments.

Polarization in Elite Politics

The scholars and other commentators who speak about polarization in American politics today are not referring to a single phenomenon. Rather, the term has been used to apply to several related but conceptually distinct attributes of politics.

One important distinction is between mass and elite politics. Although the two levels of politics shape each other in powerful ways, their attributes do not necessarily coincide. Indeed, in at least one respect, it can be argued that political elites in the United States today are considerably more polarized then the general public.[1] Because we think that the Supreme Court is shaped primarily by elites rather than the public as a whole, we focus on polarization at the elite level.

Even more important are distinctions among different characteristics of political attitudes and behavior, distinctions that are not always recognized by those who discuss polarization. For the most part, people who speak about political polarization are referring to three characteristics.[2]

The first is *extremism*. This term refers to a tendency for political views and positions to move away from the middle and toward the poles on one side or the other. On specific issues, extremism is reflected in movement away from moderate stances toward full support for one side. On abortion, for instance, extremism would be manifested in a clustering of opinions or actions by policymakers into two sides that reflect the agendas of the prochoice or pro-life movements rather than reflecting the agendas of each movement in part.[3]

The second characteristic has been called *affective polarization*.[4] That term refers to development of a strong sense of identification with one partisan or ideological camp and a corresponding hostility toward the opposing camp. To return to a concept that we used in chapter 2, affective polarization makes political affiliations increasingly important as an element of people's social identities, and that importance arouses negative attitudes toward people who have competing affiliations.

The third characteristic is *partisan sorting*.[5] In partisan sorting, the major political parties become more homogeneous ideologically. More specifically, with partisan sorting, people in the Democratic Party are overwhelmingly liberal, while Republicans are overwhelmingly conservative. The term *sorting* implies that people move into the party that better represents their ideological positions, and this appears to be the dominant process by which parties become more homogeneous. But people's partisan affiliations may also shape their issue positions and thus their places on the ideological spectrum, as they are drawn to take the positions that they identify with their party.

Although these three types of polarization are conceptually distinct, they can be expected to covary to some degree, in part because of causal relationships among them.[6] At the elite level, there is strong evidence that all three characteristics have become unusually strong in the current era. We discuss that evidence in chapter 4, but observation of the political process makes it clear that we are in an era of high polarization no matter how that term is defined. Partisan sorting at the elite level is nicely illustrated by the ideological distance between members of the two parties in Congress. Figure 3.1 shows trends in this aspect of polarization in the House and Senate from the late nineteenth century to the early twenty-first century. Most striking is the growth in polarization since the mid-twentieth century, growth that has been most pronounced since the 1980s. Compared with earlier and later

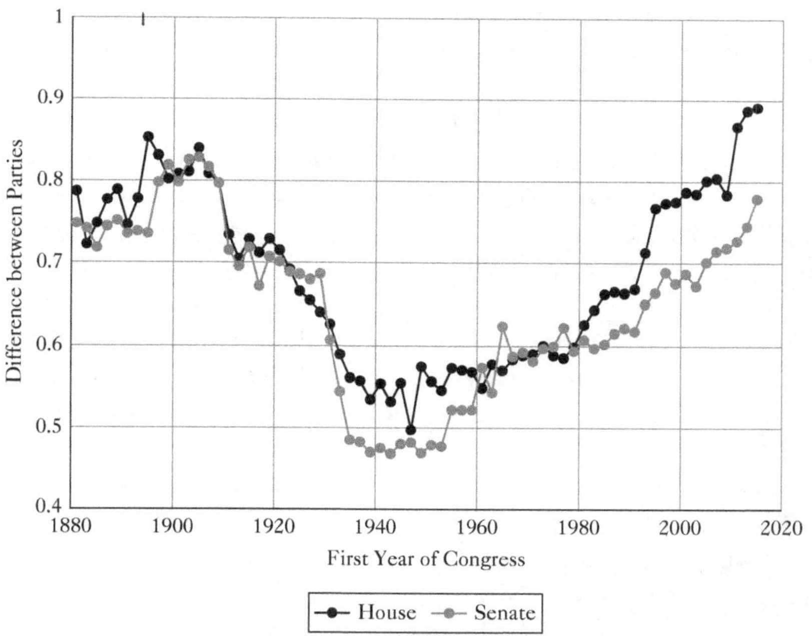

FIGURE 3.1. Differences between median scores of congressional Republicans and Democrats, first ideological dimension, 1881–2016.

The chart was created from data in Jeffrey B. Lewis, Keith Poole, Howard Rosenthal, Adam Boche, Aaron Rudkin, and Luke Sonnet, *Voteview: Congressional Roll-Call Votes Database*, https://voteview.com/.

periods, Congress featured low levels of partisan sorting in the period from the Roosevelt Court to the Burger Court.

Inevitably, elite polarization in the current era has had a significant impact on the Supreme Court—and, indeed, on other courts.[7] Because polarization is so pervasive, it could affect the Court in a variety of ways. For instance, two legal scholars have argued that polarization in Congress and the general public has brought about an increase in advocacy by the Justices at oral argument.[8]

Based on the multiple measures that scholars have used, it is uncertain whether the level of extremism on the Court has substantially increased in recent decades.[9] But there certainly has been an increase in partisan sorting. That increase culminated in the coinciding of ideological and partisan lines that has existed since Elena Kagan's appointment to the Court in 2010, a coinciding that makes today's Court distinctive. Affective polarization has also changed the Court. In terms of the conception of elite networks that we presented in chapter 2, two important things have happened. First, political networks, those based on ideology and partisanship, have become more salient to the Justices. Second, the left-centrist network that had been dominant among legal elites has fragmented and has been supplanted by separate legal networks that are associated with the competing ideological and partisan camps.

In this chapter and the next, we track developments in the elite world that have brought about these changes in the Court and other changes that are associated with them. Polarization came to the elite world and some types of polarization came to the Supreme Court in a lengthy process rather than abruptly, so any line of division between past and current eras is arbitrary. But one arbitrary line is useful for understanding changes that have occurred in the Court. In 1985, the beginning of President Ronald Reagan's second term, the Department of Justice under Attorney General Edwin Meese sought aggressively to advance conservative goals in the legal system. That campaign was a key to the process by which polarization among political elites shaped the judiciary and, a quarter century later, produced a Supreme Court that was divided between blocs of conservative Republicans and liberal Democrats.

This chapter focuses on the pre-1985 period, though it moves forward to 2010 in discussing how the Court was affected by the relatively limited polarization of the elite world prior to the mid-1980s. It starts with a selective survey of the Court's history before the inception of the "Roosevelt Court" in 1937, a survey that focuses primarily on the limited partisan sorting on the Court. It then looks more closely at the era that began with the Roosevelt

Court and continued for several decades after that time. Chapter 4 turns to the current era of high polarization in the elite world around the Court.

From the Founding to the New Deal

Political polarization in its various aspects is hardly unique to the current era in American politics. Deep and bitter divisions have been a recurring feature of the political system, and these divisions have often fallen largely along party lines. Strong as affective polarization appears to be today, it has not resulted in a civil war. Even so, the overall level of polarization in the Supreme Court was considerably lower through most of American history than it has been in the past few decades. This is especially true of partisan sorting, our primary focus. Changing patterns in elite polarization explain both today's partisan divide and the absence of such a divide in the Court in earlier periods.

The Absence of Partisan Divisions

Certainly the polarization that characterized elite politics in some eras had an impact on the Supreme Court. Yet there was one striking attribute of the Court in the period from its founding in 1790 until 1936: at no time were there liberal and conservative blocs that fell along partisan lines as defined by the party of the president who appointed a Justice. (We will refer to Justices—for most of our history, as Republicans and Democrats—on the basis of the party of their appointing president, not a Justice's own affiliation.) In that one important respect, there was a sharp difference between that long era and the current era.

In some periods, one-party dominance of presidential elections worked against the development of partisan blocs on the Court. It was not until 1807, for instance, that a second non-Federalist Justice joined the Court. But more fundamental were some interrelated practices that effectively muted ideological disagreement on the Court.

One important practice was the infrequency of dissent. Starting with Chief Justice John Marshall at the beginning of the nineteenth century and continuing with varying strength for most of the Court's history,[10] a successful push toward consensus was an important institutional characteristic of the Court. From the 1801 term through the 1936 term, there were at most four terms in which more than 20 percent of the Court's decisions included dissenting opinions, and in most terms this dissent rate was below 10 percent.[11] As a result, sharp and consistent lines of division between subsets of the Court were absent.

The infrequency of dissent was partly a product of a second characteristic, the Court's mandatory jurisdiction over the great majority of cases that came before it during its first century of operation. Mandatory jurisdiction left the Justices overwhelmed with their caseloads in some periods, and Congress rescued the Court by giving it discretionary jurisdiction over some sets of cases in 1891 and then over most cases in 1925.[12] Caseload pressures left Justices with less time to write dissenting opinions, and those pressures likely gave the Justices greater interest in processing cases than in issuing multiple opinions that debated broader legal principles. Moreover, because the Court had only limited power to screen the cases that were brought to it, high proportions of the cases that it decided were narrow and legally "easy." These cases were unlikely to evoke disagreements among the Justices, especially disagreements that reflected ideological or partisan considerations.

Even so, partisan blocs could have appeared on the Court during at least some eras. Alongside the routine cases that dominated the Court's docket, the Court addressed issues of major importance on which the political parties differed. This was especially true of questions related to federalism before the Civil War and questions related to government intervention in the economy after that time.[13] Yet the available evidence indicates that divisions among the Justices on these and other cases did not follow party lines.

One piece of evidence is derived from the coding of Justices' votes on case outcomes in ideological terms in the Supreme Court Database, a dataset on attributes of the Court's decisions throughout its history.[14] The coding of decisions and votes as liberal or conservative is subject to disagreement even in the period since the Roosevelt Court,[15] and application of coding rules for ideological direction that were developed for that period to earlier eras can be problematic because definitions of conservative and liberal positions on issues change over time.[16] Even so, the patterns of Justices' votes in the database tell us something about the relationship between party and ideology.

Before the inception of the Chase Court in 1864, the dearth of dissents makes it difficult to analyze differences in the Justices' voting patterns. But during the Marshall and Taney eras, there were five "natural Courts"—periods of stable membership—in which there were at least twenty nonunanimous decisions. All but one of these natural Courts occurred under Chief Justice Taney. Democratic appointees dominated the Court in all five of the natural Courts, with only one or two Federalists or Whigs in each. Still, it is noteworthy that in none of those periods was there ideological separation between appointees of the two parties.

In the period from the beginning of the Chase Court in 1864 to the end of the Fuller Court in 1910, dissent—though still uncommon—became somewhat more frequent. Voting in every natural Court in that period in which there were at least forty nonunanimous decisions was analyzed. Eleven natural Courts met that criterion. Because of the success of Republican candidates for president during that period, every natural Court was dominated by Republican appointees, but in seven of those Courts there were at least two Democratic appointees. In none of those Courts were all the Democratic Justices separated from all the Republicans on an ideological scale that was based on their votes, and typically Justices from the two parties were quite intermixed in their positions on that scale.[17]

Measures of Justices' ideological positions based on their voting agreements and disagreements with each other are available from the beginning of the White Court in 1910 until the present. Because these measures do not require the coding of votes as liberal or conservative, they avoid the potential problems that arise in creating and applying coding rules for ideological direction.[18] Donald Leavitt's study of the White Court (1910–1921) used data on agreements and disagreements to calculate scores on ideological scales for the 1910–1915 and 1916–1920 terms.[19] In neither period were the Court's Republican- and Democratic-appointed Justices separated from each other ideologically. Most notably, Justice James McReynolds—appointed by Democratic president Woodrow Wilson—took positions that were relatively and increasingly conservative.[20]

Eloise Snyder analyzed patterns of agreements among Justices in an important subset of cases to identify ideological blocs that she called "cliques" for each natural Court from 1921 to 1937.[21] There was no natural Court in which all the Justices appointed by Democratic presidents were in separate cliques from all the Justices appointed by Republicans. The best known of the natural Courts in that period was the Court that sat in the 1932–1936 terms, the one that collectively came into severe conflict with President Franklin Roosevelt during his first term in office. That Court, like its predecessors, split along lines that cut across party. Of the Court's two Democratic appointees, one (Louis Brandeis) was firmly in the liberal bloc of three Justices, and the other (James McReynolds) just as firmly part of the conservative bloc of four Justices.[22]

Of course, ideological considerations are more relevant to some Supreme Court decisions than to others. Analyses of Justices' voting patterns in recent eras have found that the tendency of Justices to vote along ideological lines is strongest in the cases that are the most important, based on newspaper coverage of decisions.[23] The same probably was true of past eras as well. The *Guide to the U.S. Supreme Court* includes a list of the Court's most important decisions across its history.[24] The list was compiled by different people over time, and there undoubtedly are biases and idiosyncrasies in the selection of cases. Still, the list in the *Guide* is a meaningful set of decisions that can be considered important.[25]

Between 1790 and 1937, there were seventy-five decisions on the list in which at least two Justices cast dissenting votes. In only one of those cases were all of the Justices on one side appointed by presidents of one party and all of the Justices on the other side appointed by presidents of the other party.[26] Of course, the Court did not always have two or more Justices from both parties. Even so, the nearly complete absence of divisions along party lines is striking.

This pattern is exemplified by two of the most noteworthy cases from this period, *Dred Scott v. Sandford* (1857) and *Lochner v. New York* (1905).[27] In *Dred Scott*, the two dissenters were the Whig-appointed Benjamin Curtis and the Democratic-appointed John McLean. In *Lochner*, Justices appointed by Democratic and Republican presidents were each on both the majority and dissenting sides. Similarly, the major decisions reviewing New Deal programs in which the Justices divided cut across party lines just as the Court's ideological blocs did during that period.[28]

The absence of strong partisan sorting on the Court in the pre–Roosevelt Court period is puzzling. Although the relevance of various policy issues and the positions of the parties on some issues changed over time, there were always strong ideological disagreements between the Democratic and Republican parties (and earlier, between Democrats and Whigs).[29] As Figure 3.1 shows, ideological differences between the congressional parties were quite substantial—about as substantial as in the current era—throughout the period from the late 1870s to the early 1920s.

Further, issues that divided the parties appeared in the Supreme Court, and the Court's decisions had an impact on the resolution of those issues. For this reason, presidents sometimes appointed Justices with an eye toward advancing their party's policy agenda or their own agenda. An especially clear example is President U. S. Grant's appointments of two Supreme Court Justices (Joseph Bradley and William Strong) who supported Grant's view that paper money was acceptable under the Constitution. With the backing of Bradley and Strong, the Court in 1871 voted 5–4 to overturn an 1870 ruling that the federal government was without authority to issue paper money.[30]

Explaining the Lack of Partisan Division

Beyond the infrequency of dissent that worked against the development of ideological blocs on any basis, the relatively weak relationship between party and ideology on the Court prior to the New Deal era seems to reflect two related factors. The first is that presidents did not always give a high priority to selecting Justices whose views reflected the distinctive orientation of their party. In choosing Supreme Court nominees, presidents historically have considered prospective nominees' ideological positions and policy views. But they have also taken "objective" qualifications into account, used nominations as a reward for service to the president and the president's party, thought about political benefits that may be gained through a nomination, and considered the prospects for confirmation of a nominee.[31] Over the Court's history, the relative weights given to policy and other considerations have varied considerably from president to president and even from nomination to nomination.[32]

Some presidents gave close attention to the policy preferences of at least some of their nominees, but prior to the current era those Justices were distinctly in the minority. That certainly was true of the late nineteenth and early twentieth centuries. "Political" considerations such as personal acquaintanceship and regional representation often played central roles in the selection of Justices. In a remarkable episode in 1932, pressure from people within and outside the legal system left President Herbert Hoover with little choice but to nominate Benjamin Cardozo, whose views diverged considerably from those of Hoover and the Republican Party.[33] Even when presidents sought to choose nominees whose orientations accorded with the party's positions, their choices were subject to error. That may have been the case when Woodrow Wilson nominated James McReynolds in 1914.[34] In part, such errors reflected the fact that policy considerations were only a moderately strong priority even for some presidents who took them into account. Moreover, with ideology playing a subordinate role, it does not appear that there were any groups—the equivalents of today's Federalist Society—to groom and vet potential nominees.

The lack of a consistent emphasis on policy considerations was also reflected in senatorial responses to nominees. The period from the 1840s to the 1890s was a bad one for nominees, with a substantial number of failed nominations. A few of those failures reflected disagreements about policy. But in most, other considerations were dominant. In the post–Civil War era, a half-dozen nominations failed because the president had not acceded to senatorial courtesy, senators had personal objections to the nominee, or they questioned the nominee's qualifications.[35]

Moreover, presidents did not necessarily share their party's distinctive ideological orientation. In the late nineteenth century the Democratic Party was divided into a populist faction and a conservative faction whose positions on economic issues were not very different from those of the Republican Party. Grover Cleveland, the only Democratic president between 1861 and 1913, appointed Justices who reflected his own conservatism.[36] Those appointments blurred the ideological distinction between the two parties' appointees on the Court for multiple decades. For his part, Theodore Roosevelt, whose presidency brought progressive leadership to the Republican Party "by accident,"[37] appointed a set of Justices who were more liberal than the party as a whole.[38]

The second factor working against a close relationship between party and ideology was that most Justices appointed by presidents of both parties came from higher-status families and had legal careers that made them part of an economic and social elite. Elites were not separated by partisan ideology at this time; instead, class status transcended party and ideology. According to one analysis, 43 percent of the Justices who joined the Court before 1920 had upper-class backgrounds, and another 29 percent came from the upper middle class.[39] An analysis by John Schmidhauser suggests an even stronger tendency for Justices to come from elite backgrounds.[40] Schmidhauser concluded that this tendency was clear in the period from 1862 to 1919, when appointments to the Supreme Court matched "the general historical descriptions of the era of corporate ascendancy—in family background the justices almost invariably were drawn from the 'better' classes of society."[41] That pattern is hardly surprising, in part because people who were economically and socially advantaged had the greatest access to education at prestigious schools and to apprenticeships with leading lawyers.[42] But it is nonetheless striking in light of the small proportions of Americans who fell into those classes for most of the nation's history.

In their careers, the Justices who were appointed to the Court in the late nineteenth and early twentieth centuries were part of a legal profession in which conservative values were dominant, especially in the elite segment of the profession. In particular, legal elites embraced social Darwinism, the idea that government "should not interfere with the normal activities of people in their struggle for existence" and that an "immoral political system would be one in which one class assigned the rights to themselves while throwing the duties on others."[43] Correspondingly, "conservatives, often of the moneyed classes, viewed the rise of social movements, labor unrest, and the resultant legislation as a direct threat. Property was under attack. To their cause they mustered an individualistic laissez-faire mentality that, while having long roots in American thought, nonetheless conflicted fundamentally with the popular impetus for state-driven solutions."[44] That conservatism was symbolized by the opposition of leaders of the bar to the confirmation of liberal nominee Louis Brandeis in 1916.[45] The future Justices who spent much of their careers as practicing lawyers typically had large businesses as clients, and some served on corporate boards.[46]

These backgrounds and associations did not guarantee that Justices would take conservative positions on the economic issues that dominated the Court's constitutional jurisprudence in that era. Consider, for example, Justice Brandeis, a progressive who often ruled against business interests. Brandeis came from an upper-class family, and his early legal practice was centered on business clients. Nonetheless, the Justices' backgrounds, especially their professional associations, had a significant impact on their thinking. Justice Samuel Miller complained to a family member in 1875 about this influence.

> It is vain to contend with judges who have been at the bar the advocates for forty years of rail road companies, and all the forms of associated capital, when they are called upon to decide cases where such interests are in contest. All their training, all their feelings are from the start in favor of those who need no such influence.[47]

Moreover, the Justices of that era—whatever their backgrounds and predilections might be—existed in an environment in which advocacy of laissez-faire economics was a powerful theme in legal and social commentary, a theme that inevitably shaped the Justices' thinking.[48] That environment was linked to the Court most directly through the powerful arguments that leading members of the bar made to the Court, "propagating and defending laissez-faire before the courts" and extolling limits on government power over economic activity.[49] The pervasiveness of this theme likely helped to suppress differences between the appointees of the two parties who were influenced by it.

During the so-called *Lochner* era (from 1897 to 1937), Democratic and Republican appointees to the Court often sided with business interests to strike down government regulation of the economy. For Robert McCloskey, Court decision making reflected the "unadorned endorsement of the strong and wealthy at the expense of the weak and poor"; for Archibald Cox, "the Lochnerian decisions flowed partly from the willful defense of wealth and power."[50] In their own time, the Justices collectively were viewed as allies of wealthy business elites, the very social class that they came from. In that era, "populists, progressives, and labor leaders subjected both state and federal courts to vigorous and persistent criticism and numerous proposed plans to abridge judicial power," culminating in President Roosevelt's 1937 Court-packing plan to increase the number of Justices sitting on the Court.[51]

These characterizations of the *Lochner* Court as little more than an agent of business have been criticized for failing to recognize both the Court's willingness to uphold governmental power in many cases and the individual liberty origins of the *Lochner* era.[52] To a considerable degree, that criticism is well taken. But to the extent that the Court played an assertive role in policymaking, that assertiveness was primarily in the service of corporations that sought to limit government regulation of economic activity. In turn, that powerful theme in the Court's work reflected both the Justices' backgrounds and the elite environment around them before and during their service on the Court.

From Roosevelt to Reagan

The Supreme Court's 1937 term represents a break in the Court's history in several important respects. With the series of decisions in the spring of 1937 that upheld government regulations of economic activity, the Court put behind its confrontation with the other branches over the scope of regulatory power.[53] The retirement of Justice Willis Van Devanter in June 1937 allowed President Franklin Roosevelt to make his first appointment to the Court, and his appointment of Senator Hugo Black was the first of the series of eight by Roosevelt that established a solid liberal majority on issues of economic regulation. Moreover, since disputes regarding the power of government to regulate the economy were fading, the Court turned its attention to individual rights issues. Thus, it is not surprising that historians, political scientists, and law professors typically treat 1937 as the beginning of the "modern" Supreme Court.[54] For these scholars, "1937 marks a major divide . . . in the decisional philosophy of the Supreme Court," and "future histories of the Supreme Court may very well divide the Court's development since 1790 into two fundamental periods, pre- and post-1937."[55]

Another important change in the Court occurred around that time. Congress acted in 1925 to expand the Court's discretionary jurisdiction to cover most of the cases that came to the Court, giving the Justices freedom to limit the size of their agenda and to focus their energies primarily on the cases that they deemed most important.[56] In so doing, the Justices were less interested in resolving disputes and more interested in establishing enduring legal principles.[57] By embracing a "law declaration" model that sees "articulating public norms" as critical, the Justices often look beyond litigants' arguments to advance their legal policy preferences.[58] This change in jurisdiction facilitated an increase in the frequency of disagreement among the Justices in decisions. That increase developed after 1937 with the arrival of new members who were more prone to dissent than their predecessors had been and the 1941 accession of a new Chief Justice (Harlan Fiske Stone) who was less committed to achieving consensus than his predecessors.[59]

The growth in dissensus on the Court reflected and strengthened a new expectation that Justices would no longer suppress their disagreement with the Court's decision or opinion. As a result, dissent is not only more common but also a clearer reflection of the Justices' views about cases. For both reasons, it has become easier to trace patterns of disagreement within the Court.

We look at those patterns primarily in terms of "Martin-Quinn" scores, developed by two scholars to place the Justices along an ideological scale based on patterns of agreement and disagreement in decisions. In this respect they are similar to the scores we used to analyze the 1910–1936 terms. However, they are based on a more complex statistical procedure, one that is designed to minimize the impact of fluctuations in the Justices' voting that result from the specific mix of cases that the Court hears in any given term.[60]

The Relationship between Party and Ideology

Table 3.1 shows the ordering of the Justices by Martin-Quinn scores for the terms from 1937 to 2017, with Republican appointees in boldface.[61] (The 1946–1952 terms are omitted because there were no Republican appointees on the Court during that period.) As the arrays of Justices show, until the 2010 term there was no time during this period that the Justices divided into clear ideological blocs solely by party. The Court came closest to a full split between Republican and Democratic appointees in the 1941–1944 terms. Seven of the nine Justices had been appointed by Democrat Franklin Roosevelt; Owen Roberts and Chief Justice Stone had been appointed by Republican Calvin Coolidge (although Stone was elevated to Chief Justice by Roosevelt). Throughout that period, Roberts was the Court's most conservative Justice. In all but one of the four terms (and again in 1945, after Roberts's retirement), Stone's score was more conservative than that of any Justice who had initially

Table 3.1. Ordering of Justices by Martin-Quinn Scores from Most Liberal to Most Conservative, 1937–2017 Terms

1937	Black	**Card.**	Reed	Stone	Bran.	**Hugh.**	**ORob.**	**Butl.**	McRe.
1938	Black	Fran.	Reed	**Stone**	Bran.	**Hugh.**	**ORob.**	**Butl.**	McRe.
1939	Black	Doug.	Murp.	Fran.	Reed	**Stone**	**Hugh.**	**ORob.**	McRe.
1940	Black	Doug.	Murp.	Reed	Fran.	**Stone**	**Hugh.**	**ORob.**	McRe
1941	Black	Doug.	Murp.	Reed	Byrn.	Fran.	Jack.	**Stone**	**ORob.**
1942	Black	Doug.	Murp.	Rutl.	Reed	Jack.	Fran.	**Stone**	**ORob.**
1943	Black	Doug.	Murp.	Rutl.	Jack.	Reed	**Stone**	Fran.	**ORob.**
1944	Black	Doug.	Murp.	Rutl.	Reed	Jack.	Fran.	**Stone**	**ORob.**
1945	Black	Doug.	Murp.	Rutl.	Reed	Burt.	Fran.	**Stone**	
1953	Doug.	Black	**Warr.**	Fran.	Clark	Jack.	Mint.	Burt.	Reed
1954	Doug.	Black	**Warr.**	Clark	Fran.	**Harl.**	Mint.	Burt.	Reed
1955	Doug.	Black	**Warr.**	Clark	Fran.	Mint.	Reed	**Harl.**	Burt.
1956	Doug.	Black	**Warr.**	**Bren.**	Clark	Fran.	Reed	Burt.	**Harl.**
1957	Doug.	Black	**Warr.**	**Bren.**	Clark	Fran.	**Whit.**	Burt.	**Harl.**
1958–1959	Doug.	Black	**Warr.**	**Bren.**	Clark	**Stew.**	**Whit.**	Fran.	**Harl.**
1960–1961	Doug.	Black	**Warr.**	**Bren.**	**Stew.**	Clark	**Whit.**	Fran.	**Harl.**
1962	Doug.	Black	**Warr.**	**Bren.**	Gold.	White	Clark	**Stew.**	**Harl.**
1963	Doug.	**Warr.**	Black	Gold.	**Bren.**	White	Clark	**Stew.**	**Harl.**
1964	Doug.	**Warr.**	**Bren.**	Black	Gold.	White	Clark	**Stew.**	**Harl.**
1965–1966	Doug.	Fort.	**Warr.**	**Bren.**	Black	White	Clark	**Stew.**	**Harl.**
1967	Doug.	Fort.	**Warr.**	**Bren.**	Mars.	**Stew.**	Black	White	**Harl.**
1968	Doug.	**Warr.**	Fort.	Mars.	**Bren.**	White	Black	**Stew.**	**Harl.**
1969	Doug.	Mars.	**Bren.**	Black	White	**Stew.**	**Harl.**	**Burg.**	
1970	Doug.	**Bren.**	Mars.	Black	White	**Stew.**	**Harl.**	**Blmn.**	**Burg.**
1971–1973	Doug.	**Bren.**	Mars.	**Stew.**	White	**Powe.**	**Blmn.**	**Burg.**	**Rehn.**
1974	Doug.	**Bren.**	Mars.	**Stew.**	White	**Blmn.**	**Powe.**	**Burg.**	**Rehn.**
1975–1976	**Bren.**	Mars.	**Stev.**	White	**Stew.**	**Blmn.**	**Powe.**	**Burg.**	**Rehn.**
1977	**Bren.**	Mars.	**Stev.**	White	**Blmn.**	**Stew.**	**Powe.**	**Burg.**	**Rehn.**
1978	Mars.	**Bren.**	**Stev.**	White	**Blmn.**	**Stew.**	**Powe.**	**Burg.**	**Rehn.**
1979–1980	Mars.	**Bren.**	**Stev.**	**Blmn.**	White	**Stew.**	**Powe.**	**Burg.**	**Rehn.**
1981	Mars.	**Bren.**	**Stev.**	**Blmn.**	White	**Powe.**	**O'Con.**	**Burg.**	**Rehn.**
1982	Mars.	**Bren.**	**Stev.**	**Blmn.**	White	**Powe.**	**Burg.**	O'Con.	**Rehn.**
1983	Mars.	**Bren.**	**Stev.**	**Blmn.**	White	**Powe.**	**O'Con.**	**Burg.**	**Rehn.**
1984	Mars.	**Bren.**	**Stev.**	**Blmn.**	**Powe.**	White	**O'Con.**	**Burg.**	**Rehn.**
1985	Mars.	**Bren.**	**Blmn.**	**Stev.**	**Powe.**	White	**O'Con.**	**Burg.**	**Rehn.**
1986	Mars.	**Bren.**	**Blmn.**	**Stev.**	**Powe.**	White	**O'Con.**	**Scal.**	**Rehn.**
1987–1988	Mars.	**Bren.**	**Blmn.**	**Stev.**	White	**Kenn.**	**O'Con.**	**Scal.**	**Rehn.**
1989	Mars.	**Bren.**	**Stev.**	**Blmn.**	White	**Kenn.**	**O'Con.**	**Scal.**	**Rehn.**

Table 3.1. Continued

1990	Mars.	**Stev.**	**Blmn.**	White	**Sout.**	**O'Con.**	**Kenn.**	**Scal.**	**Rehn.**
1991	**Stev.**	**Blmn.**	White	**Sout.**	**O'Con.**	**Kenn.**	**Rehn.**	**Scal.**	**Thom.**
1992	**Stev.**	**Blmn.**	**Sout.**	White	**O'Con.**	**Kenn.**	**Rehn.**	**Scal.**	**Thom.**
1993	**Stev.**	**Blmn.**	**Sout.**	Gins.	**Kenn.**	**O'Con.**	**Rehn.**	**Scal.**	**Thom.**
1994	**Stev.**	Gins.	**Sout.**	Brey.	**O'Con.**	**Kenn.**	**Rehn.**	**Scal.**	**Thom.**
1995	**Stev.**	Gins.	Brey.	**Sout.**	**Kenn.**	**O'Con.**	**Rehn.**	**Scal.**	**Thom.**
1996–1997	**Stev.**	Brey.	Gins.	**Sout.**	**Kenn.**	**O'Con.**	**Rehn.**	**Scal.**	**Thom.**
1998	**Stev.**	Gins.	Brey.	**Sout.**	**Kenn.**	**O'Con.**	**Rehn.**	**Scal.**	**Thom.**
1999	**Stev.**	Gins.	**Sout.**	Brey.	**O'Con.**	**Kenn.**	**Rehn.**	**Scal.**	**Thom.**
2000	**Stev.**	Gins.	Brey.	**Sout.**	**O'Con.**	**Kenn.**	**Rehn.**	**Scal.**	**Thom.**
2001–2004	**Stev.**	Gins.	**Sout.**	Brey.	**O'Con.**	**Kenn.**	**Rehn.**	**Scal.**	**Thom.**
2005–2008	**Stev.**	Gins.	**Sout.**	Brey.	**Kenn.**	**JRob.**	**Alito**	**Scal.**	**Thom.**
2009	**Stev.**	Gins.	Soto.	Brey.	**Kenn.**	**JRob.**	**Alito**	**Scal.**	**Thom.**
2010–2011	Gins.	Soto.	Kagan	Brey.	**Kenn.**	**JRob.**	**Alito**	**Scal.**	**Thom.**
2012	Gins.	Soto.	Kagan	Brey.	**Kenn.**	**JRob.**	**Scal.**	**Alito**	**Thom.**
2013–2014	Soto.	Gins.	Kagan	Brey.	**Kenn.**	**JRob.**	**Scal.**	**Alito**	**Thom.**
2015–2016	Soto.	Gins.	Kagan	Brey.	**Kenn.**	**JRob.**	**Alito**	**Thom.**	
2017	Soto.	Gins.	Brey.	Kagan	**Kenn.**	**JRob.**	**Gors.**	**Alito**	**Thom.**

been appointed by Roosevelt. But the differences between him and the most conservative Roosevelt appointee in each of those terms were small.[62]

In contrast with today's partisan divide on the Court, in the first half of the 1940s there was widespread agreement among the Justices on issues that had previously divided the Court. Most notably, the Justices recognized broad power in both the federal and state governments to regulate the economy. Stone and Roberts, for example, joined the Court's Democratic-appointed Justices in *Wickard v. Filburn*, embracing an extraordinarily broad interpretation of congressional power to regulate interstate commerce.[63] Indeed, Stone and Roberts—after the Court initially determined only that Congress must engage in fact finding to back up economic regulation—supported the Court's reversing course to craft a ruling without a logical stopping point according to its author Robert Jackson.[64]

Moreover, substantial differences in the positions of the seven Democratic-appointed Justices on the 1941–1945 Court developed, whether gauged by the Justices' Martin-Quinn scores or by doctrinal disagreements. In several landmark rulings involving the First Amendment rights of Jehovah's Witnesses, for example, the Court's Democratic-appointed Justices were bitterly divided.[65] Beyond disagreements over legal doctrine, enmities among the Roosevelt appointees—particularly Hugo Black and William Douglas on one side versus Felix Frankfurter and Robert Jackson on the other side—ultimately reached a level that has had few if any parallels in the Court's history.[66]

After Stone's death in the spring of 1946, the Court was composed entirely of Democratic (Roosevelt and Truman) appointees for seven terms. The enmities between some of those Justices became even stronger during that period. Disagreements among the Justices also increased because of the relative conservatism of the four Justices whom Truman appointed to the Court—Chief Justice Fred Vinson (appointed in 1946) and Associate Justices Harold Burton (1945), Tom Clark (1949), and Sherman Minton (1949).

Like the Roosevelt and Truman appointees, the five Justices appointed by Republican Dwight Eisenhower were ideologically heterogeneous. Three of those appointees (John Harlan, Charles Whittaker, and Potter Stewart) established relatively conservative records, but William Brennan and Earl Warren (who served as Chief Justice from 1953 to 1969) were distinctly more liberal. President John Kennedy made two appointments in 1962. Byron White, who proved to be a moderate conservative, had little impact on the Court's ideological balance. But Arthur Goldberg became the Court's fifth liberal, and his appointment initiated a seven-year period in which the Court almost surely was more liberal by the current meaning of that label than in any other time in the Court's history. Certainly the Court of that period was more favorable to broad interpretations of constitutional protections of civil liberties than any of its predecessors or successors.

One striking attribute of the Warren Court's expansions of constitutional rights in the 1960s is that the set of Justices who were most supportive of those expansions and the set that was more skeptical were both mixed in party terms. The first group included Democratic appointees Black, Douglas, and Goldberg (who was succeeded in 1965 by Abe Fortas) along with Republican appointees Warren and Brennan. The second group included Democratic appointees Clark and White alongside Republican appointees Harlan and Stewart. That was the Court's lineup in what may have been the most controversial of its civil liberties decisions, *Miranda v. Arizona*.[67]

The relationship between party and ideology remained complicated in the Burger and Rehnquist Courts and in the first five terms of the Roberts Court. While party and ideology have lined up in appointments to the Court since 1991, the earlier appointments of two relatively liberal Republicans—John Paul Stevens and David Souter—maintained a divergence between party and ideological lines on the Court until 2010. Based on the Martin-Quinn scores shown in Table 3.1, Eisenhower appointee William Brennan was one of the two most liberal Justices in each of his last twenty terms on the Court between 1970 and 1990. President Gerald Ford's appointee John Paul Stevens was to the left of the Court's center throughout his tenure from 1975 to 2010, and from 1991 to 2010 he was the most liberal Justice. President George H. W. Bush's appointee David Souter was at the center of the Court in the 1991 term, his first year as a Justice, and to the left of center for the remainder of a tenure that ended in 2009. For his part, John Kennedy's appointee Byron White was near the Court's ideological center throughout his tenure on the Court from 1962 to 1993. In the Burger and Rehnquist Courts he stood to the right of Brennan, Stevens, and (from the 1979 term on) Harry Blackmun, a Richard Nixon appointee.

During this long period the Court's Republican appointees as a group were usually more conservative than its Democratic appointees, but the two groups did not fully separate until the retirements of Souter in 2009 and Stevens a year later. Later in this chapter, we will explain why partisan identity and ideology did not link up in the Court before 2010. In chapter 4, we will highlight how party polarization and the rise of the conservative legal network explain both the growing role of ideology in Supreme Court appointments and the hardening of ideological positions.

As in the Warren Court, the lack of a sharp division between Republican and Democratic appointees in the post-Warren era is illustrated by the Court's most visible decisions. For instance, *Roe v. Wade* (1973) was decided by a 7–2 vote, with five Republican appointees and two Democratic appointees in the majority and one dissenter from each party.[68] Two decades later, when the Court revisited *Roe* in *Planned Parenthood v. Casey* (1992), the Court's seven Republican appointees were divided almost evenly between four who voted to maintain *Roe* fully or for the most part and three who voted to overturn it; the two Democratic appointees were split between the opposing camps.[69]

As in the period from 1790 to 1937, the lack of a partisan divide in the Court from 1937 to 2010 is underlined by the divisions of the Court in important cases. Of the 322 decisions in that period that the *Guide to the U.S. Supreme Court* classifies as important and in which at least two Justices dissented,[70] only one case divided all the Court's Republican-appointed Justices from all of their Democratic-appointed colleagues—and the division in that decision is ambiguous.[71] That is a remarkable record.

Explaining the Deviation from Partisan Division: Appointments

Any explanation of the imperfect relationship between party and ideology in the Court that prevailed from the Roosevelt Court through the first decade of the twenty-first century must start with appointments to the Court. In thinking about the impact of appointments, we need to take into account the slow process by which appointments shape the Court. The fictional character Mr. Dooley opined that "the Supreme Court follows the election returns."[72] But because each president can select only a limited number of Justices, legal scholar Fred Rodell suggested in 1955 that the aphorism should refer to the election returns "of ten or twelve years before."[73] Since the average tenure of Justices has increased considerably since Rodell wrote,[74] his time span might be lengthened to twenty or twenty-five years. The lack of a clear ideological division between Republican and Democratic appointees in the modern Court before 2010 reflects appointments made up to 1990 and primarily those made by the presidents from Franklin Roosevelt to Gerald Ford.

The period from the 1930s to the 1970s was not one of strong partisan polarization among political elites. In particular, ideological differences between the parties were limited in comparison with earlier and later eras. From the 1930s to the 1970s, Democratic presidents were certainly more liberal than their Republican counterparts.[75] But their parties were ideologically heterogeneous coalitions. This was largely because of regional differences, especially the division between North and South in the Democratic Party. In Congress, as Figure 3.1 shows, the ideological distance between the parties declined dramatically in the 1920s and 1930s, and it was only in the 1980s that this distance began its ascent to the current very high levels.

This is one reason that presidents typically did not give the highest priority to choosing nominees who were on their party's side of the ideological spectrum. Further, as in earlier eras, presidents also sought to use nominations to reward friends and serve other goals. That was especially true in periods when the policy stakes in the Court seemed to be relatively low.

Democratic Presidents. Among the Democratic presidents from Franklin Roosevelt through Lyndon Johnson, the stakes were highest for Roosevelt's early appointments to the Court. Roosevelt's first appointment, of Hugo Black in 1937, came after the switch of the Court's pivotal Justices to support New Deal programs that were challenged under the Constitution. But the close division on the Court gave Roosevelt good reason to seek a Justice who was a reliable supporter of government power to regulate the economy.

Indeed, in filling this vacancy and the series of vacancies that followed, Roosevelt gave priority to choosing liberals who could be expected to support the New Deal.[76] By the time that Roosevelt's sixth opportunity to fill a Court seat arose in 1941, the Court's majority was sufficiently secure that he could choose the relatively conservative James Byrnes for a set of political reasons.[77] Ultimately, Roosevelt chose eight Justices, along with his elevation of Harlan Fiske Stone to Chief Justice.

When the Roosevelt appointees came into conflict with each other, the sources of the conflict—aside from personal ambitions and animosities—were disagreements not over New Deal issues but over civil liberties issues that were becoming increasingly important to the Court's work in the 1940s. In particular, after the New Deal Court decimated *Lochner*-era precedents (overturning a staggering thirty-two decisions from 1937 to 1946, by one count)[78] and made clear that the federal and state governments had sweeping power to regulate the economy, there was little left to say about economic matters under the Constitution. The Justices then turned their attention to race and social issues that divided the nation, often along regional and not partisan lines. The Court heard relatively few civil rights and liberties cases before 1937; in contrast, "after 1937, the most significant matters on the docket were civil liberties and other personal rights."[79]

Roosevelt could not have anticipated how quickly the Court's agenda would shift toward civil liberties. The "horse and buggy" Court he criticized when proposing his Court-packing plan had been replaced by a modern Court that assumed broad governmental power over business and an expansive administrative state to manage ever-growing governmental programs.[80] Even if Roosevelt could have imagined the Court's transformation, he would have focused more on economic issues. His last appointment in 1943 came at a time when the agenda shift was becoming apparent, and his appointee Wiley Rutledge joined the Justices who favored expansive interpretations of constitutional protections of individual liberties. The prospect that Rutledge would do so may have played some role in his appointment, but it does not appear that this was a major consideration.[81]

Rutledge was not personally acquainted with the president, and this made him an exception to the rule among Roosevelt appointees. Indeed, all four Democratic presidents between the 1930s and the 1960s were close to most or all of the people they chose as nominees. According to Robert Scigliano, "Nearly all of the justices chosen by Presidents Franklin Roosevelt, Truman, Kennedy, and Johnson had at least a fairly confidential relationship with them prior to their appointment."[82]

What stood out in President Harry Truman's four nominations to the Court was the emphasis on personal ties as a criterion for nominations. In one leading analysis of presidents' appointment strategies, the chapter on Truman is entitled "Truman Rewards Loyalty and Friendship."[83] Although other considerations were important to some nomination decisions, all four of Truman's ultimate choices were close to him. Sherman Minton, Truman's last nominee, exemplifies this pattern. Minton was a good friend of the president. Having chosen Tom Clark for a vacancy in which Minton was interested a few months earlier, Truman quickly fixed on Minton after Justice Rutledge died in 1949. According to Justices William O. Douglas and Tom Clark, Minton traveled from Indiana to Washington, DC, when he learned of Rutledge's death, went to the White House, asked Truman for the nomination to fill Rutledge's seat, and got Truman's immediate assent.[84] Whether or not this story is accurate, the Truman-Minton friendship was clearly the key criterion for this appointment.

As it turned out, the Truman appointees all established relatively conservative records on the Court, especially on civil liberties issues.[85] It is uncertain how disappointed Truman was with these records, but years later he did express considerable unhappiness about Justice Clark: "He hasn't made one right decision that I can think of. And so when you ask me what was my biggest mistake, that's it. Putting Tom Clark on the Supreme Court of the United States."[86] To the extent that Truman was disappointed with the performance of the people he appointed to the Court, that disappointment resulted primarily from his emphasis on acquaintanceship as a criterion for nominations.

In comparison with Truman's appointees, the two Justices chosen by John F. Kennedy may have had stronger legal credentials. But like Truman, Kennedy chose nominees with whom he had significant personal ties.[87] Kennedy and Byron White had been acquainted for more than twenty years, and White served in the Kennedy Justice Department. Arthur Goldberg had been an important political supporter of Kennedy's, especially in helping him win support in the labor movement, and he served as secretary of labor. Goldberg was more or less an immediate choice, while White was chosen after the administration considered a range of candidates. Personal and political considerations favored White over the other two finalists for his nomination.

Policy considerations may have played a small part in ruling out one of those finalists. William Hastie, a federal court of appeals judge, would have been the first African American Justice if he had been appointed to the Court. Chief Justice Earl Warren and Justice William O. Douglas both objected to him on the ground that he was too conservative.[88] But with that possible exception, prospective positions on the issues that the Court addressed apparently had no impact on the Kennedy appointments.[89] As one scholar put it, "JFK considered the [Supreme Court], like all judicial appointments, a sideshow."[90]

Lyndon Johnson's two successful nominees for Associate Justices, Abe Fortas and Thurgood Marshall, both had distinguished careers in the legal profession.[91] Marshall may have been the most important practicing attorney of the twentieth century. But in selection processes that Johnson personally dominated to an unusual degree, personal ties played the key role in the Fortas nomination and a substantial part in Marshall's nomination. Fortas had served Johnson as a lawyer and personal adviser for many years, beginning with the episode in which he helped Johnson win a legal battle over the vote count in a 1948 Senate primary election in Texas. Johnson engineered a vacancy on the Court for Fortas in 1965 by putting heavy pressure on Justice Goldberg to resign and take a position as US ambassador to the United Nations.

Two years later Johnson did the same thing for Marshall, appointing Ramsey Clark to be attorney general and using that appointment to more or less force Ramsey's father Tom Clark to retire from the Court. Marshall did not have a close relationship with Johnson, but he had sacrificed his position as a federal court of appeals judge to join the Johnson administration as solicitor general. Probably more important, Johnson liked the idea of naming the first African American Justice, and Marshall was the logical candidate for that honor.

When Chief Justice Earl Warren announced in 1968 that he would retire from the Court once a successor was confirmed, Johnson again knew what he wanted to do: elevate Fortas to Chief Justice and name federal court of appeals judge Homer Thornberry to fill Fortas's current seat. Thornberry was a childhood friend of Johnson's, and Johnson had been quite important to his political and legal careers. Ultimately, the Fortas and Thornberry nominations failed through a successful Senate filibuster against Fortas. The close ties between Johnson and the nominees, including Fortas's continued work as a Johnson adviser even while he sat on the Court, were at least a minor factor in that failure.

Johnson undoubtedly had a good sense of Fortas's and Thornberry's policy views when he nominated them, and it seems unlikely that he would have chosen either if he had perceived them as conservative. And in a conversation with his attorney general, Johnson "seemed almost to delight in Marshall's potential for extreme liberalism."[92] To that extent, ideology was one consideration for Johnson even if personal acquaintanceship dominated his choices.

As a Justice, Marshall fulfilled Johnson's expectations. Goldberg and Fortas also established liberal records in their short careers on the Court. The same was not true of White, who was to the right of center in the late Warren Court and stood near the ideological middle of the more conservative Courts that followed it. Arguably, White's record was not very distant from Kennedy's own moderate liberalism. But like the conservatism of the Truman appointees, White's record reflected his appointer's limited interest in ideology rather than intention.

Across the whole period from 1937 to 1968, appointments to the Court by Democratic presidents had a mixed effect on the Court's ideological position. The Roosevelt appointees produced a solidly liberal Court on economic issues, but they split on the civil liberties issues that soon became a major part of the Court's agenda. The four Truman appointees moved the Court to the right in civil liberties, and only because of the relatively brief tenure of three of those Justices (all but Clark) did the Court of the 1960s become the most liberal Court in history. That development was the result most directly of Kennedy's appointment of Goldberg in 1962 and Johnson's appointment of his successor Fortas in 1965, but the Kennedy appointment of White added weight to the conservative side of the Court on most civil liberties issues during the Burger and early Rehnquist years.

This mixed record has multiple sources, but at its heart was the lack of a consistent commitment to choose Justices with strongly liberal views on the kinds of issues that the Supreme Court addressed. That lack of commitment reflected the divergence of ideological positions within the Democratic Party, especially the critical role played by conservative Southern Democrats throughout this period.

Republican Presidents. Dwight Eisenhower was the first Republican president in what we have called the modern era of the Supreme Court, taking office in 1953 after twenty years of Democrats in the White House. Eisenhower made five nominations of Justices, all successful in the Senate. Eisenhower was a moderate conservative who had won the Republican nomination in 1952 over Robert Taft, who represented the more conservative wing of the party. Eisenhower wanted to select Justices who would reflect his own views, but his appointees were a mixed group ideologically. To a considerable degree, this result followed from the low priority that he gave to policy considerations in his first-term nominations.

Earl Warren won Eisenhower's first appointment in 1953 primarily because of his support for Eisenhower in the 1952 Republican convention and in the general election campaign that followed.[93] In announcing his choice of Warren, Eisenhower referred to his "middle-of-the-road philosophy,"[94] a characterization that had some basis in his record as governor of California and one that at least reassured the president about the Warren appointment. But Warren himself seemed to have a clear vision of the direction he would take on the Court. As one reporter recalled, Warren told the reporters at a farewell party in California that "I am glad to be going to the Supreme Court because now I can help the less fortunate, the people in our society who suffer, the disadvantaged."[95]

Three years later, shortly before the 1956 presidential election, Eisenhower appointed William Brennan to the Court.[96] For political reasons Eisenhower wanted to choose a Democrat and a Catholic, and Brennan was among the very few credible candidates who met those criteria and who also fell within the age range that Eisenhower had set. The administration focused on Brennan, and when inquiries about him produced positive findings, he was appointed.[97] Brennan later recalled that in his interview with the president, his views on legal issues never came up.[98] Brennan's record on the New Jersey Supreme Court provided clear clues to his liberalism. Indeed, a contemporary legal commentator predicted with considerable accuracy the kinds of positions that he would take as a Supreme Court Justice.[99] But the officials who vetted Brennan seem to have missed those clues.

Eisenhower became unhappy with the Court's direction on civil liberties issues and the contributions of Warren and Brennan to that direction, so his second-term nominations were made with greater attention to ideology.[100] The result was the appointments of Charles Whittaker and Potter Stewart, both of whom stood on the conservative side of the spectrum once they joined the Court. Whittaker served on the Court for only five years, but over his twenty-three-year tenure Stewart established a record of moderate conservatism that likely would have pleased Eisenhower.

The next Republican president, Richard Nixon, had sharply criticized the decisions of the Warren Court as a candidate.[101] Once elected, he made six nominations to the Court, two of them unsuccessful. All of his nominees were perceived to be conservative.[102] With the important exception of Harry Blackmun in the later part of his Court tenure, the four successful nominees all established records that were more consistent than not with that perception.

Understandably, the standard narrative of the Nixon nominations is that he was a conservative who chose certain nominees to create a more conservative Court. Yet as Kevin McMahon has shown, the reality was more complicated than that.[103] For one thing, Nixon himself was a moderate conservative—considerably more moderate than some of the Republican presidents who have followed him. Further, Nixon's primary interest in the Court as candidate and then president was to woo conservatives to the Republican Party by emphasizing concerns about a limited set of Court policies, primarily criminal justice and school busing. At the same time, though, Nixon was careful not to alienate northern moderates who were still important to his party.

In choosing nominees, Nixon certainly cared about their policy views, primarily in the areas that were important to him for political reasons. (Outside those areas, he once said, an appointee "can do as he pleases.")[104] But Nixon did not closely scrutinize evidence about what those views were. "With perhaps the exception of Burger," his successful nominee for Chief Justice, "Nixon knew little about the ideological positions of his nominees and did not seem to care as long as they came across as conservative to the public."[105] And an insider's account of the chaotic process through which several of the Nixon nominations were made underlines the absence of a systematic effort to choose nominees on the basis of their policy positions.[106] The lack of thorough vetting of candidates for nominations—again, with the partial exception of Burger—was striking. Like the Johnson administration, the Nixon administration "investigated potential nominees carelessly."[107]

Nixon probably gave greater emphasis to traditional political considerations relating to ethnicity, religion, and region. He was especially interested in putting a southerner on the Court to appeal to voters in that region. McMahon's analysis "suggests that politics far more than ideology drove all six of his choices for the Court."[108] Faced with a Democratic majority in the Senate, Nixon also had to take into account a prospective nominee's prospects for confirmation. This was especially true after the defeats of Clement Haynsworth and G. Harrold Carswell for the seat that Abe Fortas vacated in 1969 under pressure from the Nixon administration. Those defeats occurred in part because of the administration's shallow research into the nominees' records.[109]

The Court that resulted from the four Nixon appointments was distinctly more conservative than its predecessor. Yet the differences were not as substantial as most observers would have expected. Indeed, the Burger Court embraced quantitative evidence of race discrimination, blocked state support of religion, and authorized abortion rights. One set of essays on the Burger Court came in a book subtitled "The Counter-Revolution That Wasn't."[110]

The primary reason is that among the Nixon appointees, only William Rehnquist established a strongly conservative record on the Court.[111]

Gerald Ford's nomination of John Paul Stevens reflected ideological considerations to a degree, in that he wanted to choose a conservative. But other considerations were also important.[112] In the wake of Watergate, and with a large Democratic majority in the Senate, Ford and his attorney general Edward Levi gave emphasis to selecting a nominee who was highly regarded and uncontroversial. In a way, the Stevens nomination strongly reflected personal considerations, in that Stevens (whom Ford did not know personally) had a friendship with Levi that dated back to elementary school.[113] Of course, Stevens ultimately became a liberal mainstay on the Court, one whose presence prevented the establishment of ideological blocs along party lines until his retirement in 2010.

As we will discuss in the next chapter, Ronald Reagan's administration marked the beginning of a new era. Under Attorney General Edwin Meese, the administration helped to institutionalize conservative legal groups and to advance their views in the legal world. Reagan also brought a new emphasis to ideology in the selection of Justices. But all that occurred primarily in Reagan's second term, beginning in 1985, which was also the year that Meese became attorney general. In his first term Reagan made one appointment to the Court, and that appointment reflected existing patterns of nomination decisions rather than ushering in a new era.

The appointment was of Sandra Day O'Connor. Although there was a wide-ranging search for potential nominees, Reagan was constrained by his campaign promise to choose a woman for "among the first Supreme Court vacancies in my administration."[114] Reagan and others involved in the search for a nominee wanted to choose a conservative, but there were few conservative women serving in high judicial positions. Chief Justice Burger, who was acquainted with O'Connor, called her to the administration's attention. Gradually she became the focus of the search for a nominee. Although considerable effort was given to ascertaining her policy positions, the available evidence was limited and, on the key issue of abortion, ambiguous. In nominating her, Reagan settled for someone who did not have a clear record of strong conservatism.[115] Consistent with perceptions of her at the time of her appointment,[116] O'Connor established herself as a moderate conservative on the Court.

Taken together, the nominations of Supreme Court Justices by Republican presidents from 1953 to 1985 reflected a real but limited concern with ideology. The goal of putting conservatives on the Court varied in the priority that was given to it, and the care with which that goal was pursued also varied considerably. In part, the lack of a stronger commitment reflected the relative moderation of Republican presidents prior to Reagan. In part, it reflected the limited importance of Supreme Court policy to some presidents.

The absence of a more concerted and more consistent effort to staff the Court with strong conservatives goes far toward explaining why the Court was not more conservative during the second half of the twentieth century and the first decade of the twenty-first. We next consider another explanation for that outcome.

Explaining the Deviation from Partisan Division: Elite Influence

We argued in chapter 2 that the Justices live in a world of social and political elites, elites that serve as a key audience for them and thus as the most powerful external influence on their choices as decision makers. More than anything else, the weak relationship between party and ideology during most of the Court's history is reflected in the appointment process. But the attributes of the elite world around the Court also weakened that relationship by exposing the Justices to influences that eroded partisan differences. In the late nineteenth and early twentieth centuries, as we have suggested, a largely conservative elite may have moved both Republican and Democratic appointees toward support for limits on government power to regulate the economy. In particular, the Justices were part of elite social networks dominated by the well-to-do and by lawyers who embraced laissez-faire.

In the period from Roosevelt to Reagan, elite influence came to exert an effect in the opposite direction. As elite groups that were relevant to the Justices became more liberal, they began to serve as a force favoring liberal positions on the issues that the Supreme Court addresses. This was especially true of the kinds of rights that liberals generally favor more than conservatives, which we will call civil liberties. For Justices who already supported a broadening of civil liberties, these groups reinforced their position. For Justices who did not come to the Court with that position, elite groups had the potential to shape their evolving views.

Elite Attitudes. It is difficult to characterize the policy positions of elite groups in any given era, in part because there is always considerable diversity in the views of people who fall into those groups. However, it seems clear that support for liberal legal policies became the preponderant position of elites around the Court.

In the first half of the twentieth century, the elite segment of the legal profession leaned clearly in a conservative direction. For instance, although the American Bar Association (ABA) took mixed positions on economic issues, it generally opposed federal regulation of economic activity.[117] The ABA's economic conservatism was reflected in its involvement in issues relating to selection of judges.[118] The National Lawyers Guild was founded in 1937 by lawyers on the political left because of their dissatisfaction with the ABA.[119]

Gradually, the ideological leaning of legal elites shifted leftward. Steven Teles described the various threads of this evolution in the development of what he called "the liberal legal network."[120] Lawyers who participated in the New Deal later moved into leading positions in the profession. Indeed, the growth of government during this era incentivized a new generation of lawyers to engage in civic life.[121] The American Civil Liberties Union and the National Association for the Advancement of Colored People (NAACP) also had an impact on the thinking of new generations of lawyers. The ABA moved more slowly, maintaining its traditional conservatism into the 1950s, but eventually its orientation began to change as well.[122] The civil libertarianism of the late Warren Court both reflected and contributed to these changes.

Law professors shared in the liberalism of other legal elites. For college faculty as a whole, there has been a substantial liberal skew since at least as far back as the 1950s.[123] For law professors specifically, a 1969 survey showed a strong leaning to the left among law professors, with more than three times as many who described themselves as "left" or liberal as there were conservatives.[124] With generational change, in part reflecting the Warren Court's inspiration, the legal academy moved even further to the left.[125] In the past three decades, evidence indicates that legal scholars—including those in the most prestigious law schools—are overwhelmingly on the political left.[126] For example, a 2005 study of the top twenty-one law schools found that 81 percent of political contributions by law school faculty were made to Democrats (as compared to 15 percent for Republicans).[127] Another reflection of the preponderantly liberal perspective of prominent legal scholars is their ratings of Supreme Court Justices, which indicate more favorable evaluations of Justices with liberal records on the Court.[128]

Law clerks in the Supreme Court are of particular interest, because clerkships have increasingly served as a step to prestigious and influential positions in the legal profession.[129] Surveys of former law clerks who served up to 2000 indicate that during their clerkships, most were liberal and identified with the Democratic Party.[130] If clerks generally maintained those orientations during their careers, as seems almost certain, they contributed to the liberal tinge of legal elites.

Journalists in elite news media also leaned to the liberal side of the spectrum. Surveys of journalists in "prominent" news organizations in 1971 and 1982–1983 found that there were far more on the political left than on the right and far more Democrats than Republicans.[131] Similarly, a survey of journalists working at the leading national newspapers, newsmagazines, and television networks in 1979–1980 found a strong pattern of liberal attitudes on social issues, though attitudes on economic issues were more mixed.[132] And from the 1960s on, the most prominent Supreme Court reporters, such as Anthony Lewis and Linda Greenhouse of the *New York Times* and Nina Totenberg of National Public Radio, reported and assessed the Justices' positions primarily from a liberal perspective. This does not necessarily mean that the content of news coverage was skewed in a liberal direction, and measurement of ideological bias in news coverage is a difficult task.[133] But Justices interacted primarily with journalists who had liberal views, and that in itself is significant.

Our analysis of editorials in the most visible newspapers provides additional evidence both that media elites typically favored liberal outcomes in Supreme Court cases and that most journalists and publishers had center-left preferences. We analyzed the content of editorials from several newspapers about a sampling of thirty-two major Supreme Court decisions.[134] The newspapers were the *Washington Post*, the *New York Times*, the *Wall Street Journal*, the *Chicago Tribune*, the *Los Angeles Times*, the *Boston Globe*, and the *Dallas Morning News*. These newspapers were chosen for their prominence and for ideological diversity.[135] These decisions concerned race, religion, speech, election law, enemy combatants, criminal procedure, abortion, gay rights, gun rights, and health care. The earliest decision was *Brown v. Board of Education* (1954); the most recent were *Burwell v. Hobby Lobby Stores* (2014) and *Riley v. California* (2014).[136] Although we were interested in editorials across the whole period and in decisions that took liberal, conservative, and mixed positions, we focused primarily on pro-civil liberties decisions in the early part of the period—a time in which there was a degree of elite consensus on left-center positions on the kinds of issues that the Supreme Court addressed.

In general, the editorials reflected the newspapers' ideological orientations. It is not surprising that during the Warren and Burger Courts (and more recently), the *New York Times* and *Washington Post*, both liberal in their orientations, almost invariably supported liberal decisions on civil liberties even when those decisions took unpopular positions on issues such as criminal justice and religious exercises in public schools.[137] Still, this support in two newspapers that were especially visible to the Justices is noteworthy. Moreover, support for pro-civil liberties decisions extended to other major newspapers, and even those with a conservative orientation sometimes editorialized in favor of those decisions.[138] On the whole, then, editorial reactions to the Court's decisions in the most prominent newspapers reinforced liberal positions on civil liberties issues.

Of course, there is no concrete evidence on the attitudes of people in the Washington community with whom the Justices interacted. But there is reason to think that with the expansion of the federal government during the New Deal era, Washington increasingly was populated with elites who supported an activist government. Moreover, the highly educated people in Washington elites could be expected to share the liberal views of their counterparts elsewhere on social issues. Indeed, President Nixon complained about what he perceived as a liberal "Washington-Georgetown social set."[139]

For Justices who came to the Court as liberals, then, there was a politically congenial social environment. That environment provided reinforcement for the direction that these Justices were inclined to take on the basis of their personal views. They could expect to receive primarily praise for liberal votes and opinions from Supreme Court reporters and legal scholars.

In the second half of the twentieth century there were no liberal organizations of lawyers comparable to the American Constitution Society and the Federalist Society, its conservative counterpart, in the current era. There was no need for such organizations on the liberal side, because the elite segment of the legal profession—like the larger elite world around the Justices—was favorable to liberal positions. To take one example, the Madison Lectures at New York University, initiated in 1960, served as a forum for liberal federal appellate judges to be honored and to express their views on legal issues (which were then published in the *NYU Law Review*). The first five lectures were given by Hugo Black, William Brennan, Earl Warren, William O. Douglas, and Arthur Goldberg—the liberal core of the Warren Court in the period from 1962 to 1965.[140]

It is impossible to ascertain the impact of this elite environment on the Justices who were already inclined to take liberal positions on most issues before the Court. It seems reasonable to posit that the Court's environment strengthened Justices' liberal inclinations to some degree by giving them another reason to take liberal positions in their votes and opinions. In any event, there was no conflict between the policy preferences that liberal Justices brought to the Court and the dominant direction of the ideological signals they were receiving from relevant sets of people outside the Court.

The Justices who joined the Court as liberals included both Republican and Democratic appointees. As we have discussed, the presence of liberal Republican appointees such as Warren and Brennan reflected the limited and variable role of ideology in presidential nominations prior to the mid-1980s. But what of the Republican appointees who seemed to be at least moderately conservative when they joined the Court? Several of those Justices, from the Eisenhower era forward, compiled records on the Court that could best be characterized as moderate to liberal—at least in the field of civil liberties, which has constituted the most contentious portion of the Court's agenda since the 1940s and the largest portion since the 1960s.[141] The result was to further muddle the relationship between party and ideology on the Court for several decades. In light of the liberal leanings of elites around the Court for so long, it is at least possible that the difference between expectations of those Republican appointees and their actual records reflected the influence of the elite world.

Ideological Shifts by Justices over Time: The "Greenhouse Effect" Hypothesis. As it happens, several commentators on the Court have argued that liberal elites exerted a powerful impact on a series of Republican appointees to the Court. Those commentators are primarily conservatives who were disappointed because the Court did not move more sharply to the right after the end of the Warren Court. Their disappointment is understandable. Because Jimmy Carter did not have the opportunity to choose any Justices, there was a string of ten consecutive appointments by Republican presidents between 1969 and 1991. These appointments certainly created a more conservative Court. But in civil rights and liberties the Court remained relatively moderate. Conservatives were frustrated by the Court's refusal to overturn disfavored precedents; Reagan Attorney General Edwin Meese, for example, spoke of the need to challenge these rulings and of the difference between the Constitution and Supreme Court interpretations of the Constitution.[142] Conservatives were particularly upset with decisions such as the Court's refusal to reconsider its school prayer rulings, its continuing approval of affirmative action, and, most notably, its 1992 ruling in *Planned Parenthood v. Casey* that largely ratified *Roe v. Wade*.

The fact that the Court did not change as much as conservatives had hoped reflected the unexpected records of some Justices who had been appointed by Republican presidents. Leaving aside Warren and Brennan, Ford appointee John Paul Stevens, George H. W. Bush appointee David Souter, and (in the later years of his Court tenure) Nixon appointee Harry Blackmun took primarily liberal positions that had been unexpected when they were appointed. Other Republican appointees had records that were primarily conservative, but not to the degree that conservatives would have hoped. These included Eisenhower appointee Potter Stewart, Nixon appointee Lewis Powell, and Reagan appointees Sandra Day O'Connor and Anthony Kennedy. Republican Senator Ted Cruz expressed a common lament in one of the Republican presidential debates in 2016: "Democrats bat about 1.000. Just about everyone they put on the court votes exactly as they want. Republicans have batted worse than .500, more than half of the people we put on the court have been a disaster."[143]

That outcome—or a less exaggerated version of it—might be ascribed to simple bad luck or poor judgments by Republican presidents. But some conservatives, while criticizing appointment decisions, have pointed to what they see as another source of the problem: the influence of left-leaning elites on Justices once they sit on the Court.

Concern about the influence of liberal elites on Supreme Court Justices was expressed by one leading conservative even when the string of consecutive Republican appointments was just beginning. That conservative was President Nixon. When Nixon complained about a liberal "Washington-Georgetown social set," it was partly because he thought that Justice Stewart had been "overwhelmed" by it.[144] As he was talking about one potential nominee to the Court, he worried that if the candidate had "a social wife," she might get involved with "that [expletive deleted] Georgetown set."[145] And after letting Harry Blackmun know that his nomination would be announced a few days later, Nixon warned Blackmun "that the 'Georgetown crowd' will do their best to elbow in on you. You will be wined and dined and approached. I suspect that two of the Justices have fallen victim to this kind of thing."[146] Telling Chief Justice Warren Burger that he was pleased about his appointee William Rehnquist, Nixon said that "he isn't going to be moved by the Georgetown set."[147]

As Republican appointees in the post-Warren era established records on the Court, concern about this kind of influence continued. In 1981, one official in the Reagan administration who formulated questions to be asked about prospective Supreme Court nominees posed this question: "Is this person strongly convinced of his/her own philosophy? Will they likely be unduly swayed by liberal, academic, media, peer or other pressures?"[148]

Conservative disappointment with the string of Republican appointments intensified in the 1990s, and concern about the influence of liberal elites spread more widely. That influence also received a label, alluding to what some commentators saw as the baleful influence of *New York Times* Supreme Court reporter Linda Greenhouse: the "Greenhouse effect." Economist and political commentator Thomas Sowell coined the term, based on his view that Greenhouse was "the most prominent practitioner" of reporters' efforts to sway Justices in a liberal direction.[149] Federal court of appeals judge Laurence Silberman also helped to popularize the term.[150]

Since that time other conservatives, some adopting the label of the Greenhouse effect, have made similar arguments. Frequently they go beyond the news media, pointing to other liberal-leaning elite influences that include legal scholars, leaders of the legal profession, and—sharing President Nixon's concern—Washington social circles.[151] Sowell, for instance, argued that "all the influences and incentives are to move leftward. That is how you get the applause of the American Bar Association, good ink in the liberal press, acclaim in the elite law schools and invitations to tony Georgetown parties."[152] For that matter, Justice Antonin Scalia wrote in several dissenting opinions about what he saw as his colleagues' undue responsiveness to the views of a liberal elite.[153] Conservatives have singled out some Republican appointees for criticism, especially Blackmun and (more recently) Kennedy.[154]

It is tempting to dismiss this commentary as nothing more than an expression of unhappiness and bitterness about the Supreme Court's direction. Certainly the idea that an interest in acclaim from certain elites in itself transformed the jurisprudence of a series of Justices might seem questionable. But the possibility that left-leaning elites influenced the thinking of those Justices is not unreasonable.[155] As we discussed in chapter 2, based on the perspective of social psychology, Justices can be expected to seek the positive regard of the individuals and groups that are most salient to them—and those audiences are primarily in political and social elites. And as we have discussed in this chapter, for several decades the elites that were most relevant to the Justices were primarily liberal.

Commentators who argue that elites have a liberalizing influence on Justices have no difficulty making the case that several Republican appointees had moderate or liberal records as Justices. These commentators typically emphasize major decisions such as *Planned Parenthood v. Casey* (in which Justices O'Connor, Kennedy, and Souter co-wrote the decisive opinion maintaining most of what the Court had ruled in *Roe v. Wade*), *National Federation of Independent Business v. Sebelius*[156] (in which Chief Justice Roberts's vote and opinion upheld the "individual mandate" in the health care program sponsored by President Obama), and a series of decisions involving gay rights (in which Justice Kennedy wrote the Court's opinions that announced liberal outcomes).[157] These commentators also point to Justices' overall records on the Court.

The idea of a Greenhouse effect rests heavily on the existence of movement to the left during a Justice's Court career. If a Justice appointed by a Republican president immediately adopts a liberal position on the Court and maintains that position over the years, it is unlikely (though not impossible) that the Justice was heavily influenced by elites in the Court's environment. But if a Justice's record moves to the left over the course of the Justice's Court's tenure, it is more likely (though far from certain) that elite influence occurred.

As we will discuss shortly, such movement can be difficult to ascertain. Justice Blackmun's movement to the left during his Court career was so decisive that it clearly reflected a fundamental change in his policy positions.[158] But other Justices have not made such decisive shifts. Adherents to the Greenhouse hypothesis generally have relied on impressionistic evidence of Justices' positions on the ideological scale over time.

The most difficult element of this hypothesis to probe is the sources of the relatively liberal records of some Republican appointees. There can be no definitive judgment about the impact of the elite world around the Court on the Justices' thinking and policy positions. Adherents to the hypothesis have argued for its plausibility, and they have also used comparisons of Republican appointees who took different paths on the Court to support the hypothesis. We will examine the relevant evidence on this question, as well as the more tractable question of whether several Republican appointees moved to the left during their tenure on the Court.

Probing the Evidence. We can start with change in Justices' positions. As we have said, measurement of such change is a difficult task. The most straightforward approach is to analyze the proportions of liberal and conservative votes cast by a Justice over time. But there are significant limitations to this approach. For one thing, definitions of liberal and conservative sides on the issues that the Court addresses are subject to change over time, and to a degree they are arbitrary.[159]

More important, the mix of cases that the Court hears on an issue or on a set of issues such as civil liberties changes over time. As a result, a Justice who voted for civil liberties claims 60 percent of the time in one term and whose underlying ideological position remains exactly the same might vote for those claims 50 percent or 70 percent of the time in another term. To some extent changes in the mix of cases are idiosyncratic, but there is also systematic change that reflects the Court's overall ideological position.[160] Methods of identifying Justices' ideological positions based on patterns of agreement between them avoid the problem of defining liberal and conservative sides, but the ideological scores they produce are not necessarily comparable over time.[161]

The best solution to these difficulties that has been developed so far is the set of ideological scores for the field of civil liberties devised by political scientist Michael Bailey.[162] Bailey's method is complex, but one key element of his approach is using pairs of cases from different Court terms as bases for comparison. If a Justice writes an opinion that explicitly agrees or disagrees with an earlier decision, we know how the Justice thinks he or she would have voted in that earlier decision. There are also cases in which a Justice's vote allows us to infer the Justice's view of an earlier decision. If a Justice voted to strike down a substantial state restriction on abortion after *Roe v. Wade*, that vote implies support for the majority position in *Roe*.[163] That information could then be used to control for change in the Court's agenda over time and thereby calculate scores for each Justice for each year (Bailey used calendar years rather than Court terms) that are comparable across years.

Bailey limited his analysis to what he called social policy: crime, civil rights, free speech, religion, abortion, and privacy.[164] That domain serves our purposes well, since those who argue that certain Republican appointees have adopted more liberal positions over time focus on these civil liberties issues. The scores are available for the years 1950 to 2011.

Table 3.2 presents information on change in the Justices' positions over time. Justices are included if they were appointed by Eisenhower or a later president and if they had served ten years on the Court by 2011.[165] Scores for Justices in a single Court term range from −1.87 (the most favorable to civil liberties claims) to +1.22 (least favorable); the mean is −0.09 and the standard deviation 0.82. We compared the Justices' mean scores for their first two years with the means for their fifth through tenth years and for their last six years on the Court (or, for Justices who continued to serve after 2011, the years 2006–2011). The figures in the two "change" columns are not the Justices' ideological scores in those periods but rather the difference between the scores for those periods and the scores for Justices' first two years. Thus a negative figure in those columns indicates that a Justice changed in a liberal direction after the first two years; the larger the score, whether positive or negative, the greater the magnitude of the change. In interpreting the scores and changes in the scores, it should be kept in mind that the scores for individual Justice-years are estimates with a fairly wide variance. Combining terms reduces random variation but does not eliminate it.

Table 3.2. Changes in Bailey Scores for Civil Liberties Votes over Justices' Tenure on the Court, Selected Justices

Justice	1st Year	Score for Years 1–2	Change to Years 5–10	Change to Last 6 Years
		Republican Appointees		
Warren	1954	0.11	−0.85	−1.15
Harlan	1955	0.32	0.04	0.00
Brennan	1957	−0.73	−0.16	−0.62
Stewart	1959	0.19	−0.30	−0.21
Burger	1970	0.49	0.20	0.14
Blackmun	1970	0.41	−0.11	−1.03
Powell	1972	0.27	−0.05	0.05
Rehnquist	1972	0.96	0.18	−0.07
Stevens	1976	−0.36	−0.10	−0.48
O'Connor	1982	0.59	−0.03	−0.26
Scalia	1986	0.58	0.22	0.36
Kennedy	1988	0.56	−0.17	−0.20
Souter	1991	0.11	−0.40	−0.73
Thomas	1992	0.87	0.15	0.20
		Democratic Appointees		
White	1962	−0.30	0.05	0.72
Marshall	1967	−1.27	−0.05	−0.23
Ginsburg	1994	−0.47	−0.08	−0.67
Breyer	1995	−0.37	−0.03	−0.15

To a considerable degree, the results are consistent with the perceptions of Republican appointees by conservative commentators. Justice Blackmun's shift to the left came relatively late in his Court career, but it was quite substantial. Justices Brennan and Stevens, already on the liberal side of the spectrum in their first two years, grew distinctly more liberal after their first ten years on the Court. Justice Souter moved from a relatively neutral position to one distinctly on the liberal side. The changes for Justices Stewart, O'Connor, and Kennedy were small enough to require caution in interpretation, but all were in the expected direction.

Not all Republican appointees moved to the left, and Justices Scalia and Thomas moved somewhat to the right. Among the Democratic appointees,

Justice Ginsburg became substantially more liberal after her first ten years on the Court, but Justice White became substantially more conservative. He was the one Justice in this group whose positions became far less favorable to civil liberties claims by this measure.

Because conservatives' disappointment with the records of Republican appointees to the Court has focused heavily on highly visible decisions, it is useful to consider those decisions separately. One widely used measure of "salience" for Supreme Court decisions is whether those decisions receive front-page coverage in the *New York Times*.[166] Although this measure does not necessarily capture the importance of cases to the Justices, it does identify decisions that one set of editors sees as consequential. It has the advantage of including cases across the full range of the Court's work, though civil liberties decisions are overrepresented.

For the Justices who were included in Table 3.2, we analyzed temporal change in voting patterns in civil liberties decisions that met the *Times*-based criterion for salience. Of course, the salient cases in two different periods are not fully comparable with each other, and we would expect some differences in liberal and conservative voting based on changes in case content.[167] Still, the comparison is instructive. The results are shown in Table 3.3. In this table, in contrast with Table 3.2, higher scores are more liberal and positive changes indicate a move toward greater liberalism.

The patterns in the Justices' voting in the most salient cases help to explain the disappointment of conservative commentators with several Republican appointees to the Court. Chief Justice Warren and Justices Brennan, Stewart, Stevens, and Souter were already more liberal in these cases than would be expected of a Republican appointee in their first two terms. Warren and Souter became even more liberal in salient cases later in their tenure. And the proportions of liberal votes by Justices Blackmun, Powell, O'Connor, and Kennedy also increased substantially. In Blackmun's case, that increase predated the increase in liberal voting across all cases. The change in Kennedy's record was quite dramatic.

The Bailey measure of Justices' ideological positions and the proportions of liberal and conservative votes in salient cases differ quite substantially in both methodology and the sets of cases on which they are based. But both show meaningful movement in a liberal direction by several Republican appointees to the Court. Moreover, the two measures agree to a considerable extent about the identities of the Justices who moved ideologically. Among the Justices chosen by Republican presidents, the correlation between the two measures of change from the first two terms to the fifth through tenth terms is .592.[168]

Table 3.3. Percentages of Liberal Votes in Civil Liberties Decisions Reported on Front Page of the *New York Times*, for Selected Periods of Justices' Tenure

Justice	Terms 1–2	Terms 5–10	Change
	Republican Appointees		
Warren	71.4	88.0	+16.6
Harlan	60.0	39.3	−20.7
Brennan	88.0	82.0	−6.0
Stewart	50.0	56.6	+6.6
Burger	32.6	22.6	−10.0
Blackmun	35.4	50.5	+15.1
Powell	28.6	40.6	+12.0
Rehnquist	15.4	12.4	−3.0
Stevens	60.0	66.7	+6.7
O'Connor	20.0	34.3	+14.3
Scalia	31.8	22.1	−9.7
Kennedy	11.9	45.6	+33.7
Souter	56.3	76.7	+20.4
Thomas	37.5	16.9	−20.6
	Democratic Appointees		
White	63.2	55.9	−7.3
Marshall	89.2	95.9	+6.7
Ginsburg	77.8	87.1	+9.3
Breyer	76.2	80.8	+4.6

This brings us to the difficult question of why some Republican appointees moved to the left. Some commentators have addressed that question by comparing those Justices with other Republican appointees who did not seem to move to the left during their tenure on the Court. They have pointed to prior experience in Washington, DC, and in the executive branch as explanations of the difference between the two sets of Justices, because lawyers who have gone through those experiences and who have adhered to their conservatism can be trusted to remain conservative as Justices:

> Republican Presidents should appoint lawyers of demonstrated invulnerability to the Greenhouse Effect—a virtue possessed by Rehnquist, Scalia, and Thomas, all three of whom had worked in the executive

> branch, been through confirmation and oversight hearings, been denounced in the press and by members of Congress, and not "grown." Newcomers to Washington are risks, as Kennedy, O'Connor, and Souter have demonstrated.[169]

Those explanations are largely consistent with the patterns shown in Tables 3.2 and 3.3. Chief Justice Burger and Justices Rehnquist, Scalia, and Thomas stood out from the other Justices chosen by Republican presidents between Eisenhower and the first Bush in that they worked in DC prior to their appointments (albeit only for two years in Rehnquist's case) and all had worked in Republican administrations. None of the four showed any evidence of leftward movement after they joined the Court. But this evidence should be interpreted with considerable caution, because it is easy to impose an explanation after the fact on a pattern of data that is actually random.[170]

Moreover, it is highly unlikely that any single factor could account for the changes that occurred in the policy positions of some Republican appointees—or for the fact that those Justices changed and other Republican appointees did not. Certainly that is true of the influence of liberal-leaning elites. It is not at all clear, for instance, that the famously self-directed David Souter was moved powerfully by his social and political environment.[171] But for some other Justices, there is more reason to conclude that elite influence played a significant part in their ideological evolution. The two Justices who stand out in this respect are Harry Blackmun and Anthony Kennedy, both subjects of considerable disappointment and disapproval among conservatives.

Blackmun and Kennedy. We begin with Blackmun. The data in Tables 3.2 and 3.3 make it clear that the widely shared perception of a movement to the left on his part in civil liberties cases was accurate. Another indication of that movement is the relative frequency with which Blackmun joined the same opinions as his liberal and conservative colleagues across all fields. Figure 3.2 shows the trend in agreements between Blackmun and William Rehnquist and William Brennan.[172] Although the trend is uneven, over time Blackmun moved from having a substantially higher agreement rate with Rehnquist to having a higher agreement rate with Brennan.

Blackmun's shift in a liberal direction has received a great deal of attention, including a book-length analysis by reporter and scholar Linda Greenhouse.[173] Understandably, there has been considerable interest in the sources of that shift. Scholars and other commentators have pointed to a

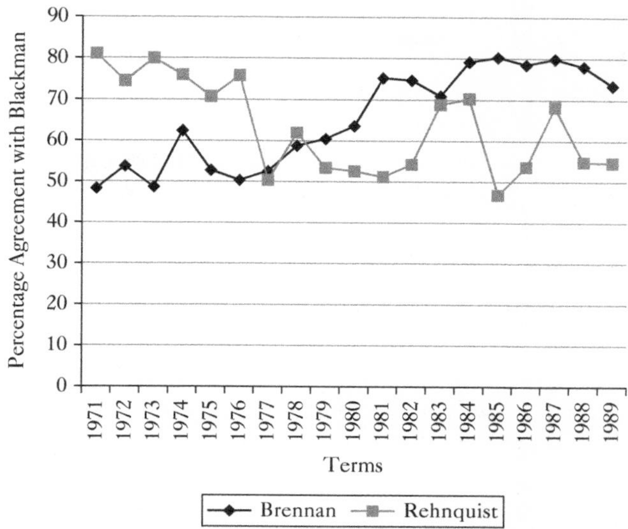

FIGURE 3.2. Rates of agreement on opinions between Justice Harry Blackmun and two colleagues, in percentages, by Court term.

range of possible explanations such as Blackmun's relationship with his childhood friend Warren Burger and his authorship of the Court's opinion in *Roe v. Wade*.[174]

One of these possibilities is the influence of the elite world with which Blackmun interacted. For conservative commentators, he has been a leading example of the influence of liberal elites on Justices.[175] Indeed, there is evidence that the approval of those elites at least reinforced his movement away from his initial conservatism and that it may have been an important source of that movement.

Blackmun did seem to be more attentive to the world outside the Court than most other Justices. He gave considerable attention to mail praising or denouncing his work as a Justice.[176] He had close relationships with several reporters.[177] He also stood out in his era for his willingness to express candid views in public or through the news media.[178] Certainly he was sensitive to how he was viewed by people outside the Court.

Roe was important to Blackmun: he identified strongly with the decision, and its continued vitality was a major concern for him.[179] Looking back at his time on the Court, he implied that *Roe* had helped to bring about his movement in a liberal direction.[180] The decision received heavy and even vitriolic criticism, and even some people who favored the substance of the decision criticized Blackmun's opinion. But many liberals gave the decision strong approval, approval that undoubtedly was important to him. And other signs of liberalism on his part also garnered approval.

It would be understandable if Blackmun responded positively to that approval by moving in a liberal direction. He liked being recognized as someone who fought for civil liberties.[181] In appearances before predominantly liberal groups, he sometimes made statements about his role as a supporter of civil liberties that were certain to draw loud approval.[182] Notably, Blackmun's movement away from William Rehnquist and toward William Brennan, shown in Figure 3.2, was driven by civil liberties issues. In civil liberties, his voting record (as measured by percentages of conservative and liberal votes) moved much closer to Brennan's and much further from Rehnquist's between his early and late terms on the Court. In contrast, there was no such movement in economic cases.[183]

Of course, it is impossible to ascertain the role of liberal audiences in Blackmun's ideological shift. And to the extent those audiences had an impact on him, that impact might have occurred even if the elite world around the Court did not lean to the left. But this leaning meant that approval of Blackmun's moves toward liberalism was more widespread than it would have been otherwise. Praise from the elite news media, for instance, would not have been as substantial if he had remained on the Court's conservative side. That praise was exemplified by the editorials in the *Washington Post* and the *New York Times* after Blackmun died.[184] Thus, there is some reason to think that the ideological state of the Court's elite environment made a difference in the course of Blackmun's career on the Court.

The course of Justice Anthony Kennedy's career as a Justice is more complicated. As the Bailey scores show for civil liberties cases, any overall movement to the left on his part was relatively small. Over time he came to stand more firmly in the Court's ideological center rather than its right center, but that is only because of changes in the Court's membership. As Figure 3.3 shows, there were fluctuations in Kennedy's agreement rates with Antonin Scalia and John Paul Stevens over his first twenty-two terms on the Court, but throughout that period Kennedy was closer to Scalia than to Stevens—sometimes by a small margin, sometimes by a substantial one.

His overall voting record aside, Kennedy supported conservative positions on a number of significant issues, including regulation of campaign finance, procedural rights for criminal defendants, voting rights, and an array of economic questions. To take one example, Kennedy dissented from the Court's 2012 ruling that upheld the Affordable Care Act (ACA) mandate for certain

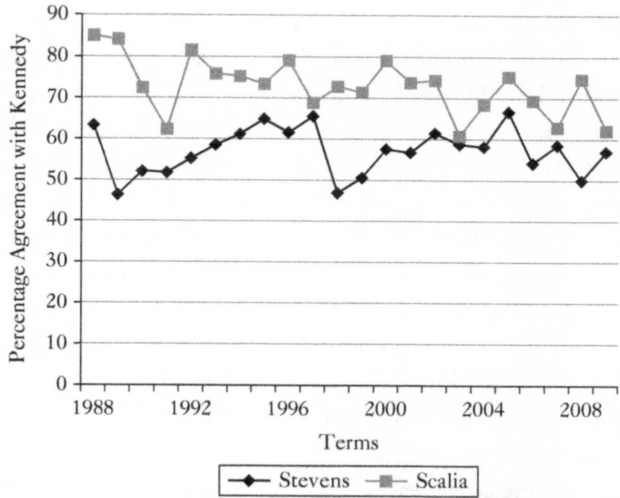

FIGURE 3.3. Rates of agreement on opinions between Justice Anthony Kennedy and two colleagues, in percentages, by Court term.

individuals to buy health insurance, and he took the conservative side on the three other issues involving the ACA that the Court decided in that case and its successors.[185] In his voting on economic issues as a whole, he stood firmly on the conservative side of the Court.[186]

Yet Kennedy received considerable criticism from conservatives for his work on the Court, criticism that seems even more intense than Blackmun received. One reason is that his relative moderation postponed the establishment of a strong and consistent conservative majority on the Court after 2006, when Samuel Alito became the fourth strong conservative. But there is a more specific reason for the criticism: although conservatives would agree with most of the positions Kennedy took on the Court, he was on the liberal side in a series of civil liberties decisions that were a high priority for conservatives in the legal community. Moreover, as Table 3.3 shows, after his first two terms on the Court, he became substantially more likely to support liberal positions on high-profile issues.

It is some of these issues that stand out for Kennedy's conservative critics. In *Planned Parenthood v. Casey,* he coauthored the opinion that maintained the heart of *Roe v. Wade,* after joining an opinion three years earlier that had hinted at support for overruling *Roe* when an appropriate case came to the Court.[187] He voted to prohibit death sentences for intellectually disabled defendants in *Atkins v. Virginia* (2002) and for defendants who were younger than eighteen when they committed murders in *Roper v. Simmons* (2005), writing the Court's opinion in *Roper*. In each instance he took a position that he had directly rejected in a 1989 decision.[188] As noted earlier, Kennedy wrote the Court's opinions in all four decisions between 1996 and 2015 that favored gay rights on important questions, culminating in the ruling in *Obergefell v. Hodges* that struck down state prohibitions on same-sex marriage.[189] And after indicating considerable skepticism about affirmative action in earlier decisions, in *Fisher v. Texas* (2016) he provided the decisive vote and wrote the Court's opinion that upheld the affirmative action plan used for undergraduate admissions to the University of Texas.[190] Even before some of those decisions were handed down, one conservative critic referred to Kennedy multiple times as "the most dangerous man in America."[191]

What accounts for the votes and opinions that disappointed conservatives? Writing in 1996, one conservative journal explained that Kennedy "sold out once he was safely on the court for life in order to curry favor with the liberal establishment, especially the social elite in the Nation's Capital." It added that on three key social issues "Kennedy has gone with the flow of elite liberal opinion, rather than to endure the slings and arrows that adherence to his moral and juridical principles would bring in Georgetown salons."[192] Other conservative commentators offered similar explanations.[193]

As with Blackmun, it seems unlikely that such a simple explanation can fully account for Kennedy's unexpected liberalism on some major social issues. Yet Kennedy's desire for elite approval may well have shaped some of those positions. It appears that he gave more attention to the Court's audiences than do most other Justices. One of his former law clerks said that in considering cases, "he would constantly refer to how it's going to be perceived, how the papers are going to do it, how it's going to look."[194] He was willing to talk with reporters on the record about his decision-making process, seemingly in an effort to foster a favorable impression from readers.[195] He was an active participant in Washington social life.[196] Thus, it is not unreasonable to posit that his positions were shaped by reactions and prospective reactions from liberal elites. And on the one position that has been most closely identified with Kennedy—equality based on sexual orientation—it would be surprising if he did not enjoy his status as a hero to supporters of gay rights.[197]

Summing Up. It is impossible to reach anything like a definitive judgment about the impact of left-leaning elites on the Republican appointees who joined the Supreme Court between 1953 and 1990. It does seem quite unlikely that this impact was as strong as some conservative commentators have contended; the Justices are more complex and more autonomous than that.

Yet we also think that a meaningful impact for those elites is quite plausible. As people who are part of a social elite and who are oriented toward elite groups, the Justices are subject to influence by those groups. In times when there is a strong tendency in elite opinion, as there was on civil liberties issues in and after the Warren Court era, at least some Justices may be drawn toward positions that enjoy strong support among elite groups. Both the quantitative evidence of changes in the Justices' policy positions and qualitative evidence about some Justices point to the existence of that influence.

Conclusions

In this chapter we have examined aspects of the Supreme Court's history prior to the current era of high political polarization, with particular attention to the era from Franklin Roosevelt to Reagan. Our key descriptive finding was that until quite recently, there were never ideological divisions on the Court that coincided with partisan lines: at no point before 2010 was there one substantial bloc of Justices who were appointed solely by presidents of one party and another substantial bloc of Justices appointed solely by presidents of the other party.

Undoubtedly, there was an element of chance to that surprising record. But as we showed, it reflected systematic forces. Through most of the Court's history, presidents did not make a consistent and careful effort to choose Justices whose views on issues of legal policy reflected the distinctive ideological orientation of their party. As a result, there were a good many Justices whose policy preferences did not put them firmly on the correct side from the perspective of most people in their party. The conservative Truman appointees and the two Eisenhower "mistakes"—Earl Warren and William Brennan—had a good many counterparts in other eras.[198]

The other systematic force was the elite environment in which the Justices worked. In the late nineteenth and early twentieth centuries, an elite that was predominantly conservative likely helped to move both Republican and Democratic Justices to support laissez-faire economic policies. More recently, a predominantly liberal set of elite groups may have helped to move Justices appointed by Republican presidents to the left during their careers on the Court, thereby weakening the relationship between party and ideological position on the Court.

We are now in an era of political polarization. In chapter 4 we discuss how that polarization has affected both appointments to the Court and the influence of elites on sitting Justices. The most visible result has been the development for the first time of ideological blocs that coincide with party lines, and we examine how that result has come about.

4

The Court in a Polarized World

IN CHAPTER 2, WE critiqued the dominant political science models of Supreme Court decision making and, in their place, advanced a social psychology model that also takes into account basic human motivations relating to power, status, and the esteem of other people. In chapter 3, we applied that model to explain Court decision making, including the shift of some Republican appointees to the left during the Warren and Burger Court eras. In this chapter, we consider developments during the Rehnquist (1986–2005) and Roberts Courts (starting in 2005).

Our analysis will explain how the social psychology perspective that helps to account for the earlier shift of some Justices to the left also helps in understanding the partisan divide that now separates Democratic and Republican appointees to the Court. Starting with the 2010 appointment of Democrat Elena Kagan to fill the seat of liberal Republican John Paul Stevens, the Court has been divided along partisan lines. That divide was reinforced with the 2017 appointment of Republican Neil Gorsuch and, even more, by the 2018 appointment of Republican Brett Kavanaugh. It is likely to persist for considerable time. While this divide is generally recognized, the circumstances that propelled it and are likely to make it persist are not generally understood. In this chapter, we will analyze those circumstances.

Along with the broad effects of political polarization, we give attention to more specific developments in the legal system. One development was especially important. Starting in 1985, the Reagan administration took concrete steps to develop both a conservative perspective on legal issues and an elite network of conservative lawyers who could assume positions of power within the government and, ultimately, become federal court of appeals judges and Supreme Court Justices. Correspondingly, the Reagan administration took steps to emphasize ideology in judicial appointments. These efforts and their long-term effects help to account for the current divide between conservative Republicans and liberal Democrats on the Court.

At the same time, we will also build on points made in chapter 2 to explain why partisanship on the Supreme Court is fundamentally different than partisanship in Congress. The Supreme Court is still a court, and norms of collegiality and law-oriented decision making remain important to the Justices. A partisan Supreme Court will still issue unanimous opinions, and Democratic and Republican Justices will still cross party lines to form coalitions in individual cases. Nonetheless, the frequency of party-line voting is far greater on a partisan Court, especially on those salient cases that largely define the Court's image. The perspective of social psychology can help in explaining both the development of a partisan divide and the limits of partisanship on the Court.

We begin by detailing the rise of elite polarization in Congress, the media, and the academy, and among the wealthy and well educated. We then track somewhat parallel developments in the White House and the Justice Department, particularly the efforts of Republican administrations to increasingly emphasize ideology in judicial appointments and to cultivate the conservative legal movement. We will then shift our focus to Supreme Court decision making. Initially we will document the partisan divide among Democratic and Republican appointees; we will then explain how partisanship on the Court manifests itself differently than partisanship in Congress.

The Rise of Elite Polarization

Starting in the 1980s, there has been a substantial increase in polarization in government and among political elites outside government. As we have discussed, polarization has multiple elements. Through partisan sorting, ideological views and partisan identifications may be more closely related than they were at any time since Reconstruction. Through affective polarization, Democrats and Republicans increasingly see themselves as members of opposing teams and increasingly hold negative attitudes toward members of the other party. Through extremism, attitudes about issues move away from the middle of the ideological spectrum toward the two ends of that spectrum.

In the Supreme Court, the key element of polarization has been partisan sorting. As we see it, that sorting results in part from affective polarization among the Justices. Partisan sorting and extremism among other political elites, including the other branches of government, have contributed to sorting on the Court through the appointment process. They have also created the conditions for affective polarization among the Justices. As yet, there is no clear movement toward extremism on the Court itself,[1] though such movement may occur in the future as a result of polarization among elites as a whole.

It is inevitable that the growth in political polarization would affect the Court, both directly and indirectly. In chapter 3, we examined the consequences for the Court of the relative homogeneity of elite opinion during the Warren Court and much of the Burger Court. In particular, we explained how the ideological drift of some Justices toward center-left positions could be explained in part by the dominance of center-left elite social networks among political and social elites. In this chapter, we will consider the ramifications of elite polarization. We start by examining the growth of polarization in government, giving primary attention to partisan sorting. We then consider polarization in the larger elite world, including media outlets, the legal profession, and the academy.

Government

The growing ideological separation between the two parties is reflected in both the federal and state governments. Democratic and Republican officials have grown more distinct and more distant from each other ideologically and more hostile toward each other.

Mapping Changes in Congress. In terms of partisan sorting, today's Congress is a much different place than Congress during the era of the Warren and Burger Courts. In that era differences between the two parties in median scores on a liberal-conservative scale were relatively low by the standards of the late nineteenth and early twentieth centuries.[2] In 1968, for example, Democrats occupied every ideological niche and there were several liberal Republicans. Exaggerating somewhat, George Wallace justified his third-party bid for the presidency in 1968 by claiming that there was not a "dime's worth of difference between Democrats and Republicans."[3]

Today, however, the liberal "Rockefeller Republicans" and conservative Southern Democrats have given way to an era of partisan polarization in Congress. This development has multiple sources, and the relative importance of those sources is uncertain.[4] Certainly one key factor was the political realignment in the South that was tied to civil rights reforms in the 1960s, one in which conservative Democrats in Congress were replaced by conservative Republicans.[5] Following Ronald Reagan's victory in 1980, the moderate-to-liberal wing of the Republican Party began to dissipate. There has also been a broader partisan sorting among voters, which pushes both Republican and Democratic members of Congress toward more extreme positions. Growing extremism among party activists and campaign contributors exerts a similar push. Although the impact of gerrymandering is sometimes exaggerated,[6] computer-driven districting has helped produce high proportions of safe seats in the House, in turn giving candidates an incentive to appeal primarily to partisans who vote in primaries.[7] Strategic and tactical decisions by congressional leaders have also played an important part in this development.

Whatever the sources of these changes may be, the results are striking. In every Congress since 2005, on the primary dimension of congressional voting, every Democratic senator has had a more liberal voting record than every Republican senator, and nearly the same has been true of the House.[8] By 2009, the ideological distance between the Democratic and Republican Parties was greater than it had been at any time since Reconstruction.[9] By 2012, the growth of the Tea Party had pushed the divide even further (as moderates like Texas senator Kay Bailey Hutchinson were replaced by strong conservatives like Ted Cruz).[10]

In chapter 3, we illustrated these developments through Figure 3.1, showing the ideological distance between the two parties in the House and Senate over time. That figure underlines the sharp increase in polarization that has occurred in recent decades. Congress from the 1930s to the 1970s featured relatively limited polarization between the parties. The sharp partisan sorting that has occurred in recent decades has resulted in a Congress that is even more polarized now than the Congress of the late nineteenth and early twentieth centuries.

As our discussion thus far suggests, partisan sorting has been accompanied by a growth in extremism. Indeed, the dearth of moderates is one of the most striking features of today's Congress.[11] By one definition, in 1980, moderates made up around 40 percent of Congress; in 2015, moderates were nearly extinct, making up less than 5 percent of Congress.[12] There is little prospect of moderates returning to Congress. With the growth in extremism among party activists and contributors, moderates have difficulty winning primary elections. For the House, as we have noted, that difficulty is exacerbated by redistricting that essentially guarantees a high proportion of safe seats for one party or the other. For safe House and Senate seats, candidates have an incentive to appeal to partisans who vote in primaries. One consequence is that retiring legislators have been replaced by new ones who are both more ideological and more loyal to their party.[13]

Even casual observers of Congress can attest to the growth of the third aspect of polarization, affective polarization. Members' loyalty to their own party and their animosity toward the opposing party are constantly in view. As we will discuss later, this development is part of a broader trend toward affective polarization at both the elite and mass levels.

The Consequences of Polarization in Government. The ideological divide between Democrats and Republicans has increased steadily and substantially since 1980. In Congress, where lawmakers have little reason to appeal to moderate voters, party leaders have capitalized on the fact that lawmakers are apt to see themselves as members of a party, not as independent power brokers. In the early Trump administration, for instance, Republicans in Congress as a group gave overwhelming voting support to the president's positions.[14] More significantly, party leaders have played an ever-growing role in shaping the party's agenda through party caucuses, speaker-appointed task forces, and other techniques.[15] Correspondingly, House and Senate party leaders increasingly engage in "message politics," a process by which Democrats and Republicans alike see the lawmaking process as a way to stand behind a unified party message and, in this way, to distinguish their party from the other.[16]

One area in which polarization in Congress and the executive branch has had a particularly powerful effect is in the process of nominating and confirming federal judges. As we will discuss later in this chapter, Ronald Reagan presided over a substantial increase in the role of ideology in judicial appointments. Since that time, presidents—especially Republican presidents—have increasingly taken ideology into account when appointing Supreme Court Justices and federal court of appeals judges.[17] Correspondingly, party polarization has dramatically impacted Senate consideration of Supreme Court and lower federal court nominees.[18]

Polarization has transformed the process of confirming lower federal court judges, resulting in a dramatic upswing in the amount of time it takes for the Senate to confirm judges and an equally dramatic downswing in the percentage of lower court nominees whom the Judiciary Committee approves, especially when the president's party lacks a Senate majority.[19] Before the 1990s, lower court judges waited less than two months to be confirmed, on average, and confirmation rates were well above 50 percent. Starting in the 1990s and especially after 2000, the number of failed nominees sharply increased, and failed nominees for the courts of appeals typically lingered in the Senate for over a year.[20] It was this change that spurred Senate Democrats in 2013 to invoke the so-called nuclear option—allowing for a simple up-or-down majority vote on presidential nominations to lower courts, independent agencies, and executive branch positions.[21] The success of President Trump's judicial nominees in winning confirmation during his first two years in office reflects that rule change and, more broadly, the ability of a determined majority party—even one with a small majority—to unify on behalf of its agenda.

Senate voting on judicial nominees, especially Supreme Court nominees, has also become increasingly partisan. In the three decades prior to 2005, most nominees to the Court received overwhelming support from both parties. John Paul Stevens, Sandra Day O'Connor, Antonin Scalia, and Anthony Kennedy were all confirmed by unanimous votes. There were three votes against Ruth Bader Ginsburg and nine votes against David Souter and Stephen Breyer. Robert Bork was defeated in 1987 on a vote that mostly followed party lines, and the votes against confirmation of William Rehnquist (as chief justice) in 1986 and Clarence Thomas in 1991 came overwhelmingly from Democratic Senators. But these were exceptions to the rule.

Starting with John Roberts, however, party-line voting and explicit considerations of ideology have been the norm in Senate confirmation votes. Consider, for example, then senator Barack Obama's statement (in explaining his no vote on Chief Justice Roberts) that he had "absolutely no doubt" that Roberts was qualified to sit on the Court but that he was concerned about Roberts because a Justice's positions in difficult cases reflected "one's deepest values" and "the depth and breadth of one's empathy."[22] Roberts, Samuel Alito, Sonia Sotomayor, and Neil Gorsuch all had unanimous support of the president's party in the Senate, while one Democrat voted against Elena Kagan. Democrats split evenly in the Roberts confirmation vote; Alito, Sotomayor, and Kagan were opposed by a majority of members of the opposition party.[23] Neil Gorsuch was opposed by all but three (out of forty-eight) Democratic senators. Brett Kavanaugh by all but one (of forty-nine).[24]

In today's polarized Senate, it is unimaginable that Antonin Scalia would be unanimously confirmed or that Ruth Bader Ginsburg would receive all but three (out of forty-three) Republican votes. Indeed, following Scalia's death in 2016, Democrats and Republicans locked horns in a bitter partisan feud. Senate Republicans blocked any consideration of President Obama's nomination of DC Circuit judge Merrick Garland to fill Scalia's seat. Garland was nominated in March 2016, eight months before the November 2016 presidential elections. Garland was a highly regarded judge with a moderate-liberal voting record; he had impeccable credentials, was unanimously confirmed as a federal court of appeals judge, and had been widely praised by Senate Republicans both before and after his nomination.[25] Nonetheless, Republicans claimed that a Supreme Court vacancy should not be filled during an election year—so that voters could decide the Court's future direction.[26] Democrats claimed foul, castigating Republicans for what they depicted as an unprecedented assault on the Court and the rule of law. Unlike

2013 (when Democrats were in the majority and could invoke the nuclear option to break Republican filibusters of lower court nominees), Republicans were in the majority and Garland's fate was largely in the hands of Majority Leader Mitch McConnell and Judiciary Committee Chair Charles Grassley.

Donald Trump's 2017 nomination of Neil Gorsuch tells a similar story. Following a party-line vote in the Senate Judiciary Committee, Senate Democrats sought to derail the nomination by filibustering Gorsuch. Democrats claimed both that Gorsuch was out of the mainstream and that the nomination rightly belonged to Merrick Garland. Republicans responded by invoking the nuclear option, changing Senate rules to allow for an up-or-down vote on Supreme Court nominees.[27] For Republican Majority Leader Mitch McConnell, "Our Democratic colleagues have done something today that is unprecedented in the history of the Senate, and unfortunately it has brought us to this point"; for Democratic leaders Dick Durbin and Chuck Schumer, McConnell and Gorsuch would "enter the history books with asterisks by their names" and the demise of the filibuster was also "the end of a long history of consensus on Supreme Court nominees."[28]

As we discussed in the Preface, the charges of sexual misconduct against Brett Kavanaugh led to an extraordinary battle over his confirmation. Yet in other respects, Kavanaugh's confirmation illustrated what has become the standard pattern in the current era. Democratic senators had particular reason to oppose Kavanaugh's confirmation, which seemed certain to create a stronger conservative majority on the Court. Democrats argued that Kavanaugh's accession to the Court would have dire consequences for judicial policy. They also criticized the nominee for his activities in the George W. Bush administration and charged that some documents related to those activities were being withheld. As much attention as the charges of sexual misconduct received, they had very little effect on the confirmation vote. Ultimately, the vote fell perfectly along party lines except for Democrat Joe Manchin's vote to confirm; Republican Lisa Murkowski had announced a vote against confirmation but abstained in courtesy to a fellow Republican who could not be present to cast his vote for Kavanaugh.

Polarization and the States. Polarization in state government has also grown over time. As measured by Republican–Democratic differences in voting, polarization in state legislatures as a whole has increased considerably, although with wide variation in trends among states.[29] Polarization became more visible following the 2004 presidential election and the related rise of the Tea Party, especially as it was manifested in divergence between red Republican states and blue Democratic states. As one commentator described it in 2014, Republicans in Midwestern and southern states "are determined to eviscerate liberal policies and to entrench the political power of the right."[30] Abortion regulation is key to this effort, as are voter identification laws and other election rules, tax reform, and the weakening of public sector unions.

Abortion is a good illustration of this change.[31] There have been dramatic changes both in the number of laws enacted and in the severity of state restrictions as Republican control of governorships and state legislatures has grown. According to the Alan Guttmacher Institute, thirteen states were hostile toward abortion in 2000; in 2010, the number was twenty-two with five considered very hostile; in 2017, twenty-nine states were considered hostile and twenty-four of them very hostile.[32]

Another measure of increasing polarization at the state level is the practices of state attorneys general. Starting around 2008, state attorneys general increasingly refused to defend laws unpopular with their political base.[33] For example, twelve Democratic attorneys general refused to defend state bans on same-sex marriage from 2008 to 2014.[34] For their part, Republican attorneys general refused to defend campaign finance regulations and gun control measures.[35] Equally significant, Republican and Democratic attorneys general play an active role in seeking to check the opposition party president. Republican attorneys general helped to lead the effort against Obamacare and successfully blocked President Obama's immigration initiative.[36] Democratic attorneys general have taken aim at President Trump; the effort to repudiate President Trump's immigration orders was spearheaded by Democratic attorneys general, and two Democrats also challenged President Trump's ownership of his company after he became president.[37] The centerpiece of fundraising efforts for the Democratic Attorneys General Association is claims that the Association is "lead[ing] the charge against Trump," "suing Trump at a record pace."[38]

The Larger Elite World

Inevitably, the polarization that is so evident among elected officials has permeated the public as a whole to a considerable degree. For instance, polarization in Congress has clarified the parties' ideological positions and thereby increased party importance and salience.[39] Survey data confirm the existence of partisan sorting: Democrats and Republicans are further apart than ever before. In 1994, 23 percent of Republicans were more liberal than the median Democrat and 17 percent of Democrats were more conservative than the median Republican; in 2017, those numbers had shrunk to 1 and 3 percent respectively.[40] In that year the median Republican in the general public was more conservative than nearly all Democrats (97 percent).[41] Similarly, differences between Republicans and Democrats in positions on political issues have grown enormously, more than doubling between 1994 and 2017 by one measure.[42]

There is also considerable evidence of affective polarization in the general public. In particular, there is a growing trend among Republicans and Democrats to feel anger and a sense of rivalry toward each other.[43] Correspondingly, the information that voters seek out has little to do with educating themselves; instead, information is typically sought out to back up pre-existing policy preferences.[44] More telling, even when there is not sharp ideological disagreement, Americans misperceive the views of the opposing party and thereby create a false divide.[45] Relatedly, partisan identity stands apart from ideology, that is, separate and apart from ideological differences. "Republicans and Democrats increasingly dislike, even loathe, their opponents."[46]

The level of animosity along partisan lines is suggested by the 2014 Pew survey, finding that 23 percent of people with consistently liberal views would be unhappy if an immediate family member were to marry a Republican, and 30 percent of their conservative counterparts would be unhappy about marriage to a Democrat.[47] In 1960, in contrast, 5 percent of Republicans and 4 percent of Democrats said they would be "displeased" if their son or daughter were to marry outside of their party.[48] Perhaps more telling, 2017 research revealed that "Americans are less likely to have the kind of interpersonal contact across party lines that can dampen harsh beliefs about each other. Neighborhoods, workplaces, households and even online dating lives have become politically homogeneous."[49] The most ideological people are the most likely to agree with their friends on social networking sites; 52 percent of the very liberal and 45 percent of the very conservative agree nearly always with their friends (as compared to 18 percent for moderates).[50]

Similarly, people's rankings of their own and the opposition party on a one-hundred-point thermometer changed dramatically between 1980 and 2012. In 1980, on average voters gave their own party a seventy-two and the opposing party a forty-five on the thermometer; in 1992, the opposing party dropped to forty; in 2012, it had fallen to twenty.[51] Views of their own party held steady between seventy and seventy-two.[52]

Still, at the mass level, there is stronger evidence of some forms of polarization than others, and there is considerable disagreement about the extent of polarization that has occurred.[53] A 2016 study indicates that the various forms of polarization are all evident among partisans, but not among other Americans.[54]

The picture is much clearer in the world of elites, including the affluent and well educated as a whole, as well as the news media, the legal profession, and the academy. For the balance of this section, we will discuss this divide among today's elites. In the next section, we will further explore the divide within the legal profession, chronicling the rise of the conservative legal network as part and parcel of a larger Republican effort to prioritize ideology in the appointment of judges and Justices.

The Affluent and Well Educated. As we discussed in chapter 3, during the 1960s and 1970s, Democratic and Republican elites tended to agree with each other on civil rights and other social issues.[55] Although the distribution of elite opinion still differs from that of the mass public on some social issues, the level of consensus in this segment of society has declined. Unlike elites in the Warren and Burger Court eras, today's elites are sharply divided along partisan lines. Polling data make clear that the political class is dominated by polarized elites and, as such, the "extremes are overrepresented in the political arena and the center underrepresented."[56] Strong conservatives have become even more conservative and strong liberals have become even more liberal. In fact, today's Democratic and Republican elites are at opposite ends of the spectrum—Democratic elites are more liberal than other Democrats; Republican elites are more conservative than other Republicans.[57]

These sharp divisions of opinion are more pronounced among elites than they are in the general population. Surveys by the Pew Research Center support these claims.[58] By correlating income and education to political beliefs, the Pew studies make clear that the most liberal Americans are affluent, well-educated Democrats and the most conservative Americans are affluent, well-educated Republicans.[59] "On almost every issue surveyed, the greatest percentage of respondents taking the most conservative position were from the most affluent and highly educated group of Republicans and the greatest percentage of respondents taking the most liberal positions were from the most affluent and highly educated group of Democrats."[60] These studies also highlight growing polarization among elites.

Most significant (and tracking the hardening of the Right on today's Supreme Court), these studies call attention to dramatic changes among strong political conservatives since the 1980s. In the 1980s, conservatives divided between two groups: economic and social conservatives. By 2011, economic and social conservatives had "coalesced into a single, highly activated group of Staunch Conservatives"; indeed, the most educated and affluent Republicans were the most conservative on issues that were likely to come before courts.[61]

Liberal Democrats too became even more liberal during this period. The Pew survey in 2011 showed that on same-sex marriage, abortion rights, and restrictions on civil liberties tied to the War on Terror, "members of the most affluent well educated group of Democrats tended to be far more liberal on all issues than members of other Democratic groups."[62] The 2011 survey likewise showed that "solid liberals," a subset of Democratic-leaning voters who ranked high in education and economic status, "were more likely than any other group to favor liberal immigration laws, support health care reform, [and] maintain that racial discrimination is the main barrier to Afro-American progress."[63]

As the data in Table 2.2 showed, elite attitudes on some civil liberties issues continue to differ from those of the mass public. But there is now a divide not just between elites and nonelites but also between Republicans and Democrats.[64] Table 4.1 shows patterns of support for the Supreme Court decisions expanding civil liberties that were covered in Table 2.2, as well as the Court's 2012 decision upholding the mandate for certain individuals to purchase health insurance in the Affordable Care Act.[65] The Second Amendment, gay rights, enemy combatants, the Affordable Care Act, campaign finance, and affirmative action all highlight that disjunction. Indeed, in

Table 4.1. Relationships between Support for Selected Supreme Court Decisions and Partisan Affiliation and Education

	% Consistent with Supreme Court Decision			
Issue	Democrats	Republicans	Postgraduate Education	Bachelor's Degree or Less
School prayer	13.7	12.4	41.4	14.9
Flag burning	16.8	11.2	44.1	14.3
Regulation of internet speech	63.8	69.1	76.3	66.9
Homosexual relations	61.5	41.4	75.6	51.6
Affirmative action in school admissions	46.4	13.5	43.0	25.4
Juvenile death penalty	72.0	51.3	64.8	60.2
Rights of enemy combatants	45.0	17.4	50.0	32.7
Second Amendment	60.0	84.9	60.1	75.0
Campaign finance	13.8	28.2	21.2	19.2
Affordable Care Act	87.3	11.3	59.0	46.9
Same-sex marriage	71.9	34.6	70.9	52.5

several instances partisan differences were distinctly stronger than differences based on education.

We can compare the impact of party identification and graduate education more directly by analyzing responses to two questions related to Supreme Court decisions in the 2016 American National Election Study (ANES).[66] One question asked respondents whether same-sex couples should be allowed to marry, whether civil unions only should be allowed, or whether there should be no legal recognition of same-sex relationships.[67] Among both Republicans and Democrats, respondents with graduate degrees were more likely to favor the marriage option, with a difference of about 15 percentage points. But among people with graduate degrees, the difference between Republicans and Democrats was twice as large. The inter-party difference was about the same for respondents with graduate degrees and for other respondents.

A similar pattern appeared for a question about when abortion should be allowed, with possible responses ranging from "by law, abortion should never be permitted" to "by law, abortion as a matter of personal choice." Republicans with graduate degrees were more likely than other Republicans to support the "personal choice" option, by a difference of 12 percentage points; the impact of graduate degrees was twice as large for Democrats. But the inter-party difference for people with graduate degrees was much larger, 43 percentage points. And that difference was somewhat greater than the difference between Republicans and Democrats without graduate degrees (32 percentage points). On a similar question in the 1976 ANES, there was only a small difference between the proportions of Democrats and Republicans who favored the equivalent of the "personal choice" option, either among people with graduate degrees or among other respondents. But those with graduate degrees were far more likely to support that option than other people in their party—by a margin of about 30 percentage points in each party.[68]

Thus it remains true that educated elites as a whole are more liberal than people with lower levels of education, at least on most controversial civil liberties issues. But Republicans with high levels of education now diverge substantially from their Democratic counterparts. On social issues such as abortion and same-sex marriage, those partisan differences outweigh differences in education.[69]

Republican-Democratic differences are also revealed in Gallup Polls on Supreme Court job approval. The 2016 election of Donald Trump and appointment of Neil Gorsuch resulted in a surge of Republican approval of "the way the Supreme Court is handling its job" (65 percent support in September 2017 as compared to 26 percent in 2016) and a dramatic decline in Democratic support (40 percent in 2017 as compared to 67 percent before the 2016 elections).[70] By July 2018 (immediately after Anthony Kennedy's resignation but before the nomination of Brett Kavanaugh), Republican support jumped to 73 percent and Democratic support plummeted to 24 percent.[71]

In chapters 1 and 2, we explained that Supreme Court Justices are elites and are likely to be drawn from a pool of candidates that reflect prevailing attitudes among elites. As underscored by our discussion of elite homogeneity before the so-called Reagan Revolution and the growing elite polarization over the past thirty years, it is little wonder that elites were able to cross party lines, often to expand civil liberties protections. This situation was reflected in the work of the Warren and Burger Courts. Likewise, the partisanship on today's Court reflects prevailing elite norms. Later in this chapter, we will explain the importance of elite social networks to Supreme Court decision making. For the balance of this section, we will highlight manifestations of polarization in the social networks that the Justices come from and remain in after joining the Court and in the sectors of the elite that are especially relevant to them.

The Media, the Legal Profession, and the Academy. As we discussed in chapter 2, Supreme Court Justices care about their reputations among the elites they interface with, especially lawyers, legal academics, and the media.[72] In chapter 3, we showed that in the time of the Warren and Burger Courts these elite groups leaned to the left, a leaning that we think helps to account for the leftward movement of some Justices. In this chapter, we consider dramatic shifts in the media, the academy, and the bar starting in the 1980s. As we will now explain, elite polarization has fueled and been fueled by increasing polarization in the media, the academy, and the bar.

Partisanship in today's news media is a near-perfect mirror image of increasing polarization among political elites. During the Warren and Burger Court eras, moderate-to-liberal network television and daily newspapers dominated public discourse.[73] Over the past thirty years, the proliferation of cable television, the internet, and the blogosphere has transformed the public discourse. As a result, "it is much easier that it once was to select media consistent with one's ideology and to avoid a source whose message is opposed."[74] For example, the rise of social media sites such as Facebook and Twitter allows individuals to share "their favorite stories with hundreds of their contacts."[75] In addition to technological change, polarization was also fueled by changes in federal regulatory policy, most notably the repeal of the Fairness Doctrine in 1987, and the related proliferation of conservative and liberal media outlets that allowed consumers to get their news and opinion programming from stations that reinforced pre-existing ideological commitments.[76]

With the repeal of the Fairness Doctrine, media consumers were increasingly "exposed to louder echoes of their own voices."[77] And with so many media outlets, there has been a personalization of media consumption as consumers are forced to consume different media selectively. This "filter bubble" steers people toward information that appeals to their preconceptions; news outlets respond by embracing either pro-Democratic or pro-Republican positions.[78] Leaving aside stories connected with elections, one study found that the liberal *Daily Kos* featured anti-Republican stories 45 percentage points more often than anti-Democratic stories; the conservative *FreeRepublic* was 20 percentage points more likely to feature anti-Democratic stories.[79] The skew in coverage in outlets such as Fox News and MSNBC is even stronger.

Lack of exposure to competing viewpoints augments polarization as conservatives and liberals gradually shift to the dominant viewpoint within their ideological group. As Cass Sunstein points out, "People want to be perceived favorably by other group members, and also to perceive themselves favorably. Once they hear what others believe, they often adjust their positions in the direction of the dominant position."[80]

This assertion is backed up by 2010 and 2014 Pew studies on news audience demographics and statistics about the voting preferences of Fox and CNN viewers.[81] In 2010, conservative viewers made up around 80 percent of the audience who watched *Hannity* and the *O'Reilly Factor* on Fox; among these viewers who identified with a party, the overwhelming majority were Republicans.[82] In sharp contrast, around 75 percent of the audiences for NPR and the *Rachel Maddow* and *Hardball* shows on MSNBC were liberals or moderates, and Democrats far outnumbered Republicans in these audiences.[83] In 2014, respondents classified as consistent conservatives expressed more distrust than trust of twenty-four of thirty-six news sources measured by Pew; at the same time, 88 percent of conservatives trusted Fox News and nearly half of all conservatives named Fox as their main source for news about government and politics.[84] For their part, consistent liberals expressed more trust than distrust of twenty-eight of the thirty-six news sources measured by Pew, citing NPR, PBS, and the BBC as the most trusted news sources.[85]

This general shift to personalized, polarized media among elites corresponds to changes in the legal academy and the leadership of the legal profession. During the Warren and Burger Court eras, as we discussed in chapter 3, these legal elites leaned to the left.

Starting in the 1980s, conservative interests sought to transform lawyers' networks. One reflection of their efforts was the establishment of public interest law firms representing conservative positions on legal issues.[86] "Conservative lawyers learned from their liberal counterparts how to use

Supreme Court litigation to advance their political agendas," including the development of "networks of personal connections that promoted coordination."[87] According to Ann Southworth, "The investment in conservative public interest law groups reflected a critical strategic decision to enlist lawyers—especially idealistic and ambitious young lawyers—to help articulate the conservative agenda and lend it credibility."[88] Correspondingly, "the growth and success of conservative public interest law is closely tied with the conservative movement's improved record of recruiting elite lawyers and creating attractive career paths for them"[89]

At the very same time, conservative interests also helped establish a conservative beachhead in American law schools through efforts to fund and legitimize law and economics. Conservatives saw law and economics as both "a powerful critique of state intervention in the economy, and a device for gaining a foothold in the world of elite law schools."[90] In particular, the Olin Foundation provided infusions of money at elite law schools to be used for workshops, journals, student scholarships, and fellows; Olin also funded programs to provide incentives for law professors to do law and economics scholarship. Through these efforts, Olin sought to legitimize law and economics and facilitate the credentialing of conservative legal academics.[91]

Most significant, the creation and growth of the Federalist Society fueled an emerging conservative legal network at law schools and throughout the legal profession. In 1982, law students at Yale and the University of Chicago came together to provide a counterweight to the perceived liberal bias of elite law schools.[92] Initially, the Federalist Society was an attempt to bring conservative speakers to law schools to debate members of the academic Left; the initial efforts were so popular that the group secured funding and chapters were established at law schools throughout the country.[93] Today, the Federalist Society serves as a reference group for conservative law students and lawyers, each with their own groups and activities under the society's umbrella.[94] The Federalist Society is also a leading propagator of textualism and originalism, two linked theories of legal interpretation that have reshaped Supreme Court decision making and strengthened the conservative legal movement.

Changes in the legal academy and legal profession are now reflected in the emergence of distinct career paths for conservatives and liberals in the elite segment of the legal profession. To an increasing extent, outstanding students at the most prestigious law schools move into clerkships with federal appellate judges who share their ideological orientations, and then into presidential administrations, law firms, and other institutions that also share their liberal or conservative identifications.[95] Later in this chapter, we will provide details of the pivotal role the Federalist Society played in establishing a conservative legal network that has proved to be quite important in creating today's partisan divide on the Supreme Court. We will also examine the American Constitution Society, created in response to the success of the Federalist Society, which serves a similar though far less critical function for liberals.[96]

Even with the development of conservative institutions in the news media and the legal profession, those sectors as a whole continue to lean to the left. A 2002 survey of journalists found that they were disproportionately liberal and Democratic, and a 2016 analysis based on campaign contributions found that professionals in the print media as a group were quite liberal.[97] The same analysis found that lawyers were not as liberal as journalists, but most of them were also on the left, and a similar analysis of law professors found them to be sharply liberal as a group—and somewhat more so at the most prestigious schools.[98] Because of the continued leaning to the left, conservatives in the media and legal elites can continue to feel beleaguered despite their growing power, and that feeling strengthens the salience of organizations such as the Federalist Society to them.

Explaining the Growth in Supreme Court Polarization

As we documented in chapter 3, there was a striking lack of partisan sorting among the Justices until quite recently: in no Court prior to 2010 were there competing ideological blocs that coincided with political party. Rather, during periods when both Republican and Democratic appointees had substantial representation on the Court, there were always appointees of Republican presidents who were on the liberal side of the Court's ideological spectrum, Democratic appointees who were on the conservative side of the spectrum, or both. In contrast, since President Obama's appointment of Elena Kagan in 2010, the Democratic and Republican appointees on the Court have been ideologically distinct from each other.

Before turning to the forces that perpetuate today's ideological divide, we want to re-emphasize that the partisan divide is a story both about the separation of Democrats from Republicans and about ideological conformity among Republicans and Democrats. As Figure 1.1 showed, both Democratic Justices as a group and Republican Justices as a group have become more homogeneous in their ideological tendencies. To a considerable degree, this is because centrists have become more scarce in the Court as they have in Congress.

That growth in homogeneity came in the mid-1990s for the Court's Democrats. From the 1975 term through the 1992 term, the only Democratic appointees on the Court were the very liberal Thurgood Marshall and the moderate conservative Byron White.[99] In the long period from the 1994 term through the 2008 term, in contrast, the two Democratic Justices were the like-minded Ruth Bader Ginsburg and Stephen Breyer. The Court's Democrats continued to have similar voting tendencies when Ginsburg and Breyer were joined by Sonia Sotomayor and Elena Kagan.

The change came later for the Court's Republicans. The standard deviation in proportions of conservative votes among the Republican appointees remained high so long as relatively liberal John Paul Stevens and David Souter remained on the Court. After Souter retired at the end of the 2008 term, the standard deviation fell by almost half; when Stevens retired after the 2009 term, it again fell by half.[100] With a more homogeneous set of Republicans on the Court, the standard deviation has remained low since then. Indeed, the standard deviation among Republicans will likely fall again with the replacement of Anthony Kennedy (conservative but to the left of other Republicans) with the more conservative Brett Kavanaugh.[101]

At the same time, the growing partisan divide is largely a story of the hardening of the Right. As discussed earlier, there are no strong liberals on the current Court, and the average ideological position of today's Democratic appointees is similar to the average among more heterogeneous groups of Democratic appointees in the past. On the other hand, Justices Thomas, Alito, and Gorsuch, and Chief Justice Roberts are among the most conservative Justices to sit on the Court in the modern era; the same was true of Justice Scalia; and it is anticipated that Justice Kavanaugh too will be a strong conservative.[102]

The sharper divide between Republican and Democratic appointees on the current Court is underlined by the Court's decisions in major cases. As we discussed in chapter 3, throughout the Court's history up to 2010, it was rare for the Justices to divide along party lines in important decisions. Based on the list of such decisions in the *Guide to the Supreme Court*, among nearly four hundred important decisions in which there were at least two dissenting votes; in only two were all the Justices from one party in the majority and all the Justices from the other party in dissent.

The list we used for the period up to 2010 has not been updated since that time. But among the cases decided by the Court in the 2010–2014 terms, seven decisions in which the Court divided 5–4 or (in one case) 5–3 along party lines are obvious candidates for inclusion in the *Guide*'s list of important decisions.[103] During the Court's 2015 term, the Justices (after the death of Antonin Scalia) split 4–4—most likely on partisan lines—in high-visibility cases on public sector unions and on President Obama's immigration directive.[104] There were no such decisions in the Court's low-key 2016 term. But in the 2017 term, in which the Court divided along party lines in fourteen of its seventy-one decisions, at least two and perhaps four of those decisions qualify as important.[105]

This separation between the Court's Democrats and Republicans is to be expected; it tracks growing polarization in the elite world and related trends in judicial appointments, particularly the rise of the conservative legal network and the growing role of ideology in judicial appointments. Consider, for example, Thomas Keck's measure of Republican-Democratic differences on four issues that divide the parties (abortion, affirmative action, gun rights, and same-sex marriage). Looking at votes in Congress, on federal courts of appeals, and on the US Supreme Court, Keck documented a sharp party-line divide from 1993 to 2013. But the extent of this divide differed between branches. The average difference between Republicans and Democrats in support for liberal positions in their votes was 65 percentage points in the House and 64 percentage points in the Senate. In contrast, the average difference in the judiciary was 37 percentage points for the Supreme Court and 33 percent for the courts of appeals.[106] This difference between the branches is important, and we will return to it later in the chapter.

The growth of partisan sorting in the Supreme Court and a parallel growth in the political system as a whole clearly are not a coincidence; changes in the Court reflect changes in its political environment. One key linkage lies in the appointment process. In chapter 3, we examined how appointment strategies before 1986 contributed to the absence of an ideological divide on the Court. We will now link changes in appointment strategies to the rise in partisanship on the Court. In documenting the growing role of ideology in presidential appointments, we will highlight the critical role played by Reagan's second-term Attorney General Edwin Meese in both grooming conservative judges and making ideology a dominant feature of Republican appointment strategies. Correspondingly, the rise of the conservative legal movement has helped fuel this phenomenon. For Democrats, ideology is only one of several factors that presidents take into account when making Supreme Court nominations, but polarization has affected Democratic appointments as well.

A second key linkage stems from the development of distinct liberal and conservative segments of the political and social elite, segments that have a considerable degree of hostility toward each other. That development has affected the appointment process, but it has more direct effects on the thinking of the Justices themselves. After discussing appointments, we will consider the impact of this affective polarization on partisan sorting in the Court.

The Appointment Process

In nominating Supreme Court Justices, presidents consider much more than the "objective" qualifications of potential nominees to serve on the Court, in terms of their legal abilities and their ethical behavior. In chapter 3, we identified several of these other considerations. Presidents have looked to advance particular policy priorities, to reward service to the president and the president's party, to gain future political benefits, and to enhance the prospects for confirmation of a nominee.[107]

The president's policy priorities are of particular interest. Before the 1980s, presidents did not see Supreme Court appointments as a vehicle to advance a comprehensive ideological agenda. Franklin Delano Roosevelt appointed Justices who would uphold New Deal initiatives but paid no mind to emerging civil rights and liberties issues; Richard Nixon cared about law and order when he selected nominees to the Court but not about abortion or affirmative action.[108] Other presidents gave even less attention to policy considerations when they chose nominees.

Starting in the 1980s, in contrast, presidents have sought nominees who share the prevailing ideological positions of their increasingly divergent parties—reliable conservatives for Republican presidents, reliable liberals for Democratic presidents. Moreover, in pursuing this goal, they have been more careful than their predecessors in identifying reliable nominees. This change has been spurred in part by presidents' fellow partisans outside government. The change has been especially marked for Republicans; Democrats have paid attention to ideology while also advancing diversity and rewarding constituent interests.[109] Nomination strategies aside, partisan sorting has resulted in greater homogeneity within each political party, especially at the elite level. Democrats are overwhelmingly liberal and Republicans conservative—so much so that credible candidates from either party are likely to reflect the ideological gap that separates the parties.

All of this has helped to create a Court in which the Justices appointed by Republican presidents and those appointed by Democrats are separated by ideology. The growing emphasis on policy considerations in the selection of Justices parallels the growth in partisan polarization, and it is largely an effect of that polarization.

Republican Presidents. Ronald Reagan's 1980 victory set in motion the forces that have resulted in the sharp split between conservative Republicans and liberal Democrats on the Court, though the Reagan administration's departures from past practices were not fully instituted until Reagan's second term. Among other initiatives, the Reagan administration broke ranks with its predecessors by making ideological considerations "the most important criteria" in the screening of judicial candidates, seeking to reshape the face of Supreme Court decision making by sponsoring "ardently conservative candidates for the high court."[110] In particular, rather than focus on a narrow band of policy issues (Roosevelt and economic regulation, Nixon and crime), Reagan sought to fundamentally transform the role of the Supreme Court.[111]

By elevating the status of the Federalist Society in the identification and grooming of its judicial appointees, for example, the administration sought to fill the bench with conservatives.[112] The nominations of Antonin Scalia, Robert Bork, and Douglas Ginsburg, and the elevation of William Rehnquist to Chief Justice were made to advance the conservative legal policy agenda.[113] Scalia, Bork, and Ginsburg had markedly conservative records on the federal appellate courts; Rehnquist had a similar record as an Associate Justice.[114]

These Reagan initiatives were linked to the 1985 appointment of Attorney General Edwin Meese and related efforts to strengthen the burgeoning conservative legal network. In Reagan's first term, as noted in chapter 3, ideology was not the only criterion that the administration took into account. In choosing Sandra Day O'Connor, Reagan honored a campaign pledge to nominate a woman.[115] Moreover, when nominating Anthony Kennedy to the bench in 1987, the Reagan administration advanced a candidate who had earlier been rejected on ideological grounds.[116] At this time, however, the administration had failed in its efforts to put either of two strong conservatives on the Court to succeed Justice Lewis Powell—Robert Bork (rejected by the Senate) and Douglas Ginsburg (forced to withdraw in the wake of charges involving drug use). Consequently, rather than risk its ability to fill a Supreme Court slot before the 1988 elections, the administration thought it better to nominate a relatively moderate conservative who would easily win Senate approval.[117]

Ideology was also the defining but not exclusive factor in the nominations by Republican president George H. W. Bush (1989–1993). Bush embraced the same general commitment to a conservative judiciary that had existed in the Reagan administration.[118] Facing a Democratic Senate, Bush paid close attention to the confirmability of Supreme Court nominees. In 1990, Bush passed over federal appellate judge Edith Jones for fear of a bitter confirmation fight, even though the administration thought she was a committed conservative.[119] Instead, David Souter was nominated, in part, because there was little prospect of a bruising confirmation battle over past decisions or writings. Clarence Thomas was also seen as highly confirmable, because he seemed politically compelling. White House officials thought that his "southern background and humble origins would trap southern Democrats into voting for him."[120]

Still, both nominees were perceived as conservative. Bush administration officials were confident that Souter was a solid conservative, and administration officials quelled the doubts of some conservatives about Souter.[121] Unlike Souter, Clarence Thomas was part of, and embraced by, the conservative legal movement. For example, Bush's legal counsel C. Boyden Gray "had gotten to know Thomas socially in Washington's conservative circles, and was struck by his adamant rejection of the principles of affirmative action."[122]

By the time of the George W. Bush presidency (2001–2009), conservatives who were frustrated by the moderate or liberal paths of prior Republican appointees emphasized the need for great care in making nominations. That emphasis was reflected in the slogan "No more Souters."[123] Staunch conservatives—especially those for whom abortion was a high priority—succeeded in preventing the nomination of Attorney General Alberto Gonzales.[124] By nominating John Roberts, Harriet Miers, and Samuel Alito, Bush sought to select the "most conservative possible Supreme Court justice."[125] Miers had served as both Bush's personal attorney and White House counsel; she was a trusted personal and political associate.[126] Bush was also confident that she was strongly conservative, making her the perfect "stealth" candidate without the risk.[127] For this reason, it is striking that well-placed conservatives who distrusted Miers were able to secure her withdrawal.

Donald Trump's nominations of Neil Gorsuch in 2017 and Brett Kavanaugh in 2018 followed a similar script. In spring of 2016, Trump sought to establish his bona fides with the conservative legal network by turning to Leonard Leo of the Federalist Society to assemble a list of potential Supreme Court nominees. Trump issued that list in May 2016, a list of additional names in September 2016, and a consolidated list with more additions in November 2017.[128] Gorsuch and Kavanaugh were each on one of those lists. And like Trump's other finalists for the two nominations, they had ties to the Federalist Society. Later in this section, we will discuss the ascendancy of the conservative legal movement in general and the Federalist Society in particular, especially with respect to the grooming and vetting of Supreme Court Justices.

These changes in appointment processes and criteria should be put in a broader context. The Reagan administration did more than transform the judicial selection process; in addition to making ideology the defining criterion in judicial appointments, it also sought to redefine the process by which judges and Justices were vetted and nurtured. Under the leadership of his second-term Attorney General Edwin Meese, Reagan took steps to groom a cadre of well-credentialed conservative lawyers and, in so doing, transform constitutional discourse and judicial decision making over an extended period of time. By using the "bureaucratic power to transform the conditions of future political conflict,"[129] Reagan's Department of Justice (DoJ) set in motion the processes that resulted in the appointments of Justices Scalia, Thomas, Alito, Gorsuch, and Kavanaugh, and Chief Justice Roberts. In this way, the ideological divide on today's Court is very much tied to the efforts of the Reagan DoJ.

Unlike first-term Attorney General William French Smith (who embraced conservative ideals but had no plan to advance those ideals), Meese sought to advance conservative goals over the long term. As one DoJ official said, the "project of getting the Constitution right was more than just appointing judges, and that we had to have a rhetoric that was persuasive, and an analysis that became talked about by pubic intellectuals."[130] Recognizing this fact, Meese—following a talk to DoJ political appointees by then DC Circuit judge Antonin Scalia—formally embraced "a jurisprudence of original intention."[131] He gave speeches, organized seminars within the DoJ so that political appointees could work through the implications of originalism for their own work, and directed his Office of Legal Policy to issue *Guidelines for Constitutional Litigation* (so that DoJ attorneys would adhere to originalism in their legal analysis and arguments).[132] In these and other ways, Meese sought to create a metric by which to measure legal arguments and judicial decisions and thereby "facilitate the orderly development of conservative legal ideas and their injection into the legal mainstream."[133] Meese also recognized the importance of reaching out to the "legal profession's elite" and "very little of this was aimed at the general public"; instead, Meese was "trying to stir up the elites," and his target was lawyers, academics, and public intellectuals.[134]

Most significantly, Meese sought to staff his department with young conservative lawyers—making "ideological commitment . . . a credential rather than a disqualification."[135] The recently established Federalist Society was an important component of this strategy. Meese hired the Society's founders as special assistants and tapped Stephen Markman, who headed the Washington, DC, chapter of the Federalist Society, to become the assistant attorney general in charge of judicial selection.[136] In so doing, the Reagan DoJ sent a signal that "you could win" by identifying as a conservative and acting "on the basis of your ideals."[137] Federalist Society cofounder and Meese special assistant Steve Calabresi put it this way: "There was a real desire to train a generation of people—a farm team—who might go on later on in future Republican administrations to have an impact and to hold more important positions."[138] Correspondingly, the Reagan administration and Federalist Society worked in tandem to foster the conservative legal network by using the Federalist Society annual meeting as a marker of status and belonging. "Of the seventy-six speakers listed on the published agendas of Federalist Society national meetings from 1981 to 1988, nineteen (25%) were serving or would serve at some time in the Reagan administration."[139]

The George H. W. Bush and George W. Bush administrations followed the Reagan administration lead, staffing top executive positions with Federalist Society members and putting a premium on fealty to the conservative legal agenda when selecting judicial candidates. The first Bush administration looked to Lee Liberman Otis, cofounder of the Federalist Society, to lead its judicial selection process.[140] The second Bush administration tapped society members Brett Kavanaugh and Viet Dinh to be in charge of judicial selection.[141] More than that, Federalist Society Executive Vice President Leonard Leo (along with Federalist Society members Edwin Meese, Boyden Gray, and Jay Sekulow) provided judicial selection advice to the George W. Bush administration.[142]

In nominating judges, all three Republican administrations embraced the mantra that judicial nominees should be "committed to the rule of law and to the enforcement of the Constitution and statutes as those were adopted by 'we the people' and their elected representatives."[143] Equally significant, membership in the Federalist Society was a proxy for adherence to conservative ideology. Ronald Reagan made all three of the society's original faculty advisers federal court judges (and two of these three—Robert Bork and Antonin Scalia—were nominated to the Supreme Court).[144] Nine of President George H. W. Bush's nominees to the federal court of appeals and US Supreme Court were society members (including Clarence Thomas, Samuel Alito, and John Roberts).[145] George W. Bush Supreme Court nominees Samuel Alito and John Roberts were society members, as were around half of the appointees of the second President Bush to the federal courts of appeals.[146] Three Society members appointed to the courts of appeals by George W. Bush (Neil

Gorsuch, William Pryor, and Thomas Hardiman) were the finalists to fill Justice Scalia's seat in 2017.[147]

The Reagan and first Bush administrations were limited in their ability to nominate reliable conservatives. These administrations could not look to a "farm team" of conservatives who had joined the Federalist Society as law students and cut their teeth either clerking for a conservative judge or as a government attorney. The Federalist Society and, more generally, the conservative legal movement were too nascent to have groomed these individuals. "These were the days," as Reagan DoJ official Richard Willard put it, "before the Federalist Society was really off the ground, so it was hard to find lawyers who had a conservative political outlook. At that time, the law schools and the professional associations were overwhelmingly liberal in their outlook, and so finding conservative lawyers who had the outlook, but also the professional competence, to do the job was a challenge."[148] Indeed, recognizing that "people are policy," the Reagan DoJ responded to the dearth of well-credentialed conservatives by hiring young lawyers as "that's where the talent was and that's where the people were that agreed with our philosophy."[149]

This lack of a deep bench of vetted conservatives contributed to Ronald Reagan's nomination of Sandra Day O'Connor and to George H. W. Bush's nomination of David Souter to the Supreme Court. The decision to interview and later nominate O'Connor—then a little-known state court of appeals judge—underscores the thinness of the pool of credentialed conservative women in the early 1980s. When Souter was nominated in 1990, the number of well-credentialed conservatives was comparably thin and the conservative legal movement was not sufficiently entrenched to demand that Republican appointees come from the pool of vetted conservatives. Consequently, doubts about Souter's lack of paper record were offset by the strong backing of Bush Chief of Staff John Sununu, who had considerable credibility with Republican conservatives.[150]

By the time George W. Bush became president in 2001, the conservative legal movement dominated DoJ and judicial appointments. Not only did people in the Federalist Society network play "key roles in selecting, vetting, and shepherding nominees" for judgeships, but also major legal positions in the administration were overwhelmingly filled by society members. Federalist Society member and Bush-appointed counsel to the US Food and Drug Administration Daniel Troy put it this way: "Everybody, I mean everybody who got a job who was a lawyer was involved with the Federalist Society. I mean everybody."[151] By 2005, moreover, the "farm team" of credentialed conservatives included John Roberts, Samuel Alito, Neil Gorsuch, Brett Kavanaugh, and many others.

The nomination and withdrawal of Bush Supreme Court nominee Harriet Miers vividly illustrates both the power of the conservative legal movement and the depth of today's pool of conservative Supreme Court nominees. Attacking Miers for both her lack of Federalist Society "credentials"[152] and her ties to the American Bar Association (which conservatives had turned against as too liberal in its screening of judges),[153] conservatives demanded that she withdraw and be replaced by a nominee from the "deep farm team of superbly qualified and talented circuit court judges primed for this moment."[154] Her replacement was Samuel Alito—a Federalist Society member and the favorite of the very conservatives who attacked Miers; the *New York Times* headline put it this way: "In Alito, G.O.P. Reaps Harvest Planted in '82."[155]

Donald Trump's 2017 nomination of Neil Gorsuch likewise exemplifies the dominant role played by the conservative legal networks in judicial appointments, especially the Federalist Society.[156] Gorsuch took the seat held by Antonin Scalia, a Federalist Society stalwart. When campaigning for president in 2016, Donald Trump claimed that his judicial nominees would "all [be] picked by the Federalist Society" and then turned to the "Federalist people"—specifically the society's executive vice president Leonard Leo—to assemble lists of potential Supreme Court nominees.[157] When the society held its annual National Lawyers Convention one week after the 2016 election, nine of the twenty-one judges on those two lists were among the speakers and nearly all the others were in attendance. And when Trump had narrowed his pool to three court of appeals judges, all three were Federalist Society members who regularly spoke at society events.[158] Indeed, when a Senate questionnaire asked Gorsuch about his experience in the selection process, Gorsuch duly noted that he "was contacted by Leonard Leo."[159]

After the White House announced five additional names on the list of potential Supreme Court nominees in November 2017, bringing the total to twenty-five, one publication "identified a Federalist Society connection, either membership or at least involvement with events, for all but one." Of the eighteen Trump nominees to the courts of appeals at that point, nominees' questionnaires and other sources indicated ties to the Federalist Society for seventeen.[160] Brett Kavanaugh's selection from the list of potential Supreme Court nominees in 2018 came after a search process that resembled the process in 2017. Once again, Leonard Leo of the Federalist Society played a key role alongside White House Counsel Donald McGahn. President Trump considered a subset of the prospective nominees on his list—by one account, five court of appeals judges, all of whom had strong conservative credentials. Senate Majority Leader Mitch McConnell advised Trump that two other finalists would have an easier path to confirmation than Kavanaugh, but Trump ultimately chose a candidate who was especially close to the Federalist Society and whose record of conservatism was voluminous.[161]

The fact that all Republican Justices who now sit on the Supreme Court have been Federalist Society members underlines the role of the society as a "mediating institution" for conservatives, a network that has maintained "channels of communication through which individuals and organizations exercise political influence."[162] An analysis of contacts among lawyers for conservative and libertarian causes suggested that the Federalist Society plays an instrumental role in bringing these lawyers together.[163] Correspondingly, society membership is critical to the credentialing of conservative lawyers. Michael Greve put it this way: "On the left there are a million ways of getting credentialed; on the political right there's only one way in these legal circles."[164]

Democratic Presidents. In the years since 1992, Democratic presidents have chosen five nominees—Ruth Bader Ginsburg (1993) and Stephen Breyer (1994) by Bill Clinton, and Sonia Sotomayor (2009), Elena Kagan (2010), and Merrick Garland (2016) by Barack Obama. More than earlier Democratic presidents, Clinton and Obama sought to select nominees whose records gave strong evidence of liberalism. Clinton, for example, drew from a pool of "mostly liberal and Democratic candidates" and seriously considered liberal criticisms of Ginsburg's position on abortion.[165]

At the same time, unlike Republican nominations in the current era, ideology has not played a determinative role in Democratic selections. Instead, Clinton and Obama emphasized the pursuit of other objectives. Clinton, for example, thought it important that Ginsburg was championed by Senator Daniel Patrick Moynihan—who would play a critical role in his pursuit of health care legislation.[166] Clinton also sought to nominate a close personal friend (Richard Arnold) but did not do so because of concerns about the prospective nominee's health.[167]

Clinton and Obama also disappointed strong liberals by veering away from nominees who would prompt confirmation battles and toward nominees who embraced the rhetoric of judicial restraint, had rich personal histories, and were less ideological.[168] When nominating Merrick Garland to fill Antonin Scalia's seat, for example, Obama was well aware of Senate Republican threats to derail any nomination. Acknowledging that Garland was "just the right nominee during such a divisive time in our politics," Obama selected a sixty-three-year-old moderate-liberal who seemed to stand a better chance of confirmation than any other candidate. Of course, the Garland nomination came in the unusual circumstance of a Republican vow to block any Obama nominee to Scalia's seat. But more generally, Obama did not seek to use his judicial appointments to appoint young lawyers who "could make significant marks on the law" to the degree that Republican presidents had done.[169]

The lack of a strong emphasis on ideology in Democratic Supreme Court nominations corresponded with the high priority that Clinton and especially Obama put on racial and gender diversity in judicial nominations, including Supreme Court appointments. Forty-two percent of Obama's appointees to federal courts were women, compared with 21 percent for George W. Bush; 20 percent were African Americans, compared with 8 percent for Bush.[170] The nominations of Ruth Bader Ginsburg, Sonia Sotomayor, and Elena Kagan also reflected the two presidents' interest in diversity. As Mark Tushnet has put it, "Democratic presidents tend to pursue a demographic strategy rather than an ideological one for Supreme Court nominations."[171]

This difference in nomination strategies reflects differences between the parties in the current era. Most fundamental is the contrast between "ideological Republicans and group interest Democrats."[172] In contrast with Republicans, held together primarily by a shared conservatism, Democrats advance the interests of myriad progovernment interest groups. Among other goals, many of these groups seek diversity in the selection of judges. Moreover, the liberal legal network is much larger than the conservative legal network and, consequently, Democratic presidents are less likely to be captured by a subset within it.[173] Accordingly, polarization has had a greater impact on the Republican Party than on the Democratic Party. Clinton and Obama had Democratic majorities in the Senate when they made their successful nominations, but they still chose relatively moderate nominees to reduce the difficulty of confirmation.

Yet the difference between the Clinton-Obama approach and the George W. Bush–Trump approach should not obscure the change that occurred in Democratic appointment strategies as well. Clinton and Obama chose nominees who seemed relatively moderate over more liberal candidates, but they were still careful to select people who were on the liberal side of the ideological spectrum. One way to characterize the Clinton-Obama appointments is that, in comparison with the appointments of earlier Democratic administrations, the average ideological position has not changed a great deal but the variation has been reduced. Unlike earlier Democrats (who appointed strong liberals, as well as conservatives), Clinton-Obama appointees are all moderate liberals.

A measure of the ideological positions taken by Justices in civil liberties cases devised by Michael Bailey underscores this conclusion.[174] By this measure, 1.22 is the most conservative score that any Justice received for a single year and −1.87 the most liberal.[175] For the Democratic appointees who served during the study period, the average of their mean scores across terms was −.55 for the Obama and Clinton appointees and −.24, somewhat less liberal, for the Justices appointed by the Democratic presidents from Roosevelt to Johnson. But the Clinton and Obama appointees were clustered together, with a standard deviation of .09 in their mean scores; in contrast, the Democrats selected in the earlier era had a standard deviation of 1.03. Of the thirteen pre-Clinton appointees, five were more liberal than any of the Clinton and Obama Justices, and the other eight were more conservative than any of them.

Thus, the Obama and Clinton appointees have contributed to partisan polarization of the Court by standing on the liberal side of the ideological spectrum, but their contribution has been limited by their adherence to moderate rather than strong liberalism. Merrick Garland conformed to this pattern; by one measure of ideology, Garland was located smack in the middle of Clinton-Obama Democratic appointees.[176] More to the point, Democratic appointees to the Court do not reflect the leftward shift of Democratic elites. Instead, by valuing interest group politics as much as ideology, Clinton and Obama did not appoint strong liberals to the Court.

The Justices' World

Changes in the appointment process, especially on the Republican side, have played a key role in partisan sorting on the Court. The increased weight of ideological considerations in the selection of nominees and increased care in screening candidates for nominations have done much to end the historic pattern in which Justices often deviated from the dominant ideological orientation of their party.

But the appointment process does not fully account for partisan sorting on the Court. After all, a significant number of Justices appointed in past eras deviated from the expectations of the presidents who chose them, and these deviations sometimes appeared well after a Justice joined the Court. Republican appointment strategies in the current era are still driven by the disappointment and bitterness of conservatives about the unexpected course taken by several Republican appointees from the 1950s through the early 1990s.

As we see it, the effects of changes in presidential nomination strategies have been reinforced by changes in the Justices' own perspectives. The development of more distinct conservative and liberal camps among social and political elites and the strengthening of the overlap between party and ideology have helped to bring about affective polarization. The people who become Supreme Court Justices inevitably have been affected in their thinking by those trends: affective polarization has reached the Court.

Republican Appointees. In contrast with an earlier time, Republicans who have served on the Court since 2010 (with the partial but consequential exception of Justice Kennedy) have remained steadfast in their conservatism: Justices Scalia for nearly thirty years, Justice Thomas for more than twenty-five years, and Justice Alito and Chief Justice Roberts for more than ten years. It is anticipated that Justices Gorsuch and Kavanaugh will maintain the same consistency.

Table 3.2 presented data on change in the Justices' Bailey scores for civil liberties voting between their first two terms and later periods. For both Scalia and Thomas, the scores became somewhat more conservative over time. Because the scores end in 2011, more limited information is available for Roberts and Alito. But neither Roberts nor Alito showed much change between their first year on the Court (2005 for Roberts, 2006 for Alito) and 2010.

Table 4.2 shows the proportions of conservative votes in civil liberties cases for those four Justices by two-term periods in the 2005–2016 terms and, for comparison, voting by the most moderate liberal (Justice Breyer).[177] Raw proportions of votes must be interpreted with caution, because the sets of cases decided in different terms are not comparable. (In contrast, the Bailey scores take changes in the mix of cases into account.) Still, the Justices' voting patterns in relation to those of their colleagues are instructive.

The table shows substantial declines in the proportions of conservative votes by the strongly conservative Justices over this time period. In all likelihood, these declines result primarily from changes in the content of civil liberties cases.[178] The key fact is that the voting records of all four Justices remained distinct even from Justice Breyer's record. For these Justices, there was no sign of the ideological drift to the left that some conservatives referred to as the Greenhouse effect.[179]

In recent terms Chief Justice Roberts's record has been less distinctly conservative than that of the Court's other strong conservatives. Indeed, he has

Table 4.2. Proportions of Conservative Votes in Civil Liberties Cases, Roberts Court, Selected Justices (Part I)

	Justice				
Terms	Scalia	Thomas	Roberts	Alito	Breyer
2005–2006	76.0	80.0	76.4	79.6	37.3
2007–2008	71.3	80.5	67.8	72.4	38.4
2009–2010	55.8	65.1	57.0	69.0	43.0
2011–2012	64.1	73.1	65.4	76.6	46.2
2013–2014	60.0	70.0	52.9	64.3	31.9
2015–2016	—	60.0	48.6	61.4	35.7
2017	—	69.0	55.2	72.4	31.0

attracted some criticism from conservatives, most visibly after his vote to uphold a key provision of the Affordable Care Act against a constitutional challenge in 2012.[180] Ted Cruz referred to his support for Roberts's confirmation in 2005 as "a mistake," and Donald Trump attacked Roberts for writing an opinion catering to those inside the "beltway."[181] On the whole, however, Roberts's record remains distinctly more conservative than those of the Court's liberals.[182] That conservatism is reflected in the voting records in Table 4.2.[183] Beyond changes in the Court's civil liberties agenda, his relatively moderate voting record in recent years is best explained by a more moderate set of conservative policy preferences than that of most other Republican appointees on the Court and by his strategic considerations as Chief Justice.[184] It may be as well that on the whole, economic issues are more salient to Roberts than civil liberties issues. If he has moved a bit to the left in civil liberties during his Court career so far, it does not appear that any such movement has occurred in economic cases.[185]

To a degree, this difference between the voting behavior of these Republican appointees and several of their predecessors probably stems from their more deeply rooted conservatism. Those roots result in part from the development of a stronger and more distinct conservative sector among elite groups, especially the rise of the conservative legal movement. Equally telling, once these Justices joined the Court, the conservative movement could continue to serve as an important reference group for them. Unlike earlier periods (when elite social networks were dominated by liberals), conservative Justices on the Roberts Court have had links with like-minded people and groups that would support and reinforce the Justices' conservative stances on issues that came before the Court. As Amanda Hollis-Brusky noted about conservative justices, "What the Federalist Society has done has created a competing judicial audience, so these justices and judges don't need to seek the applause of the liberal, Establishment media."[186] Steven Calabresi, one of the founders of the Federalist Society, went even further by arguing that the development of a conservative legal counter-elite "helps keep" conservative Justices "in check." In Calabresi's view, these Justices notice "criticism by law schools, journalists, and conservative think tanks like the Federalist Society" and take that criticism into account.[187]

In the case of Justice Thomas,[188] the elite conservative sector provided personal support during his early years on the Court, when he felt beleaguered by the criticism that he had received during the highly contentious debate over his confirmation as a Justice. In response, in the words of one reporter, Thomas "constructed a world apart from his critics."[189] He appeared at law schools with relatively conservative orientations and focused his attention on news media with similar orientations.[190] He maintained, and continues to maintain, ties with conservative leaders and organizations such as the Federalist Society,[191] and he has acknowledged that conservatives in the legal community serve as an important reference group for him.[192]

Thomas frequently appears at the Federalist Society's annual meeting. It is noteworthy that when Thomas returned to Yale Law School in 2011 after an estrangement from the law school, the two student groups with which he met were the Black Law Students Association and the law school's chapter of the Federalist Society.[193] During the 2016 term, Thomas participated in two Federalist Society events and gave a lecture at the conservative Heritage Foundation, and those three events constituted half of the public appearances identified by one source.[194] In the 2017 term he gave the keynote address at the Federalist Society's National Student Symposium.[195] Although Thomas is generally reticent about media interviews, in 2016 he engaged in a televised conversation with the editor of the conservative *Weekly Standard*.[196] And in 2017 he gave an interview on Fox News to prominent conservative commentator Laura Ingraham, a former Thomas law clerk.[197]

These links are accompanied by an antipathy toward what Thomas perceives as a liberal establishment. That antipathy was reflected in a remark that one of Thomas's law clerks reported early in his tenure about an anticipated retirement in 2034: "The liberals made my life miserable for 43 years, and I'm going to make their lives miserable for 43 years."[198]

As an original leader of the Federalist Society,[199] Justice Scalia already had deep roots in the conservative segment of the legal elite by the time he became a Justice. He maintained his ties with conservatives during his Court service, making frequent appearances before groups with a conservative orientation. He was regularly honored by the Federalist Society[200] and participated frequently in the organization's events. In 2012, for instance, Scalia traveled to give speeches or lectures at five Federalist Society events.[201] In 2013, he went to Montana to speak at a lunch aimed at building support for the creation of a state chapter of the society,[202] and in 2014, he traveled to New York City to give a speech before a Federalist Society group.[203] In 2012, he spoke before a group of Hollywood conservatives called the "Friends of Abe."[204] In 2011, he spoke to members of Congress about constitutional interpretation at an event organized by the Tea Party Caucus.[205] After his death, Federalist Society chapters throughout the country held tributes to Scalia, and Justices Thomas and Alito eulogized him at the society's November 2016 annual convention.[206]

As a court of appeals judge, Justice Alito was "particularly active at Federalist Society national meetings."[207] He was strongly backed by conservative groups at the time of his appointment to the Supreme Court and has maintained his ties with conservative groups since his Supreme Court appointment. Those ties are reflected in his appearances, between 2010 and 2012, at three meetings of the Federalist Society outside Washington, DC, and at the Manhattan Institute.[208] In 2008, Alito was the keynote speaker at the annual dinner for the conservative magazine the *American Spectator*, and his remarks included some distinctly partisan content; he also appeared at the magazine's annual dinner in 2010.[209] At a 2012 Federalist Society dinner, Alito took aim both at the Obama administration and at critics of the *Citizens United* campaign finance decision, claiming that critics of the decision were misleading and that the Obama Department of Justice was advancing a vision of society in which the "federal government towers over the people."[210] In 2014, Alito was again the featured speaker at the Federalist Society's annual dinner. Shortly after that Federalist Society appearance, Linda Greenhouse wrote that Alito has a "base" in the conservative movement.[211] During the Court's 2016 term, Alito spoke at two events of the Federalist Society, as well as an event of the conservative Claremont Institute.[212] In the Claremont speech Alito argued for what one commentator called not just a conservative judicial agenda but "the larger conservative political agenda."[213]

Justice Neil Gorsuch likewise has strong ties to the Federalist Society and other conservative interests. His mother, Ann Burford, was the head of Ronald Reagan's Environmental Protection Agency, and she was the subject of fierce criticism by left-leaning environmental interest groups and Democratic lawmakers that ultimately led her to resign. Gorsuch himself developed conservative views that he expressed frequently over the years.[214] In 2005, he criticized—for the conservative *National Review*—the "Left's . . . dependence on constitutional litigation," claiming it risked "political atrophy" and prompted backlash.[215] Gorsuch has long had "close ties to the Federalist network"; he delivered the 2013 Barbara Olson lecture at the Federalist Society annual meeting and spoke at numerous Federalist Society events.[216]

After joining the Court, Gorsuch continued to speak to conservative groups.[217] In September 2017, he was criticized for giving the keynote speech for a meeting of the conservative Fund for American Studies at the Trump International Hotel in Washington, DC.[218] In November of that year he gave a featured speech at the annual meeting of the Federalist Society in which he underlined his identification with the Society; before the speech, he embraced Leonard Leo, the society's executive vice president who played a key role in Gorsuch's nomination to the Court.[219] And while Gorsuch has served only one full term on the Court (so we cannot compare his early to later voting record), his early record strongly signals that he is a committed conservative. Just as Clarence Thomas said early in his Court tenure that "I ain't evolving," Gorsuch assured his audience at the Federalist Society that "originalism has regained its place, and textualism has triumphed, and neither is going anywhere on my watch!"[220]

Brett Kavanaugh has been a member of the Federalist Society since 1988. During the twelve years between his 2006 appointment to the federal court of appeals and his nomination to the Supreme Court in 2018, he participated formally in at least fifty Society events, primarily as a speaker or panelist. In most years he was on panels at the society's National Lawyers Convention, and he frequently spoke or served on panels at its Annual Student Symposium and at chapters of the society.[221] In addition to the Federalist Society, Kavanaugh received the Heritage Foundation's Defender of the Constitution Award in 2017, delivered the Walter Berns lecture at the American Enterprise Institute in the same year, and gave other speeches to conservative audiences.

Over his career, Kavanaugh also established a record of conservative positions. When serving as staff secretary to George W. Bush, for instance, he favored the appointment of Samuel Alito, "a known and trusted figure within the conservative legal community,"[222] over Harriet Miers. It was anything but surprising that he was on the list of potential Supreme Court nominees assembled for the Trump administration by the Federalist Society. His level of involvement undoubtedly helped to make people in the Society and other conservatives comfortable with the prospect of his elevation to the Supreme Court.

Chief Justice Roberts's ties to the conservative movement have not been as visible as those of other Republican appointees, but Roberts participated in the twenty-fifth anniversary celebration of the Federalist Society in 2007.[223] He also presented a featured lecture at the society's annual meeting that year, as Justice Scalia had done two years earlier.[224]

The linkages between conservative Justices and the conservative legal movement are symbolized by an off-hand comment by Theodore Olson, a leading advocate before the Supreme Court who supports the Barbara Olson lectures at the Federalist Society in honor of his late wife. "The lecture is always at the Mayflower [hotel], but we often have a dinner afterward . . . and usually a couple of the Justices come, and it's a good time."[225]

One other measure of the allegiance of today's Republican Justices to the conservative legal network is the tendency for Justices to choose law clerks who share their ideological tendencies.[226] Before party polarization took hold, Justices took ideology into account only to a limited degree; reflecting the dominant ideology of elites, most law clerks were left-leaning, even if their Justice was not.[227] That is no longer true today. Conservative Justices in particular give greater weight to the ideological positions of prospective clerks than in the past.[228] By one measure of law clerks' positions, Chief Justice Roberts and Justices Scalia, Kennedy, Alito, and Thomas, along with Chief Justice Rehnquist, have had the most conservative sets of clerks of all Justices who have served on the Court since 1960.[229]

Similarly, Justices have become increasingly prone to choose clerks who have served like-minded judges in the lower courts (primarily the federal courts of appeals). Again, this is especially true of conservative Justices.[230] Table 4.3 shows the Justices' selection practices for the 2005–2017 terms, the first thirteen terms of the Roberts Court.[231] The differences between conservative and liberal Justices shown in the table are far greater than those that existed in the late 1970s and early 1980s—when the highest percentage of clerks drawn from Democratic-appointed judges was around 70 percent (for Justices Marshall and Brennan) and the lowest percentage was around 40 percent (Rehnquist).[232] It is noteworthy that the tendency to choose clerks on an ideological basis is stronger among conservative Justices.

It remains true that Justices sometimes choose clerks from judges who are ideologically distant from them, just as they occasionally seek out clerks whose views differ from their own.[233] But the change over time is still striking. It may be consequential as well: federal judge Jon Newman lamented what

Table 4.3. Proportions of Justices' Clerks Who Had Served with a Democratic-Appointed Lower Court Judge, 2005–2017 Terms

Justice	Percentage
Ginsburg	76.6
Souter	75.0
Kagan	67.9
Sotomayor	62.5
Stevens	60.0
Breyer	59.6
Kennedy	20.8
Roberts	19.1
Alito	5.6
Scalia	2.3
Thomas	2.1

he called "the current unfortunate system whereby Justices re-enforce their own biases by limiting their selection of law clerks to those who have served as clerks to court of appeals judges with whom the justices tend to agree."[234]

The relationship between Justice and law clerk has changed in other ways. Today's clerks often wear the party and ideological affiliations of their Justice on their sleeves. Clerks who served Republican and Democratic Justices are more likely today than ever before to feed into social and career networks dominated by the interests of either liberal Democrats or conservative Republicans. Clarence Thomas's law clerks, for example, played an unusually visible role in the early Trump administration—several were nominated to federal courts of appeals and many more assumed high-profile positions throughout the government.[235] Clerk "alumni" have long served as supporters and guardians of Justices' reputations. More than in the past, they now serve as well as a part of a Justice's ideological team.

Democratic Appointees. The increasing ideological distance between Democrats and Republicans on the Court is largely a story of changes that have occurred in the Republican Party. Not only are there no liberal Republicans on the Court, but also today's Republican Justices are more conservative than previous Republican nominees. For their part, as we have discussed, Democratic Justices are more homogeneous than they were in the recent past, but as a group they are not a great deal more liberal. Unlike previous Democratic appointees (some of whom were very liberal and others who were either moderate or conservative), all of today's Democrats are somewhat but not extremely liberal.

The changing profile of Democratic nominees is tied to broader changes in the Democratic Party. Before the mid-1960s, the Democratic Party was long an uneasy alliance between Northern liberals and Southerners who were considerably more conservative.[236] The ideologically mixed character of the Democrats at that time is reflected in Democratic presidents' Supreme Court appointments. In a later era, people who held views like those of Stanley Reed, Fred Vinson, Sherman Minton, and Tom Clark likely would have been Republicans rather than Democrats; perhaps the same is also true of Byron White. Nor was there anything like a liberal legal establishment in that era. The leaders of the American Bar Association, for instance, were a relatively conservative group until the 1960s.[237]

Following the social changes of the 1960s, a liberal legal establishment developed. The American Civil Liberties Union and the National Association for the Advancement of Colored People (NAACP) Legal Defense and Education Fund were joined by a set of new liberal public interest law firms. Legal academia and the American Bar Association took on a more liberal cast. Because there was no competing conservative legal network at that time, the liberalism of the elite world around the Justices certainly reinforced the pre-existing liberalism of Democratic judicial appointees. Moreover, as we discussed in chapter 3, the ideological drift of some Republican appointees from the 1950s to 1990s is linked to this then-dominant liberal elite social network.

Starting around 2000, conservative legal organizations' success in shaping law and policy has made liberals more self-conscious about the functions of elite networks. In particular, liberal lawyers and law professors perceived a need for an organization that would serve as a counterweight to the Federalist Society.[238] The American Constitution Society (ACS), founded in 2001, is largely parallel to the Federalist Society in its activities and goals.[239] At the same time, neither the ACS nor any other group dominates the liberal legal network.

Democratic Justices undoubtedly see themselves as members of a different team than their Republican counterparts. The ACS accentuates and facilitates this divide. Justices Breyer, Ginsburg, and Sotomayor have all been keynote speakers at the ACS national convention, and each has spoken at another national convention.[240] Perhaps more telling is Elena Kagan's greeting to a national student convention of the Federalist Society when she was dean of the law school at Harvard in 2005: after telling the audience that "I love the Federalist Society," she added, "You are *not* my people."[241] Indeed, a 2016 study of the Justices' public appearances found "no record of a sitting, liberal Supreme Court Justice addressing the Federalist Society annual meeting," though "Justice Breyer has spoken at local Federalist Society lawyer events."[242] Correspondingly, all four Democratic Justices have some inclination to choose law clerks who have served with judges from their party.[243] To a degree, then, the Court's Democrats have joined their Republican colleagues in building ideologically compatible teams in their chambers.

Justice Ginsburg stands out for her status as a favorite of liberals who follow the Court, a status reflected in admiring books and even movies.[244] Law professor Richard Hasen described her in 2018 as "traversing the country, telling stories, fielding questions from sympathetic interviewers and generally basking in the adulation of crowds who see her as a judicial hero."[245] In this respect she has become the liberal counterpart of Justice Scalia, although Scalia's celebrity was focused more on his approach to legal interpretation and was more concentrated within the legal community. In any event, this hero status can have the effect of bonding a Justice more closely with people on one side of the political spectrum.

As Table 4.2 did for the current Court's conservative Republicans, Table 4.4 provides some perspective on the ideological positions of the current Court's Democratic appointees.[246] In their civil liberties votes in the 2005–2016 terms, all Democrats were distinctly to the left of the most liberal Republican in the post-2010 period, Anthony Kennedy. Of course, the gap between the Court's Democrats and the four more strongly conservative Republicans (represented in Table 4.4 by Justice Alito) is even more

Table 4.4. Proportions of Conservative Votes in Civil Liberties Cases, Roberts Court, Selected Justices (Part II)

	Justice					
Terms	Ginsburg	Breyer	Sotomayor	Kagan	Kennedy	Alito
2005–2006	36.0	37.3	—	—	65.3	79.6
2007–2008	29.9	38.4	—	—	59.8	72.4
2009–2010	39.5	43.0	36.5	37.9	53.5	69.0
2011–2012	30.8	46.2	32.5	31.5	53.2	76.6
2013–2014	32.9	31.9	29.0	34.8	51.4	64.3
2015–2016	35.7	35.7	29.0	31.3	41.4	61.4
2017	25.9	31.0	27.6	28.6	53.4	72.4

substantial. Although the proportions of conservative votes cast by liberal Justices fluctuate over time (especially for Justice Breyer), on the whole they have remained fairly stable—in contrast with the overall decline among conservatives during the same period. Here too, changes in the Court's civil liberties agenda likely account for the temporal pattern shown in the table.

And as was true with today's Republican Justices, the convictions of Democratic Justices are undoubtedly strengthened by the liberal elite networks that they were a part of before and after joining the Court. These networks still dominate the legal academy numerically and have clear majority status in the legal profession.[247] Journalists as a group continue to lean to the left,[248] and that appears to be true of those journalists who cover the Supreme Court. The development of a more self-consciously liberal segment of the elite, reflected in the emergence of the ACS, provides additional reinforcement for liberal Justices.

The Limits of Partisanship

Throughout this chapter, we have called attention to the split between Democratic and Republican Justices on the Supreme Court in the current era and identified the various causes of this divide. While the partisan divide is very real and very consequential, it is also important to highlight that the Supreme Court is still a court and that today's partisanship is limited by numerous factors. In chapter 2, we noted that Supreme Court Justices were attentive to norms of collegiality and law-oriented decision making. These norms and the corresponding interest of the Justices in their reputations and legacies cut against out-and-out partisanship on the Supreme Court.

The difference between the legislative and judicial branches in this respect is highlighted by the findings of Thomas Keck's study of abortion, affirmative action, gun rights, and same-sex marriage, discussed earlier in the chapter. Republican and Democratic appointees on the Supreme Court and the federal courts of appeals differ considerably in their aggregate voting behavior on those issues, but those differences are considerably more limited than the corresponding party differences in Congress. That contrast between Congress and the courts reflects differing incentives and perspectives in the two branches.[249]

On the Supreme Court, these differences are highlighted by the Justices' responses to the 2016 death of Justice Antonin Scalia and the events that followed. In the months after Scalia's death, Senate Democrats and Republicans were engaged in brutal partisan fights regarding the refusal to consider Merrick Garland and the repudiation of the filibuster. During that period the Justices sought to send two related messages: first, that they disapproved of the politicization of the Supreme Court by the other branches, and second, that they were a collegial court.

Unlike Democratic senators (who cried foul at the Republicans' successful campaign to save the Scalia seat for a Republican appointee), Democratic Justices embraced the Court as a collegial institution that operated above the political fray. Justice Sonia Sotomayor (who had earlier complained that "the world around us has politicized what we've done") bemoaned people losing confidence in judges and spoke of the Justices' efforts to "reach consensus more."[250] Justice Elena Kagan likewise critiqued the perception of judicial politicization and said that the Justices had "worked very hard to reach consensus and to find ways to agree that might not have been very obvious." (She expressed a similar view a year later while a Senate battle over confirmation of Brett Kavanaugh was developing, lamenting that the confirmation process now makes people see the Justices as political actors even though "that's not the way we think of ourselves.")[251] Justice Stephen Breyer insisted that Justices are not "junior-varsity politicians" and said that he was confident that an eight-member Court would not deadlock if there was a dispute regarding the 2016 presidential elections.[252] Even Justice Ruth Bader Ginsburg (who called Trump a "faker" before the 2016 elections) praised Court nominee Neil Gorsuch as "very easy to get along with" and called for the Senate to end the gridlock that was delaying confirmation of a ninth Justice.[253]

In pointing to the important element of collegiality in the Court, we do not mean to exaggerate that element. Certainly there are interpersonal frictions and tensions among the Justices, as there were in past eras. Ruth Bader Ginsburg said in 2018 that "I respect all of my colleagues and genuinely like most of them,"[254] a seemingly pointed reservation. And despite her close friendship with Antonin Scalia, she said that "sometimes I'd like to strangle him."[255]

The sharp criticism and even ridicule of colleagues' statements that appears in some dissenting opinions is also striking. Scalia's dissent in the Court's 2015 decision striking down state prohibitions of same-sex marriage responded to the opening of Anthony Kennedy's opinion for the Court by declaring that "the Supreme Court of the United States has descended from the disciplined legal reasoning of John Marshall and Joseph Story to the mystical aphorisms of the fortune cookie."[256] Scalia stood out for the frequency of acerbic language in his opinions, perhaps because his interest in communicating his views to his ideological allies overrode any concern for comity. But other

Justices have written harsh judgments about colleagues' opinions in their own opinions—again, at least in part as a means to appeal to like-minded elites outside the Court.

Even so, in this era of bitter political contention, the Court stands out for the extent of collegiality among its members. Certainly it stands in stark contrast with Congress.

The Court's collegiality helps to explain the degree of consensus that exists in the Court's decisions. Consensus was especially apparent during the two terms that the Justices largely operated as an eight-member Court. In its 2015 term, decisions issued after Scalia's death were "modest and ephemeral" as the Justices were "especially concerned" about reaching consensus.[257] In its 2016 term, the average share of votes in support of the majority opinion was 89 percent (the highest in at least seventy years), 57 percent of decisions were unanimous, and only 14 percent of decisions were decided by a bare five-member majority.[258] And while this consensus stemmed in part from the Court's steering clear of salient issues likely to divide the Justices, it nonetheless reflects the desires of the Justices to present themselves as a collegial Court—even if it meant issuing "exceedingly narrow decisions to avoid deadlocks."[259]

The 2015 and 2016 terms are striking but do not stand alone in the era of a Court that is divided along party lines. In its 2013 term, by one count, 62 percent of the Court's decisions were by unanimous votes (the highest percentage since 1940).[260] The average difference in size between the Court's majority and dissenting coalitions showed no decline between 2000 and 2016 suggesting that today's partisan divide did not result in pervasive party-line voting.[261]

The 2017 term featured a level of consensus that was relatively low for the post-2010 era, and it may be the harbinger of a more divided Court in the near future. Still, there was considerable agreement among the Justices. The Court reached unanimity 39 percent of the time. With one narrow exception, every pair of Justices agreed on case outcomes a majority of the time.[262]

Indeed, as Table 4.5 shows,[263] the average rate of voting agreement by term between Republican appointees and Democratic appointees in the 2010–2017 terms was 68 percent despite the substantial ideological distance between the Court's Democrats and at least four of its five Republicans.[264] In other words, notwithstanding the fact that the Court's Republicans and Democrats now constitute distinct ideological groups, today's partisan divide on the Court looks very different from the partisan divide in Congress.

Although some other Justices seem concerned with consensus as a goal,[265] Chief Justice Roberts has played an especially important role in the Court's

Table 4.5. Percentages of Cases in Which Pairs of Justices Supported the Same Outcome, 2010–2017 Terms

	Tho	Ali	Gor	Sca	Rob	Ken	Bre	Kag	Gin
Alito	88.0								
Gorsuch	84.9	84.9							
Scalia	87.7	84.1							
Roberts	82.1	86.9	83.7	87.1					
Kennedy	77.5	81.7	84.9	78.3	86.0				
Breyer	66.8	70.5	61.6	65.6	77.0	81.3			
Kagan	66.5	69.5	63.9	71.2	75.1	82.5	90.2		
Ginsburg	62.5	64.5	59.3	65.7	70.3	76.0	87.3	90.6	
Sotomayor	64.1	66.5	55.8	65.7	73.0	78.6	86.7	88.8	90.0

Mean rates of agreement:
between Democratic Justices 88.9%
between Republican Justices 84.1%
between Democrats and Republicans 68.1%

efforts to achieve consensus. In 2006, as an interviewer described it, Roberts declared that he would "make it his priority to discourage his colleagues from issuing separate opinions."[266] In his view, unanimous or nearly unanimous opinions "contribute to the stability of the law . . . [whereas] 5-4 decisions make it harder for the public to respect the Court as an impartial institution that transcends partisan politics."[267] And while the Chief Justice usually has sided with his Republican colleagues in high-salience cases that divided the Court, his efforts contributed to a rate of unanimous votes on case outcomes in the Roberts Court that is above average for the period since 1941, when the Court moved away from its traditional practice of emphasizing unanimity. The unanimity rate has been even higher since the Court's ideological lines began to coincide with partisan lines in 2010.[268]

Roberts also appears to have placed institutional concerns ahead of ideology when he broke ranks with his Republican colleagues and cast the deciding vote upholding a key provision of the Affordable Care Act.[269] Roberts, finally, has also spoken about the need for the Court to appear above politics. In an April 2017 speech, he pointed to the "real danger that the partisan hostility that people see in the political branches will affect the nonpartisan activity of the judicial branch. It is very difficult I think for a member of the public to look at what goes on in confirmation hearings these days . . . and not think that the person who comes out of that process must similarly share that partisan view of public issues and public life."[270]

None of this is surprising. In addition to norms of collegiality and law-oriented decision making, the Justices care greatly about their personal reputations. As discussed in chapter 2, Supreme Court Justices trade off income and personal freedom for status and power. This seems especially true of today's Supreme Court. Today's Justices are particularly likely to write books, give public speeches, and otherwise cultivate their reputations. Indeed, a study of publicly reported interviews and appearances from 1960 to 2014 reveals an eightfold increase since the 1970s; more striking, all nine of the Justices on the 2010–2014 Roberts Court were ranked in the top ten on a "celebrity index" (a measure of average number of speeches and public appearances per year).[271]

Reputational concerns help to explain the willingness of Justices on the Roberts Court to speak or vote against their perceived ideological interests. In particular, today's Justices are not simply part of conservative or liberal elite social networks. Those networks are critically important and are partly responsible for the partisan divide on today's Supreme Court. But the Justices are also part of a community of Supreme Court advocates, law clerks, and academics who write about the Court.

This network of Court insiders places great stock in the Court's institutional reputation as a court of law, not a court of partisans. For example, the status of Supreme Court practitioners and former Supreme Court law clerks is tied to their reputation for excellence, and that reputation is furthered when the Court acts as a court of law and not another political institution. Moreover, this network of Court insiders is more powerful today than ever before. In particular, Supreme Court practice is now dominated by an elite Supreme Court bar made up of former Supreme Court law clerks and alumni of the Office of Solicitor General.[272] A 2014 study found that sixty-six lawyers in the private sector "were involved in 43 percent of cases the high court agreed to hear."[273] For its part, the Office of Solicitor General (largely made up of former Supreme Court clerks) participates in oral argument in around three-quarters of all cases.[274] The Justices embrace this network and reinforce it, heralding its benefits in interviews and appointing former law clerks to serve as amicus curiae before the Court.[275]

Against this backdrop, it is easy to understand why today's Justices want to present themselves as not simply partisans. And while the partisan divide on the Court is real and the affinity of Justices to ideological organizations that share their views is likewise real, it is also the case that today's Justices seek outlets to demonstrate their interest in the Court's institutional reputation. Unanimous or near-unanimous opinions are the principal way that the Justices show they are a collegial body. Critical votes that conflict with the Justices' perceived ideological interests are another way. Chief Justice Roberts's vote on the individual mandate in the Affordable Care Act, for example, protected his own personal reputation from charges of partisan manipulation even while it greatly displeased some conservatives.[276] Likewise, reputational concerns may help explain the willingness of all four Democratic Justices to fight back against claims that the Supreme Court has become a partisan institution—especially in the face of the Republican Senate's failure to act on the Merrick Garland nomination.

Conclusion

Elite polarization explains the partisan division on the modern Supreme Court. The pool of Democratic nominees is liberal, the pool of Republican nominees conservative. Moreover, ideology—especially for Republicans—has become more salient in the selection of Justices. Correspondingly, prospective Justices are groomed in elite social networks that make them both more ideological and more likely to stand firm in their ideological convictions. In particular, unlike the center-left drift of several earlier Justices who were appointed by Republican presidents, today's Republican appointees have proved to be committed conservatives. The conservative legal network, especially the Federalist Society, has played a key role here—reinforcing conservative principles both before and after a nominee is selected. Correspondingly, Democratic appointees are part of an elite liberal legal network. The dominance of that network in a period of limited polarization helped to pull some Republican appointees on the Court to center-left positions. Because of the growth in affective polarization since that time, the liberal network has become even more salient to Justices who are part of it.

This chapter has highlighted this partisan divide and its causes. It has also called attention to basic differences between the Supreme Court and other political actors. The Justices care greatly about their reputations among the institutional elites who are part of the Supreme Court social network; consequently, the partisan divide is tempered by the Justices' continuing adherence to norms of collegiality and law-oriented decision making. And while the Justices will not vote regularly in ways that conflict with their sincere preferences, they also act to reduce the sharpness of the ideological and partisan lines between them. Thus they are engaged in a juggling act between policy considerations and attaining consensus. In turn, this juggling act reflects the fact that they care a great deal about both elites that are ideologically oriented and elites that also emphasize institutional considerations related to the Court.

5

Conclusions

IN THIS BOOK we have presented a perspective on the Supreme Court that differs in important respects from the ways that the Court is typically portrayed. In this chapter, after providing an overview of our perspective and findings, we draw out the implications of our perspective for an understanding of the Court and for the Court's future.

An Overview

The most fundamental premise underlying our perspective on the Supreme Court is that Justices, like other people, have social identities. Those identities lead them to seek approval and respect from individuals and groups that are important to them. As a result, which sets of people are part of a Justice's identity makes a good deal of difference for that Justice's work as a decision maker.

We have argued that Justices' social identities are oriented toward elite segments of American society. That orientation flows from several realities about the Justices.

Historically, the great majority of Justices came from families of high social and economic status.[1] That is largely true today, but Clarence Thomas and Sonia Sotomayor are notable counterexamples. At the same time, all nine Justices have been part of elite culture since their teens or twenties. Indeed, it is close to impossible for a Justice not to be part of elite culture, for getting to the Court requires that people achieve high status in their own lives. Sotomayor went to undergraduate school at Princeton, and she and Thomas both studied law at Yale. As widely noticed, every Justice appointed to the Court from 1986 to 2018 went to law school at either Harvard or Yale.[2]

Typically, Justices' careers after law school put them firmly in the elite. For most of the Court's history, many Justices had achieved high elective or appointive office in the legislative or executive branches of government. Today, that path is uncommon. Rather, future Justices most often practice in high-status law firms, teach in prestigious law schools, or do both. Of the Justices appointed between 1986 and 2017, all but one had penultimate positions on the federal courts of appeals, and the exception—Elena Kagan—was dean of Harvard Law School before becoming the federal solicitor general.

These careers connect future Justices with the elite segment of the legal profession, as well as other elites. On a day-to-day level, they interact directly and indirectly with people of high social, economic, and political status. As a result, it is those people whose regard is most important to them.

This pattern continues when someone joins the Supreme Court. Indeed, as people who hold the highest positions in the legal system, positions that carry a great deal of prestige, the Justices become more firmly rooted in social elites. Moreover, their work is judged most closely and most regularly by elites such as legal academics and news reporters who have achieved high status in their own profession.

As a result, we have argued, the strongest sources of influence on the Justices from outside the Court are the various elites with which Justices are connected. Justices are drawn toward the values of those elites, and they are likely to see the world from the perspective of the elites that are most important to them.

For this reason, the state of opinion among relevant elites at a given time can shape decision making by the Justices. In part, this is because the Justices are likely to have the same ideological predispositions as elites of their era; in part, it is because the Justices are likely to seek approval from elite audiences. We have emphasized the shift in the structure of elite opinion that has resulted from growing polarization among political elites. That polarization has multiple facets. The most important are partisan sorting, in which liberals increasingly gravitate to the Democratic Party and conservatives to the Republican side; extremism, in which people cluster more to the left and right as opposed to the ideological center; and affective polarization, in which positive feelings about one's own ideological and partisan side and negative feelings about the other side strengthen. Partisan sorting and affective polarization are quite evident among the general public; all three facets are evident among political activists and public officials.

The current high level of political polarization developed gradually, with different facets coming at different paces. For the most part, this process has occurred since the 1980s. Of course, there are always strong disagreements on political issues within elite groups. But divisions were not as sharp prior to the 1980s as they have become since that time.

Most relevant to the Supreme Court were two elements of elite attitudes in the era before the 1980s. First, highly educated people were more favorable to an array of civil liberties than was the public as a whole. This fact helps to explain why the Warren Court and its successors expanded civil liberties in ways that the mass public disapproved and on which elites were more positive. On some issues, disproportionate elite support for civil liberties continued well beyond the 1980s. When Justice Scalia complained in one case that the Court had adopted "the resolution favored by the elite class from which the Members of this institution are selected,"[3] he was capturing an important truth.

Second, elite circles that were especially relevant to the Justices leaned in a liberal direction to varying degrees. Certainly this was true of the Justices' most visible evaluators, legal scholars and Court reporters for media such as the *New York Times*. It appears to be true as well of the elite social community in Washington, DC, during that era. In our view, that leaning helps to explain the unexpected moderation or liberalism of many of the Justices who were appointed by Republican presidents between 1953 and 1990. Complaints by conservatives that some of those Republican appointees were captured by "the Georgetown social set"[4] or that their desire for approval from the news media created a "Greenhouse effect"[5] are not simply expressions of disappointment at the Court's direction. Rather, even if those complaints exaggerate the effects of the Justices' social environment on their decision making, they capture an important reality.

The era of strong political polarization has affected the Court in multiple ways, of which two are most direct. The first is a change in the criteria for nomination of Justices. Throughout American history some presidents have emphasized policy considerations in their selection of nominees to the Court, but on the whole policy has been only one of several criteria for choices of Justices. Since the beginning of President Reagan's second term in 1985, ideology has risen in importance.

This is especially true of Republican presidents. Political activists who are associated with the Republican Party have made the selection of conservative Justices a high priority, in part because of their strong disappointment with the ideological course that several prior Republican nominees followed after they joined the Court. The commitment of those activists and their influence over nominations to the Court were reflected both in the rise of ties with the Federalist Society as an important credential for Supreme Court nominees and in the related 2005 withdrawal of George W. Bush nominee Harriet Miers. Even more striking was the impact of Donald Trump's lists of prospective nominees, lists drawn up by leaders of conservative groups, in rallying conservative activists and interest groups behind his presidential candidacy in 2016.

The picture for Democratic presidents is more complicated. Even today, Democratic nominations reflect the priorities of Democratic activists in balancing policy considerations and group interests, interests centered on ethnic and gender diversity. Further, recent Democratic presidents have sought to avoid the perception that they are highly liberal. Primarily for those reasons, Democratic Justices as a group are not as liberal as their Republican counterparts are conservative.

Even so, Democratic appointment strategies have changed in ideological terms. Democratic presidents do not seek nominees who are far to the left of center, but they do seek to avoid nominees who are not on the left side of the ideological spectrum. Democrats in the current era certainly would not nominate anyone who was equivalent to the conservatives chosen by Harry Truman, and even a counterpart of John Kennedy's nominee Byron White might have difficulty securing a Democratic nomination today.

Partisan sorting among prospective nominees has had an effect as well. Increasingly, credible candidates for Supreme Court appointments are like other members of political elites: if they are conservative, they are almost certain to be Republicans, and liberals are nearly as likely to be Democrats. In today's era most if not all of the Truman nominees would be Republicans,[6] and perhaps Byron White would have been as well.

The second effect of higher polarization relates to Justices' social identities. Polarization in its various forms has changed the Supreme Court's environment, splitting that environment along ideological lines to a much greater degree than was true a few decades ago. The creation and growth of the Federalist Society is the most prominent and consequential part of the establishment of a distinct conservative segment of the elite legal community. In reaction, liberal lawyers established the American Constitution Society as a counterpart of the Federalist Society. In doing so they formalized and deepened the distinction between conservative and liberal legal elites.

In a parallel development, the news media have become more bifurcated. With liberalism dominant among elite news reporters, most national newspapers and broadcast networks in the prepolarization era adhered to what might best be characterized as moderate liberalism. Today those media have been supplemented and, to a considerable degree, supplanted by cable networks and blogs that have strongly liberal or conservative positions. One result has been the growth of Supreme Court coverage with a distinctly conservative perspective. The legal academy has contributed to this development with a growth in conservative commentary, including blogs such as the influential *Volokh Conspiracy*.[7]

To a considerable degree, Supreme Court Justices have become part of this new polarized world. Justices increasingly come to the Court with strong ties to conservative or liberal elites, ties that they maintain as Justices. To take one visible manifestation, liberal Justices go to meetings of the American Constitution Society, conservatives to Federalist Society events.[8] More fundamentally, Justices are like other Americans in that the circles of friends and acquaintances around them are more likely to have homogeneous ideological orientations than was true in prior eras. As a result, Justices are reinforced in the ideological tendencies that they bring to the Court.

In this new world, the ideological content of Justices' votes and opinions is less susceptible to change than it was in the preceding period. Democratic appointees are liberals who interact primarily with other liberals; Republicans are conservatives who are oriented toward other conservatives. This reality reinforces the appointment process in hardening ideological positions, especially on the Right. Consequently, the days when some Republican appointees drifted toward more liberal positions are behind us. Drift aside, David Souter and John Paul Stevens were the last Justices whose ideological positions differed sharply from the dominant tendency in the party of their appointing president, and their retirements produced a Court in which ideological lines coincide with partisan lines. The retirement of Anthony Kennedy—who was noticeably less conservative than other Republican Justices—is likely to create even sharper ideological differences between the Court's Republican and Democratic Justices.

All this being true, the Justices' social identities also limit the impact of political polarization in an important way. Strong as their connections to one side of the political divide might be, the Justices are still part of a legal elite with its own norms about judging. Justices routinely speak at law schools and to prominent bar groups; they interface with faculty at top law schools when hiring clerks; they are still the subject of academic commentary. Unlike earlier eras, legal practice before the Supreme Court is dominated by an elite Supreme Court bar largely composed of former law clerks to the Justices.[9]

Correspondingly, even more than in past eras, Justices' pre-Court careers tend to be concentrated in the legal system as practicing lawyers, legal academics, and judges. Their expectations of themselves and the expectations of others in the legal system include skill in the legal craft and adherence to legal ways of deciding cases. In particular, the Justices—like the legal elites they associate with—embrace norms of collegiality, judicial independence, and the related idea that the Supreme Court is a court of law and not a political body.

These expectations do not prevent Justices from following paths that reflect their positions on an ideological scale or from dividing sharply and sometimes bitterly in cases that divide conservatives from liberals. But they do create limits on ideological decision making. On the Supreme Court, as on the courts of appeals, Republican and Democratic appointees do not differ in their votes on ideologically salient issues to nearly the degree that members of Congress do.[10] The Court's high proportion of unanimous decisions and the frequency with which divisions among the Justices in decisions diverge from ideological lines are signs that the Court has not featured the severe splits between partisan and ideological adversaries that exist in the other branches of the federal and state governments.

Understanding the Court

In some important ways, our conception of the Supreme Court is in accord with the dominant models of decision making in scholarship on the Court. We agree with the consensus in political science, widely shared in the legal academy, that the Justices' policy preferences have a powerful impact on their votes and opinions on the Court. In turn, we agree with the consensus that appointments of Justices make a great deal of difference because they determine the distribution of policy preferences on the Court. We also accept the view that Justices' choices reflect their interest in law, as well as policy, a view that is strongly rejected by some political scientists and a few legal scholars but accepted to varying degrees by most students of the Court.

However, we disagree with conventional views of the Court in some important respects. That disagreement begins with our conception of the Justices' goals. The dominant theories of decision making depict Justices as people who concentrate on achieving what they see as good policy, good law, or a combination of the two. In economic terms, Justices gain utility by taking positions that accord with their conceptions of good law and policy or by moving the Court and the larger world of public policymaking toward those conceptions. With occasional exceptions, scholars do not look more broadly or more deeply for the Justices' motivations.

Working from a psychological perspective, we view Justices as having the same broad range of basic motives as other people. As scholars who study other kinds of political leaders have demonstrated, analysis of public policymakers in terms of those motives provides considerable insight on the reasons for their choices as decision makers.[11]

For Supreme Court Justices, as we have argued, the need for respect and approval is one motive that can help considerably in understanding why they do what they do. Indeed, we think that Supreme Court Justices are especially interested in being held in esteem by other people who are important to their social identities. Taking a judgeship entails accepting relatively significant constraints on personal activities and behaviors and, for most judges on higher courts, a significant reduction in monetary compensation. One of the things that Justices gain in compensation (in addition to an increase in power) is the esteem that attaches to a position on the highest court in the country. By no means would all people find this tradeoff attractive; rather, it is most attractive to people who care the most about the esteem in which they are held.

Our concern with social identity leads to a view about the relationship between the Justices and the world outside the Court that diverges from the views incorporated in the major scholarly models of decision making. The attitudinal and strategic models each view potential external influences on the Justices as stemming from their interest in the substance of legal policy. Adherents to strategic models perceive that Justices give considerable attention to potential backlash from elected officials and the general public in order to maximize the achievement of their favored legal policies. Adherents to the attitudinal model claim that the Justices have no such need and simply vote their legal policy preferences.

First of all, we disagree with the view of "attitudinalists" that the Court is essentially autonomous from the outside world. Rather, we see the world of political and social elites as a subtle but powerful force that can shape the Justices' thinking and their choices as decision makers.

Second, we disagree with the view of many scholars that the influence of the outside world stems from the Justices' interest in the substance of legal policy. Both in strategic models of decision making and in less formal conceptions offered by some scholars, this view holds that Justices take their political environment into account as a means to protect the Court's decisions and the Court's capacity to achieve implementation of its decisions. In this view,

Justices sometimes draw back from potential decisions that might be reversed by the other branches of government to avoid a result that makes policy worse from their perspective. They retreat under pressure from Congress to minimize the chances that their institutional powers and thus their capacity to shape policy will be weakened. And they bring their decisions into agreement with the attitudes of the general public to maintain the legitimacy that ensures implementation of their decisions.

We agree that these motivations sometimes come into play, though we think that their impact is often exaggerated. In particular, we doubt that mass public opinion does a great deal to deter Justices from reaching decisions that they would otherwise prefer to reach. Rather, we think that Justices respond much more to the opinions of elite segments of society than they do to the public as a whole. The influence of elites on the Justices reflects the fact that elite segments of society are the most important to Justices' social identities, so that they are the primary focus of Justices' efforts to achieve the good regard of other people.

In turn, we think that Justices' interest in the regard of elites helps to explain their choices as decision makers. To take one example that we have discussed, the leftward movement of several Republican appointees to the Court from the early 1950s to the early 1990s would be considerably more difficult to explain on the basis of models that do not take social identity into account. The recent development of ideological blocs on the Court that follow party lines is primarily the result of changes in the process of appointing Justices. But changes in the appointment process have been reinforced by changes in the elite audiences to which the Justices are oriented. As we see it, a full understanding of what the Supreme Court does requires that we take into account the elite audiences that are integral to the Justices' social identities.

Looking to the Future

What the Supreme Court will be like as an institution in the future depends on a variety of conditions that are not necessarily easy to predict. In our view, one key condition is the state of political polarization in the world of political elites.

So long as party polarization continues, it is quite likely that the current coincidence of partisan and ideological lines on the Court will also continue. Certainly it is possible that some Justice will prove to be an exception, so that party and ideology diverge to a small degree. But that exception would stand out far more than in prior eras, when it was common for nominees to deviate from the dominant ideological orientation of the nominating president's party. Moreover, powerful forces work against even occasional exceptions, both in the nomination of Justices and in the courses that Justices set for themselves once they reach the Court.

Indeed, there are reasons to expect that partisan lines on the Court will become sharper over time. New Justices increasingly will be people who have grown up politically in an era of high polarization. Even more than their older colleagues, they will be accustomed to an elite world in which there are two camps engaged in bitter competition. Like other Americans, they will live in worlds populated primarily by people who share their political views. They will have gone through career paths that are defined largely by party and ideology. Most notably, Democrats will identify with and associate with liberal groups such as the American Constitution Society; Republicans will be members of the Federalist Society. As Justices, most will use forums outside the Court—interactions with news media, public appearances, and writings—to affirm and strengthen their ties with liberal or conservative social networks. Indeed, the current Supreme Court is filled with "celebrity Justices" who increasingly make public appearances to adoring, ideologically simpatico audiences.[12] Under those circumstances, the likelihood of a movement away from their party's ideological side during their tenure on the Court would be small.

For their part, presidents and senators will increasingly look to ideology and affiliations with ideological groups in selecting and approving nominees to the Supreme Court. The Court is seen as an important political actor even more than in most past eras, and the decision to nominate and confirm a Supreme Court Justice is now seen as critical to the policy agendas of Democrats and Republicans. Witness, for example, the Senate's refusal to consider Democratic nominee Merrick Garland and the subsequent repudiation of the filibuster and party-line vote to confirm Republican Neil Gorsuch.

Against this backdrop, there is next to no chance of a Republican president selecting a moderate conservative similar to Anthony Kennedy. Even a potential nominee like John Roberts, with only a short record of judicial service to analyze, may be ruled out. On the Democratic side, presidents are likely to feel increased pressure from activists to choose nominees who are more strongly liberal than the current Democratic appointees. That will be especially true if the Court moves decisively to the right, a development that would bring to the Democratic Party the strong pressures for ideologically reliable nominees that currently exist on the Republican side. Only if the president's party lacks control of the Senate will there be incentives to choose relative moderates, and even under that circumstance those incentives may be outweighed by the forces that favor strong conservatives or liberals.

For these reasons, presidential elections will become even more important for the Court than they have been throughout American history. The ten consecutive appointments by Republican presidents from 1969 and 1991, a product of the party's success in winning presidential elections during that era,[13] moved the Court substantially to the right. But those appointments would have had much greater impact if Republican presidents during that era had given the emphasis to ideology that George W. Bush and Donald Trump have given and if most of the Justices those presidents selected had been oriented strongly toward a conservative camp in the world of social and political elites.

The rise of ideology in judicial appointments has also had spillover effects in voter attitudes toward the Court. Judicial nominations are politically salient today in ways that were not true a decade ago.[14] Voters increasingly understand that presidents pay attention to ideology when choosing Justices and senators cast party-line votes. The Republican Senate's failure to consider Merrick Garland, in particular, turned the 2016 presidential election into a referendum on the future direction of the Supreme Court for many voters.[15]

Depending on the outcomes of presidential elections and the timing of vacancies, then, in the future we can expect either of two patterns. The first is what Mark Graber called "constitutional yo-yos, dramatic swings in judicial policy making on numerous policy issues" as ideological majorities on the Court shift back and forth.[16] The second is entrenched control of the Court by one ideological side, with the result that legal doctrine moves decisively in one direction or the other.

Neil Gorsuch exemplifies the changes we have described especially well.[17] With long-standing ties to conservative elites, Gorsuch maintained those ties as a court of appeals judge while establishing a strongly conservative judicial record. Thus, he was a logical choice for the conservatives who created the lists of prospective Supreme Court nominees for Donald Trump in 2016 and ultimately for nomination to the Court.

In 2017, after he joined the Court, Gorsuch gave speeches at meetings of the Federalist Society and the Fund for American Studies, another conservative group, in effect ratifying his conservative links. Before the Federalist Society, Gorsuch delivered a speech in which he made his identification with the group clear and said he could report that "a person can both be a committed originalist and textualist and be confirmed to the Supreme Court."[18] Early in his service on the Court, his strong expression of conservative positions in opinions and in oral argument was striking. With the careful vetting that now characterizes the appointment of Justices and with the Court's new social environment, it would be very surprising if Gorsuch deviated from the ideological path that he has taken thus far in his career.

The changes that have occurred in the Court are not necessarily permanent. If the movement toward stronger polarization among political elites is reversed, that reversal can be expected to affect both the appointments of Supreme Court Justices and the partisan and ideological element of the Justices' social identities. Such a reversal seems quite unlikely in the near future. Indeed, the battle over the Court vacancy created by Antonin Scalia's death and the battle over confirmation of Brett Kavanaugh in 2018 underlined the enormous symbolic importance of ideological control of the Court for political activists in the current era, an importance that cannot be expected to decline for a long time. Further, the increased segmentation of legal elites into ideological camps will affect the thinking of lawyers who become credible candidates for the Supreme Court well into the future.

We should emphasize once more that with all the changes that have accompanied growing political polarization, the Supreme Court remains different from the other branches of government. The legal community still holds expectations about the behavior of judges that limit ideologically oriented decision making, both by shaping Justices' perceptions of the ways that legal audiences assess their performance and by shaping Justices' own values. But with the changes in the Court that have accompanied polarization, Justices now act more as adherents to one ideological side, a side increasingly identified in partisan terms, than they did for most of the Court's history. That is a consequential change.

Notes

PREFACE

1. Michael Scherer and Robert Costa, " 'Rock Bottom': Supreme Court Fight Reveals a Country on the Brink," *Washington Post*, October 7, 2018, A1.
2. Josh Blackman, "Who Do Insiders Think Trump Will Select for the Supreme Court?," *Weekly Standard,* November 23, 2016, https://www.weeklystandard.com/josh-blackman/who-do-insiders-think-trump-will-select-for-the-supreme-court.
3. Avi Selk, "McConnell Says GOP Was 'Literally under Assault'—by People Protesting an Alleged Sexual Assault," *Washington Post,* October 8, 2018, https://www.washingtonpost.com/politics/2018/10/08/mcconnell-says-gop-was-literally-under-assault-by-people-protesting-an-alleged-sex-assault/?utm_term=.3801b3b65581.
4. David A. Graham, "Lindsey Graham's Furious Defense of Brett Kavanaugh," *The Atlantic*, September 27, 2018, https://www.theatlantic.com/politics/archive/2018/09/lindsey-graham-kavanaugh-ford/571558/.
5. Ed Lilgore, "Senate Democrats Deftly Highlighted Republican Insensitivity toward Christine Blasey Ford," *Nymag.com*, September 27, 2018, http://nymag.com/intelligencer/2018/09/democrats-christine-ford-strategy-stress-gop-insensitivity.html?gtm=bottom>m=bottom.
6. Dartunorro Clark and Lauren Egan, "'Bull—Investigation,' 'Sham,' 'Horrific Cover-up': Democrats Blast FBI Kavanaugh Report," October 4, 2018, *NBC News*, https://www.nbcnews.com/politics/congress/sham-cover-so-called-investigation-democrats-blast-fbi-kavanaugh-report-n916701.
7. Peter Baker and Nicholas Fandos, "A Nomination Is Rescued by a Display of Rage and Resentment," *New York Times*, October 7, 2018, A1.
8. Jean Kirby, "Read: Brett Kavanaugh's Angry, Emotional Opening Statement," *Vox*, September 27, 2018, https://www.vox.com/2018/9/27/17911256/brett-kavanaugh-christine-blasey-ford-senate-hearing.

9. Elizabeth Dias and Jeremy W. Peters, "For Conservatives, Fight for Court Is on Their Turf and in Their D.N.A.," *New York Times*, June 29, 2018, A18. Dialynn Dwyer, "How the Massachusetts Congressional Delegation Is Reacting to Trump's Supreme Court Nominee Judge Brett Kavanaugh," *Boston Globe*, July 10, 2018, https://www.boston.com/ news/politics/2018/07/10/massachusetts-politicans-react-trump-supreme-court-nominee-judge-brett-kavanaugh.
10. Jacqueline Thomson, "Booker: Those Who Don't Oppose Kavanaugh Are 'Complicit in the Evil,'" *The Hill*, July 24, 2018, http://thehill.com/homenews/senate/398681-booker-those-who-dont-oppose-kavanaugh-are-complicit-in-the-evil.
11. 117 Cong. Rec. S4923 (daily ed. July 12, 2018) (remarks of Sen. McConnell).
12. Kate Riga, "McConnell: Blocking Garland Was 'Most Consequential Decision I Ever Made,'" *Talking Points Memo*, June 27, 2018, https://talkingpointsmemo.com/livewire/mcconnell-gloats-over-blocking-garland.
13. "'I Am a Pro-Law Judge': Excerpts of Brett Kavanaugh's Opening Remarks," *Market Watch,* September 4, 2018, https://www.marketwatch.com/story/i-am-a-pro-law-judge-excerpts-of-brett-kavanaughs-opening-remarks-2018-09-04.
14. Brett M. Kavanaugh, "I Am an Independent, Impartial Judge," *Wall Street Journal*, October 4, 2019, https://www.wsj.com/articles/i-am-an-independent-impartial-judge-1538695822.
15. "Remarks by President Trump at Swearing-In Ceremony of the Honorable Brett M. Kavanaugh as Associate Justice of the United States Supreme Court," October 8, 2018, https://www.whitehouse.gov/briefings-statements/remarks-president-trump-swearing-ceremony-honorable-brett-m-kavanaugh-associate-justice-supreme-court-united-states/.

CHAPTER 1

1. U.S. Senate, *Confirmation Hearing on the Nomination of John G. Roberts, Jr. to Be Chief Justice of the United States*, 109th Congress, 1st session, 2005, 55–56.
2. "Nomination of John Roberts," *Congressional Record* 151 (September 22, 2005): 21032 (Remarks of Sen. Obama).
3. Mitch McConnell and Chuck Grassley, "The American People Should not Be Robbed of Their Say," *Washington Post*, February 19, 2016, A21.
4. U.S. Senate, *Confirmation Hearing on the Nomination of Hon. Neil M. Gorsuch to Be an Associate Justice of the Supreme Court of the United States*, 115th Congress, 1st session, 2017, 65–66.
5. Gorsuch's rate of agreement on case outcomes with other Republican Justices was in a narrow range, from 84 percent to 85 percent; his agreement with the Democratic Justices ranged from 64 percent to 56 percent. Full information on interagreements between pairs of justices since the 2010 term is presented in Table 4.5.
6. For simplicity, at some points in the book we will refer to Justices simply as Republicans and Democrats, but what we mean is the nominees and appointees of Republican and Democratic presidents. Over the Court's history some presidents

have appointed Justices who do not share their party affiliation; the last such Justice was Lewis Powell, a Democrat appointed by President Nixon in 1971.

7. See Hans Noel, *Political Ideologies and Political Parties in America* (New York: Cambridge University Press, 2014); and Lawrence Baum, *Ideology in the Supreme Court* (Princeton, NJ: Princeton University Press, 2017).
8. These analyses are for cases decided after oral argument, based on data in the Supreme Court Database, archived at http://scdb.wustl.edu/. The criteria for coding of votes as conservative or liberal are described at http://scdb.wustl.edu/documentation.php?var=decisionDirection.
9. These measures include the Martin-Quinn scores, based on analyses of interagreements between pairs of Justices, and Bailey scores, based on comparisons of Justices' positions on the same issues with Justices who served at different times and with policymakers in the other branches of government. We will make use of both these sets of scores in later chapters. The Martin-Quinn scores are archived and described at http://mqscores.berkeley.edu/. A fuller description of the procedures for calculation of those scores is presented at Andrew D. Martin and Kevin M. Quinn, "Dynamic Ideal Point Estimation via Markov Chain Monte Carlo for the U.S. Supreme Court 1953–1999," *Political Analysis* 10 (2002): 134–153. The Bailey scores are archived at http://faculty.georgetown.edu/baileyma/Data_AJPSIdealPoints_Oct2009.htm and described in Michael A. Bailey, "Is Today's Court the Most Conservative in Sixty Years? Challenges and Opportunities in Measuring Judicial Preferences," *Journal of Politics* 75 (July 2013): 821–834.
10. Based on the coding of cases in the Supreme Court Database, the correlation between Justices' proportions of conservative votes in civil liberties cases (issue areas 1 through 6) and their votes in economic cases (issue areas 7 and 8) was +.76 in the 2010–2014 terms. The correlation may understate the relationship between the two fields somewhat because the coding rules for economic cases do not fully capture the complexity of conservative and liberal positions in that field. As in civil liberties cases, all Republican Justices had more conservative records than all Democrats in economic cases.
11. Thus, the mean standard deviation for the 1986–1993 terms is based only on the 1986–1990 terms, before Marshall's retirement.
12. As we will discuss in chapter 3, there were some terms during the Stone Court of the early 1940s in which Owen Roberts (a Republican appointee) and Harlan Fiske Stone (appointed as Associate Justice by a Republican president and promoted to Chief Justice by a Democrat) stood to the right of their Democratic-appointed colleagues. But rather than standing with Roberts and apart from the Court's Democratic appointees, Stone's position in those terms was close to that of the more conservative Democrats on the Court.
13. Most notably, Justice Roberts and Chief Justice Stone moderated earlier views on congressional power to support a broad interpretation of congressional power to regulate agriculture in *Wickard v. Filburn*, 317 U.S. 111 (1942).

14. See Dennis J. Hutchinson, "Unanimity and Desegregation: Decisionmaking in the Supreme Court, 1948–1958," *Georgetown Law Journal* 68 (October 1979): 1–96.
15. 384 U.S. 436 (1966).
16. 410 U.S. 113 (1973). Of course, Republican Harry Blackmun wrote the Court's opinion in *Roe* and played a central role in the decision. See Linda Greenhouse, *Becoming Justice Blackmun: Harry Blackmun's Supreme Court Journey* (New York: Henry Holt and Company, 2005), 72–101. Republican Lewis Powell, who joined the Court after the initial argument and vote in *Roe*, played an important role in the Court's final decision by voting to overturn the Texas law and thereby ensuring a solid majority for that position. See David J. Garrow, *Liberty and Sexuality: The Right of Privacy and the Making of Roe v Wade* (Berkeley: University of California Press, 1998), 571–576, 586–587.
17. E.g., *United Steelworkers v. Weber*, 443 U.S. 193 (1979); *Grutter v. Bollinger*, 539 U.S. 206 (2003).
18. *Planned Parenthood v. Casey*, 505 U.S. 833 (1992).
19. *Boumediene v. Bush*, 553 U.S. 723 (2008).
20. The cases are listed in David G. Savage, *Guide to the U.S. Supreme Court,* 5th ed. (Washington, DC: CQ Press, 2010), 1276–1294.
21. *United States v. Windsor*, 570 U.S. 744 (2013); *Obergefell v. Hodges*, 135 S. Ct. 2584 (2015). The votes in both decisions were 5–4.
22. *Whole Woman's Health v. Hellerstedt*, 136 S. Ct. 2292 (2016); *Fisher v. University of Texas*, 136 S. Ct. 2198 (2016). The vote in *Whole Woman's Health*, decided after Justice Scalia's death, was 5–3; the vote in *Fisher*, also after Scalia's death and with Justice Kagan recused from participating, was 4–3.
23. We will discuss these cases in chapter 4.
24. See Bailey, "Is Today's Court the Most Conservative in Sixty Years?"
25. Jeffrey A. Segal and Harold J. Spaeth, *The Supreme Court and the Attitudinal Model Revisited* (New York: Cambridge University Press, 2002).
26. Lee Epstein and Jack Knight, *The Choices Justices Make* (Washington, DC: CQ Press, 1998). More recently, Epstein and Knight have presented an alternative conception, one in which the Justices and other judges act on the basis of a broad array of goals; that conception is closer to our own perspective. Lee Epstein and Jack Knight, "Reconsidering Judicial Preferences," *Annual Review of Political Science* 16 (2013): 11–31.
27. Barry Friedman, *The Will of the People: How Public Opinion Has Influenced the Supreme Court and Shaped the Meaning of the Constitution* (New York: Farrar, Strauss and Giroux, 2009).
28. Jeffrey Rosen, *The Most Democratic Branch: How the Courts Serve America* (New York: Oxford University Press, 2006).
29. Examples include Kevin T. McGuire and James A. Stimson, "The Least Dangerous Branch Revisited: New Evidence on Supreme Court Responsiveness to Public Preferences," *Journal of Politics* 66 (November 2004): 1018–1035; Christopher Casillas, Peter K. Enns, and Patrick C. Wohlfarth, "How Public Opinion Constrains

the U.S. Supreme Court," *American Journal of Political Science* 55 (January 2011): 74–88; and Matthew E. K. Hall, "The Semiconstrained Court: Public Opinion, the Separation of Powers, and the U.S. Supreme Court's Fear of Nonimplementation," *American Journal of Political Science* 58 (April 2014): 352–366.

30. Tom S. Clark, *The Limits of Judicial Independence* (New York: Cambridge University Press, 2010).
31. William H. Rehnquist, "Constitutional Law and Public Opinion," *Suffolk University Law Review* 20 (Winter 1986): 768.
32. John C. Jefferies Jr., *Justice Lewis F. Powell, Jr.* (New York: Charles Scribner's Sons, 1994), 521–529. The quotation is from p. 521.
33. Linda Greenhouse, "Heartfelt Words from the Rehnquist Court," *New York Times*, July 6, 2003, WK3.
34. Lawrence Baum, *Judges and Their Audiences: A Perspective on Judicial Behavior* (Princeton, NJ: Princeton University Press, 2006), 10.
35. We discuss possible goals for judges and their implications in chapter 2.
36. See Neal Devins and Will Federspiel, "The Supreme Court, Social Psychology, and Group Formation," in *The Psychology of Judicial Decision Making*, ed. David Klein and Gregory Mitchell (New York: Oxford University Press, 2010), 85, 90.
37. See Roy F. Baumeister and Mark R. Leary, "The Need to Belong: Desire for Interpersonal Attachments as a Fundamental Human Motivation," *Psychological Bulletin* 117 (May 1995): 497; Thomas J. Miceli and Metin M. Cosgel, "Reputation and Judicial Decision-making," *Journal of Economic Behavior and Organization* 23 (1994): 31; Frederick Schauer, "Incentives, Reputation, and the Inglorious Determinants of Judicial Behavior," *University of Cincinnati Law Review* 68 (Spring 2000): 625–631.
38. Richard A. Posner, *How Judges Think* (Cambridge, MA: Harvard University Press, 2008), 306.
39. Posner, *How Judges Think*, 306; Michael J. Klarman, "What's So Great about Constitutionalism?," *Northwestern University Law Review* 93 (1998): 189.
40. Adam Liptak, "Justices Get Out More, but Calendars Aren't Open to Just Anyone," *New York Times*, June 1, 2015; Robert Barnes, "How Many Harvard Law School Grads Does It Take to Make a Supreme Court?," *Washington Post Blogs*, October 26, 2017, https://www.washingtonpost.com/politics/courts_law/how-many-harvard-law-school-grads-does-it-take-to-make-a-supreme-court/2017/10/26/970e5460-baa2-11e7-be94-fabb0f1e9ffb_story.html?utm_term=.9fe9a6dda247.
41. Liptak, "Justices Get Out More, but Calendars Aren't Open to Just Anyone."
42. We are not counting Harlan Fiske Stone, whom Roosevelt elevated from Associate Justice to Chief Justice.

CHAPTER 2

1. Wilfred E. Rumble Jr., *American Legal Realism: Skepticism, Reform, and the Judicial Process* (Ithaca, NY: Cornell University Press, 1968).

2. C. Herman Pritchett, *The Roosevelt Court: A Study in Judicial Politics and Values* (New York: Macmillan, 1948); Glendon Schubert, *The Judicial Mind: The Attitudes and Ideologies of Supreme Court Justices 1946–1963* (Evanston, IL: Northwestern University Press, 1965); David W. Rohde and Harold J. Spaeth, *Supreme Court Decision Making* (San Francisco: W. H. Freeman, 1976).
3. U.S. Senate, *Confirmation Hearing on the Nomination of John G. Roberts, Jr. to Be Chief Justice of the United States*, 109th Congress, 1st session, 2005, 55; U.S. Senate, *Confirmation Hearing on the Nomination of Hon. Sonia Sotomayor, to Be an Associate Justice of the Supreme Court of the United States*, 111th Congress, 1st session, 2009, 59; U.S. Senate, *The Nomination of Elena Kagan to Be an Associate Justice of the Supreme Court of the United States*, 111th Congress, 2nd session, 2010, 103.
4. Mark Tushnet, *In the Balance: Law and Politics on the Roberts Court* (New York: W. W. Norton, 2013), xiv. Tushnet was adopting a formulation by then-Senator Barack Obama. "Nomination of John Roberts," *Congressional Record* 151 (September 22, 2005): 21032 (Obama statement).
5. Joshua B. Fischman and Tonja Jacobi, "The Second Dimension of the Supreme Court," *William & Mary Law Review* 57 (April 2016): 1671–1715.
6. Jeffrey A. Segal and Harold J. Spaeth, *The Supreme Court and the Attitudinal Model* (New York: Cambridge University Press, 1993); Segal and Spaeth, *The Supreme Court and the Attitudinal Model Revisited* (New York: Cambridge University Press, 2002); Jeffrey A. Segal and Alan J. Champlin, "The Attitudinal Model," in *Routledge Handbook of Judicial Behavior*, ed. Robert M. Howard and Kirk A. Randazzo (New York: Routledge, 2018), 17–33.
7. This includes most of the research that treats the Justices as acting strategically, a perspective that we discuss shortly. One influential example is Lee Epstein and Jack Knight, *The Choices Justices Make* (Washington, DC: CQ Press, 1998).
8. Richard A. Posner, "Foreword: A Political Court," *Harvard Law Review* 119 (November 2005): 39–54; Posner, "What Is Obviously Wrong with the Federal Judiciary, yet Eminently Curable, Part II," *Green Bag 2d* 19 (Spring 2016): 263–266. Another example is Eric J. Segall, *Supreme Myths: Why the Supreme Court Is Not a Court and Its Justices Are Not Judges* (Santa Barbara, CA: Praeger, 2012).
9. Howard Gillman, "What's Law Got to Do with It? Judicial Behavioralists Test the 'Legal Model' of Judicial Decision Making," *Law & Social Inquiry* 26 (Spring 2001): 465–504; Keith E. Whittington, "Once More unto the Breach: PostBehavioralist Approaches to Judicial Politics," *Law & Social Inquiry* 25 (Spring 2000): 601–634; Mark A. Graber, "Legal, Strategic, or Legal Strategy: Deciding to Decide during the Civil War and Reconstruction," in *The Supreme Court and American Political Development*, ed. Ronald Kahn and Ken I. Kersch (Lawrence: University Press of Kansas, 2006), 33–66.
10. That point of view is reflected in many of the essays in a collection of work by historical institutionalists, Kahn and Kersch, *The Supreme Court and American Political Development*.

11. Mark J. Richards and Herbert M. Kritzer, "Jurisprudential Regimes in Supreme Court Decision Making," *American Political Science Review* 96 (June 2002): 305–320; Stefanie A. Lindquist and David E. Klein, "The Influence of Jurisprudential Considerations on Supreme Court Decisionmaking: A Study of Conflict Cases," *Law & Society Review* 40 (2006): 135–161; Michael A. Bailey and Forrest Maltzman, *The Constrained Court: Law, Politics, and the Decisions Justices Make* (Princeton, NJ: Princeton University Press, 2011).
12. A strategic perspective on the Supreme Court is presented in Epstein and Knight, *The Choices Justices Make.*
13. See, e.g., Seth Stern and Stephen Wermiel, *Justice Brennan: Liberal Champion* (New York: Houghton Mifflin Harcourt, 2010), 361–363.
14. Walter F. Murphy, *Elements of Judicial Strategy* (Chicago: University of Chicago Press, 1964); Lee Epstein and Jack Knight, "Toward a Strategic Revolution in Judicial Politics: A Look Back, a Look Ahead," *Political Research Quarterly* 53 (September 2000): 625–663; James R. Rogers, Roy B. Flemming, and Jon R. Bond, eds., *Institutional Games and the U.S. Supreme Court* (Charlottesville: University of Virginia Press, 2006).
15. Forrest Maltzman, *Crafting Law on the Supreme Court: The Collegial Game* (New York: Cambridge University Press, 2000).
16. Lee Epstein and Jack Knight, *The Choices Justices Make* (Washington, DC: CQ Press, 1997); Tom S. Clark, *The Limits of Judicial Independence* (New York: Cambridge University Press, 2011).
17. See Rogers, Flemming, and Bond, *Institutional Games and the U.S. Supreme Court.*
18. Segal and Spaeth, *Supreme Court and the Attitudinal Model Revisited*, 111–114.
19. Self-interest can be defined broadly enough to include almost any motivation, and a few scholars have referred to judges' pursuit of good legal policy as self-interested. An example is Edward P. Schwartz, Pablo T. Spiller, and Santiago Urbiztondo, "A Positive Theory of Legislative Intent," *Law and Contemporary Problems* 57 (Winter–Spring 1994): 57. But from most perspectives, acting to advance legal or policy goals is altruistic rather than self-interested.
20. One example is Mario Bergara, Barak Richman, and Pablo T. Spiller, "Modeling Supreme Court Strategic Decision Making: The Congressional Constraint," *Legislative Studies Quarterly* 28 (May 2003): 247–280.
21. Daniel Kahneman, Paul Slovic, and Amos Tversky, eds., *Judgment under Uncertainty: Heuristics and Biases* (New York: Cambridge University Press, 1982); Thomas Gilovich, Dale Griffin, and Daniel Kanheman, eds., *Heuristics and Biases: The Psychology of Intuitive Judgment* (New York: Cambridge University Press, 2002).
22. Examples of this research include Chris Guthrie, Jeffrey J. Rachlinski, and Andrew J. Wistrich, "Inside the Judicial Mind," *Cornell Law Review* 86 (May 2001): 777–830; and Jeffrey J. Rachlinski, Andrew J. Wistrich, and Chris Guthrie, "Can Judges Make Reliable Numeric Judgments? Distorted Damages and Skewed Sentences," *Indiana Law Journal* 90 (Spring 2015): 695–739.

23. Ziva Kunda, "The Case for Motivated Reasoning," *Psychological Bulletin* 108 (November 1990): 489–498. The most extensive use of this theory in the study of judicial behavior is in Eileen Braman, *Law, Politics, and Perception: How Policy Preferences Influence Legal Reasoning* (Charlottesville: University of Virginia Press, 2009).
24. Christopher Schroeder, "Causes of the Recent Turn in Constitutional Interpretation," *Duke Law Journal* 51 (October 2001): 356–359.
25. Susan T. Fiske, "Five Core Social Motives, Plus or Minus Five," in *Motivated Social Perception*, ed. Steven J. Spencer, Steven Fein, Mark P. Zanna, and James M. Olson (Mahwah, NJ: Lawrence Erlbaum, 2003), 233–246; Robert C. Beck, *Motivation: Theories and Principles* (Upper Saddle River, NJ: Pearson/Prentice Hall, 2004), 318–351; Johnmarshall Reeve, *Understanding Motivation and Emotion* (Hoboken, NJ: Wiley, 2015), 152–182.
26. David G. Winter, "Motivation and Political Leadership," in *Political Leadership for the New Century: Personality and Behavior among American Leaders*, ed. Linda O. Valenty and Oter Feldman (Westport, CT: Praeger, 2002) 25–47; David G. Winter, "Measuring the Motives of Political Actors at a Distance," in *The Psychological Assessment of Political Leaders*, ed. Jerrold M. Post (Ann Arbor: University of Michigan Press, 2003), 153–177.
27. Winter, "Motivation and Political Leadership," 27.
28. An explicit and careful presentation of the bases for this assumption is in Segal and Spaeth, *The Supreme Court and the Attitudinal Model Revisited*, 92–96.
29. Some examples of scholarship on the impact of judges' career goals are Melinda Gann Hall, "Electoral Politics and Strategic Voting in State Supreme Courts," *Journal of Politics* 54 (May 1992): 427–446; Gregory A. Huber and Sanford C. Gordon, "Accountability and Coercion: Is Justice Blind When It Runs for Office?," *American Journal of Political Science* 48 (April 2004): 247–263; and Jeffrey Budziak, "Blind Justice or Blind Ambition? The Influence of Promotion on Decision Making in the U.S. Courts of Appeals," *Justice System Journal* 34 (2013): 295–320.
30. Burton Atkins, Lenore Alpert, and Robert Ziller, "Personality Theory and Judging: A Proposed Theory of Self Esteem and Judicial Policy-Making," *Law and Policy Quarterly* 2 (April 1980): 189–220; James L. Gibson, "Personality and Elite Political Behavior: The Influence of Self Esteem on Judicial Decision Making," *Journal of Politics* 43 (February 1981): 104–125.
31. Jilda M. Aliotta, "Social Backgrounds, Social Motives and Participation on the U.S. Supreme Court," *Political Behavior* 10 (Autumn 1988): 267–284; Greg A. Caldeira, "Judicial Incentives: Some Evidence from Urban Trial Courts," *Iusticia* 4.2 (1977): 1–28; Austin Sarat, "Judging in Trial Courts: An Exploratory Study," *Journal of Politics* 39 (May 1977): 368–398.
32. James Eisenstein and Herbert Jacob, *Felony Justice: An Organizational Analysis of Criminal Courts* (Boston: Little, Brown, 1977), 24–28; Mark A. Cohen,

"Explaining Judicial Behavior or What's 'Unconstitutional' about the Sentencing Commission?," *Journal of Law, Economics, and Organization* 7 (Spring 1991): 183–199; Richard A. Posner, "What Do Judges and Justices Maximize? (The Same Thing Everybody Else Does)," *Supreme Court Economic Review* 3 (1993): 1–41; Lawrence Baum, "What Judges Want: Judges' Goals and Judicial Behavior," *Political Research Quarterly* 47 (September 1994): 749–768; Christopher R. Drahozal, "Judicial Incentives and the Appeals Process," *SMU Law Review* 51 (March–April 1998): 469–503; Ahmed E. Taha, "Publish or Paris? Evidence of How Judges Allocate Their Time," *American Law and Economics Review* 6 (Spring 2004): 1–27; Lee Epstein, William N. Landes, and Richard A. Posner, *The Behavior of Federal Judges: A Theoretical and Empirical Study of Rational Choice* (Cambridge, MA: Harvard University Press, 2013), 30–44, 48–50.

33. Richard A. Posner, *How Judges Think* (Cambridge, MA: Harvard University Press, 2008), 36.
34. Examples include Lawrence S. Wrightman, *The Psychology of the Supreme Court* (New York: Oxford University Press, 2006); and David Klein and Gregory Mitchell, eds., *The Psychology of Judicial Decision Making* (New York: Oxford University Press, 2010).
35. David Glick, "Conditional Strategic Retreat: The Court's Concession in the 1935 Gold Clause Cases," *Journal of Politics* 71 (July 2009): 800–816.
36. Rafael Gely and Pablo T. Spiller, "A Rational Choice Theory of Supreme Court Statutory Decisions with Applications to the *State Farm* and *Grove City* Cases," *Journal of Law, Economics, and Organization* 6 (Fall 1990): 263–300; William N. Eskridge Jr., "Reneging on History? Playing the Court/Congress/President Civil Rights Game," *California Law Review* 79 (May 1991): 613–684.
37. William N. Eskridge Jr., "Overriding Supreme Court Statutory Interpretation Decisions," *Yale Law Journal* 101 (November 1991): 390–415.
38. Evidence on statutory interpretation is reported in Bergara, Richman, and Spiller, "Modeling Supreme Court Strategic Decision Making"; Pablo T. Spiller and Rafael Gely, "Congressional Control or Judicial Independence: The Determinants of U.S. Supreme Court Labor-Relations Decisions, 1949–1988," *RAND Journal of Economics* 23 (Winter 1992): 463–492; Jeffrey A. Segal, "Separation-of-Powers Games in the Positive Theory of Congress and Courts," *American Political Science Review* 91 (March 1997): 28–44; and Brian R. Sala and James E. Spriggs II, "Designing Tests of the Supreme Court and the Separation of Powers," *Political Research Quarterly* 57 (June 2004): 197–208. Evidence on constitutional interpretation is reported in Jeffrey A. Segal, Chad Westerland, and Stefanie A. Lindquist, "Congress, the Supreme Court, and Judicial Review: Testing a Constitutional Separation of Powers Model," *American Journal of Political Science* 55 (January 2011): 89–104; Anna Harvey and Barry Friedman, "Pulling Punches: Congressional Constraints on the Supreme Court's Constitutional Rulings, 1987–2000,"

Legislative Studies Quarterly 31 (November 2006): 533–562; and Anna Harvey, *A Mere Machine: The Supreme Court, Congress, and American Democracy* (New Haven, CT: Yale University Press, 2013).

39. Lawrence Baum, *Judges and Their Audiences: A Perspective on Judicial Behavior* (Princeton, NJ: Princeton University Press, 2006), 73–77.
40. Roy F. Baumeister and Mark R. Leary, "The Need to Belong: Desire for Interpersonal Attachments as a Fundamental Human Motivation," *Psychological Bulletin* 117 (May 1995): 497–529; Rick H. Hoyle, Michael H. Kernis, Mark R. Leary, and Mark W. Baldwin, *Selfhood: Identity, Esteem, Regulation* (Boulder, CO: Westview Press, 1999), 31–35.
41. Mark R. Leary, *Self-Presentation: Impression Management and Interpersonal Behavior* (Madison, WI: Brown & Benchmark, 1996), 3. On self-presentation, see Erving Goffman, *The Presentation of Self in Everyday Life* (Garden City, NY: Doubleday, 1959); and Barry R. Schlenker and Michael F. Weigold, "Interpersonal Processes Involving Impression Regulation and Management," *Annual Review of Psychology* 43 (1992): 133–168.
42. Richard A. Posner, *Cardozo: A Study in Reputation* (Chicago: University of Chicago Press, 1990), 58–73; Thomas J. Miceli and Metin M. Cosgel, "Reputation and Judicial Decision-Making," *Journal of Economic Behavior and Organization* 23 (January 1994): 31–51; Frederick Schauer, "Incentives, Reputation, and the Inglorious Determinants of Judicial Behavior," *University of Cincinnati Law Review* 68 (Spring 2000): 615–636; Baum, *Judges and Their Audiences*.
43. Schauer, "Incentives, Reputation, and the Inglorious Determinants of Judicial Behavior," 625–634.
44. On social identity, see Henri Tajfel, ed., *Differentiation between Social Groups: Studies in the Social Psychology of Intergroup Relations* (New York: Academic Press, 1978); Dominic Abrams and Michael A. Hogg, eds., *Social Identity and Social Cognition* (Malden, MA: Blackwell, 1999); Marillyn B. Brewer, "The Many Faces of Social Identity: Implications for Political Psychology," *Political Psychology* 22 (March 2001): 115–125; and Richard Jenkins, *Social Identity* (New York: Routledge, 2014).
45. To take one example, observers of the Court have discussed the interest of Justice Hugh Black in his public image and have speculated about the impact of that interest on the positions he took as a Justice. See Richard Davis, *Decisions and Images: The Supreme Court and the Press* (Englewood Cliffs, NJ: Prentice-Hall, 1964), 43; William Domnarski, *In the Opinion of the Court* (Urbana: University of Illinois Press, 1996), 67; and Dennis J. Hutchinson, "Remembering Lewis F. Powell," *Green Bag 2d* 2 (Winter 1999): 167. Justice Black had lengthy experience as an elected official.
46. The evidence on possible influence is discussed in Baum, *Judges and Their Audiences*, 96.
47. Barry Friedman, *The Will of the People: How Public Opinion Has Influenced the Supreme Court and Shaped the Meaning of the Constitution* (New York: Farrar, Straus and Giroux, 2009), 374.

48. Friedman, *Will of the People*, 375.
49. Examples of scholars' emphasis on the importance of legitimacy to the Court's security and power include Jeffery J. Mondak, "Perceived Legitimacy of Supreme Court Decisions: Three Functions of Source Credibility," *Political Behavior* 12 (December 1990): 363; James L. Gibson, "Institutional Legitimacy, Procedural Justice, and Compliance with Supreme Court Decisions: A Question of Causality," *Law & Society Review* 25 (1991): 631–635; and Brandon L. Bartels and Christopher D. Johnson, "On the Ideological Foundations of Supreme Court Legitimacy in the American Public," *American Journal of Political Science* 57 (January 2013): 184.
50. A third possibility, suggested by scholars with a strategic perspective, is that Justices adhere to precedent as a means to avoid public disapproval. Epstein and Knight, *The Choices Justices Make*, 163–177.
51. Friedman, *Will of the People*; Jeffrey Rosen, *The Most Democratic Branch: How the Courts Serve America* (New York: Oxford University Press, 2006). This is also a theme of the classic history by Robert G. McCloskey, *The American Supreme Court* (Chicago: University of Chicago Press, 1960).
52. Roy B. Flemming and B. Dan Wood, "The Public and the Supreme Court: Individual Justice Responsiveness to American Policy Moods," *American Journal of Political Science* 41 (April 1997): 493–494; Christopher J. Casillas, Peter K. Enns, and Patrick C. Wohlfarth, "How Public Opinion Constrains the U.S. Supreme Court," *American Journal of Political Science* 55 (January 2011): 75–76.
53. Robert A. Dahl, "Decision-Making in a Democracy: The Supreme Court as a National Policy-Maker," *Journal of Public Law* 6 (Fall 1957): 293.
54. Dahl, "Decision-Making in a Democracy," 285.
55. The quotation is from Jean A. Briggs, "How You Going to Get 'Em Back in the Kitchen? (You Aren't)," *Forbes*, November 15, 1977, 177. On the employment increase, see Ruth Bader Ginsburg, "Gender in the Supreme Court: The 1973 and 1974 Terms," *Supreme Court Review* (1975): 2 note 10. Both sources are cited in Friedman, *The Will of the People*, 290. The decision that applied "heightened scrutiny" to laws that treat women and men differently was *Craig v. Boren*, 429 U.S. 190 (1976).
56. During oral arguments in *U.S. v. Nixon*, Nixon's lawyer, James St. Clair, equivocated on the president's willingness to accept an adverse judgment from the Court—noting that the case "is being submitted to the Court for its guidance and judgment with respect to the law. The President, on the other hand, has his obligations under the Constitution." Philip B. Kurland and Gerhard Casper, eds., *Landmark Briefs and Arguments of the Supreme Court of the United States: Constitutional Law*, vol. 79 (Arlington, VA: University Publishers of America, 1975), 872.
57. See Dennis J. Hutchinson, "Unanimity and Desegregation: Decision-Making in the Supreme Court, 1948–1958," *Georgetown Law Journal* 68 (October 1979): 34–44; S. Sidney Ulmer, "Earl Warren and the Brown Decision," *Journal of Politics* 33 (August 1971): 689–702.

58. Del Dickson, "State Court Defiance and the Limits of Supreme Court Authority: Williams v. Georgia Revisited," *Yale Law Journal* 103 (April 1994): 1476 and note 317 (quoting November 4, 1955, memo from Justice Felix N. Frankfurter to the Conference).
59. See Neal Devins and Louis Fisher, "Judicial Exclusivity and Political Instability," *Virginia Law Review* 84 (February 1998): 91–98, 100–101.
60. In *Planned Parenthood v. Casey*, the Court's willingness to moderate but not overrule *Roe v. Wade* (including the overruling of past precedent on waiting periods and informed consent requirements) is tied to the appointments of the three Justices who wrote the plurality decision (Sandra Day O'Connor, David Souter, Anthony Kennedy). In making this point, we recognize that the views of the Justices in the *Casey* plurality were shaped by a broad range of events—including but not limited to elected government resistance to *Roe*.
61. The Court may also be responding to attacks from other quarters, including elites. This is what happened in 1943, when the Court overruled a 1940 decision approving state-mandated flag salutes. This episode is discussed later in the chapter, in the section on elite opinion and Supreme Court decisions.
62. That body of scholarship is discussed in Ilya Somin, "Political Ignorance and the Countermajoritarian Difficulty: A New Perspective on the Central Obsession of Constitutional Theory," *Iowa Law Review* 89 (April 2004): 1304–1314. See Ilya Somin, *Democracy and Political Ignorance*, 2nd ed. (Palo Alto, CA: Stanford University Press, 2016); and Michael X. Delli Carpini and Scott Keeter, *What Americans Know about Politics and Why It Matters* (New Haven, CT: Yale University Press, 1996).
63. Ilya Somin and Neal Devins, "Can We Make the Constitution More Democratic?," *Drake Law Review* 55 (2007): 977.
64. Gregory Casey, "The Supreme Court and Myth: An Empirical Investigation," *Law & Society Review* 8 (Spring 1974): 388.
65. Robert Kessley, "Why Aren't Cameras Allowed at the Supreme Court Again?," *Atlantic,* March 28, 2013, https://www.theatlantic.com/national/archive/2013/03/case-allowing-cameras-supreme-court-proceedings/316876/.
66. Sixty-five percent of registered voters ranked Supreme Court appointments as one of the top issues in the 2016 elections. Pew Research Center, "2016 Campaign: Strong Interest, Widespread Dissatisfaction," July 7, 2016. Seventy percent of voters ranked the Court as an important or the most important factor in exit polling. See NBC News Exit Poll: Future Supreme Court Appointments Important Factor in Presidential Voting, November 8, 2016, http://www.nbcnews.com/card/nbc-news-exit-poll-future-supreme-court-appointments-important-factor-n680381.
67. Pew Research Center, *Moral Values: How Important? Voters Liked Campaign 2004, but Too Much "Mud Slinging,"* November 11, 2004, http://www.people-press.org/2004/11/11/voters-liked-campaign-2004-but-too-much-mud-slinging/;

Fox News/Opinion Dynamics, "The Bush Administration, Supreme Court Nominations," November 18, 2004, http://nationaljournal.com/members/polltrack/2004/todays/11/1119fox.htm. For reasons we detail in chapter 5, we think that the growing salience of the Supreme Court to 2016 voters may be a harbinger of things to come. As the president and Senate increasingly focus on party and ideology in Supreme Court nominations, voters are more likely to view the Court as electorally significant.

68. Jennifer Harper, "Superman Tops Supremes: Americans Know Pop Culture Better than Politics," *Washington Times*, August 15, 2006, A1.
69. Martin Gilens, "Political Ignorance and Collective Policy Preferences," *American Political Science Review* 95 (June 2001): 393; James L. Gibson and Gregory A. Caldeira, "Knowing the Supreme Court? A Reconsideration of Public Ignorance of the High Court," *Journal of Politics* 71 (April 2009): 434.
70. "Aye, Carumba! U.S. Fails History," *Newsday*, March 2, 2006, A15.
71. James L. Gibson and Gregory A. Caldeira, *Citizens, Courts, and Confirmations: Positivity Theory and the Judgments of the American People* (Princeton, NJ: Princeton University Press, 2009), 24–35.
72. Findings on public knowledge of decisions are summarized in David Adamany and Joel B. Grossman, "Support for the Supreme Court as a National Policymaker," *Law and Policy Quarterly* 5 (October 1983): 407; and Barry Friedman, "Mediated Popular Constitutionalism," *Michigan Law Review* 101 (May 2003): 2620–2623.
73. Elliot E. Slotnick and Jennifer A. Segal, *Television News and the Supreme Court: All the News That's Fit to Air?* (New York: Cambridge University Press, 1998), 158–188.
74. Casey, "The Supreme Court and Myth," 387.
75. Pew Research Center, *Clinton Leadership Position Enhanced*, November 13, 1998: 6, http://www.people-press.org/1998/11/13/clinton-leadership-position-enhanced/; Pew Research Center, *Campaign Incidents Have Little Punch*, December 16, 1999: 12, http://www.people-press.org/1999/12/16/campaign-incidents-have-little-punch/.
76. Among the most important of these decisions were *United States v. Lopez*, 514 U.S. 549 (1995); *City of Boerne v. Flores*, 521 U.S. 507 (1997); and *Board of Trustees v. Garrett*, 531 U.S. 356 (2001).
77. For instance, all eleven decisions received front-page coverage in the *New York Times*. Lee Epstein, Jeffrey A. Segal, Harold J. Spaeth, and Thomas G. Walker, *The Supreme Court Compendium: Data, Decisions, and Developments*, 6th ed. (Washington, DC: CQ Press, 2015), 181–185.
78. This conclusion is based on analysis of data at "Gallup Analytics," http://www.gallup.com/products/170987/gallup-analytics.aspx.
79. Doni Gewirtzman, "Glory Days: Popular Constitutionalism, Nostalgia, and the True Nature of Constitutional Culture," *Georgetown Law Journal* 93 (2005): 913–924; Neal Devins, "The D'Oh! of Popular Constitutionalism," *Michigan Law Review* 105 (April 2007): 1335.

80. John H. Kessel, "Public Perceptions of the Supreme Court," *Midwest Journal of Political Science* 10 (May 1966): 179, 185; Walter F. Murphy and Joseph Tanenhaus, "Public Opinion and the United States Supreme Court: Mapping of Some Prerequisites for Court Legitimation of Regime Changes," *Law & Society Review* 2 (May 1968): 371–373.
81. Marc J. Hetherington and Joseph L. Smith, "Issue Preferences and Evaluations of the U.S. Supreme Court," *Public Opinion Quarterly* 71 (Spring 2007): 40–66.
82. Pew Research Center, *Negative Views of Supreme Court at Record High, Driven by Republican Dissatisfaction*, July 29, 2015, http://www.people-press.org/2015/07/29/negative-views-of-supreme-court-at-record-high-driven-by-republican-dissatisfaction/. As the same report shows, in the current era both liberals and conservatives—but especially conservatives—tend to see the Court as standing on the opposite side of the ideological spectrum from themselves.
83. One study provides evidence that perceptions of the Court's ideological position are generally accurate but that "errors" in perception are overwhelmingly on the side of overestimating the Court's liberalism. Stephen Jessee and Neil Malhotra, "Public (Mis)perceptions of Supreme Court Ideology: A Method for Directly Comparing Citizens and Justices," *Public Opinion Quarterly* 77 (Summer 2013): 619–634.
84. *Brown v. Board of Education*, 347 U.S. 483 (1954); *Miranda v. Arizona*, 384 U.S. 436 (1966); *Roe v. Wade*, 410 U.S. 113 (1973); *Texas v. Johnson*, 491 U.S. 397 (1989); *United States v. Eichman*, 496 U.S. 310 (1990); *Bush v. Gore*, 531 U.S. 98 (2000); *National Federation of Independent Business v. Sebelius*, 567 U.S. 1 (2012); *United States v. Windsor*, 570 U.S. 744 (2013); *Obergefell v. Hodges*, 135 S. Ct. 2584 (2015).
85. On the Gallup Poll question about how much confidence people have in the Supreme Court, the mean proportion of respondents who said "a great deal" or "quite a lot" in six surveys in the 1980s was 51 percent; the mean in seven surveys in the 2010s (through 2018) was 35 percent. For the "very little," and "none" categories, the increase was from 12 percent to 21 percent. (The middle category, "some," showed an increase from 32 percent to 41 percent.) These figures were computed from data in the iPoll survey archive provided by the Roper Center. There has also been a decline in approval of "the way the Supreme Court is handling its job" in the Gallup polls since 2000. Justin McCarthy, "GOP Approval of Supreme Court Surges, Democrats' Slides," *Gallup News*, September 28, 2017, http://news.gallup.com/poll/219974/gop-approval-supreme-court-surges-democrats-slides.aspx.
86. Nichole Zhao, "Chief Justice Speaks at Rice," *Rice Thresher*, October 19, 2012.
87. Fox News Poll, February 2017, archived in iPOLL, Roper Center.
88. See Devins, "The D'Oh of Popular Constitutionalism," 1342–1343.
89. This body of research is discussed in James L. Gibson and Michael J. Nelson, "The Legitimacy of the US Supreme Court: Conventional Wisdoms and Recent Challenges Thereto," *Annual Review of Law and Social Science* 10 (2014): 210–219. Recent research on this subject includes Gibson and Caldeira, *Citizens, Courts, and Confirmations*; James L. Gibson and Michael J. Nelson, "Is the U.S. Supreme Court's Legitimacy Grounded in Performance Satisfaction and

Ideology?," *American Journal of Political Science* 59 (January 2015): 162–174; Dino M. Christenson and David M. Glick, "Chief Justice Roberts's Health Care Decision Disrobed: The Microfoundations of the Supreme Court's Legitimacy," *American Journal of Political Science* 59 (April 2015): 403–418; Tom S. Clark and Jonathan P. Kastellec, "Source Cues and Public Support for the Supreme Court," *American Politics Research* 43 (May 2015): 504–535; James L. Gibson and Michael J. Nelson, "Change in Institutional Support for the US Supreme Court: Is the Court's Legitimacy Imperiled by the Decisions It Makes?," *Public Opinion Quarterly* 80 (2016): 622–641; and Bartels and Johnston, "On the Ideological Foundations of Supreme Court Legitimacy."

90. There is also a degree of partisan counterbalancing in specific support for the Court, as measured by the Gallup question, "Do you approve or disapprove of the way the Supreme Court is handling its job?" People who identify with the Republican and Democratic parties sometimes move in opposite directions in their responses to this item, because many people identify the Court with the president's party and because appointment politics and high-visibility decisions lead to different reactions from adherents to the two parties. To take one example, Gallup found a 39-percentage-point increase in approval of the Court among Republicans between 2016 and 2017 alongside a 27-percentage-point decline among Democrats. McCarthy, "GOP Approval of Supreme Court Surges, Democrats' Slides."

91. Herbert M. Kritzer, "The Impact of Bush v. Gore on Public Perceptions and Knowledge of the Supreme Court," *Judicature* 85 (July–August 2001): 34–36. See also Vincent Price and Anca Romantan, "Confidence in Institutions before, during, and after 'Indecision 2000,'" *Journal of Politics* 66 (August 2004): 949–953.

92. Jeffrey L. Yates and Andrew B. Whitford, "The Presidency and the Supreme Court after *Bush v. Gore*: Implications for Institutional Legitimacy and Effectiveness," *Stanford Law & Policy Review* 13 (2002): 113. About 30 percent of all respondents said they had lost confidence in the Court.

    Republican and Democratic attitudes toward the Court were similarly impacted by Senate Republicans' blocking the Merrick Garland nomination and Donald Trump's subsequent nomination of Neil Gorsuch. "Republicans' Views of Supreme Court Now More Favorable than Democrats'," Pew Research Center, April 25, 2018, http://www.people-press.org/2018/04/26/1-democracy-and-government-the-u-s-political-system-elected-officials-and-governmental-institutions/1_13-5/.

93. Gibson and Caldeira, *Citizens, Courts, and Confirmations*, 45–47; James L. Gibson, Gregory A. Caldeira, and Lester Kenyatta Spence, "The Supreme Court and the US Presidential Election of 2000: Wounds, Self-Inflicted or Otherwise?," *British Journal of Political Science* 33 (October 2003): 539–545. An analysis of a set of surveys before and after the Supreme Court's 2012 decision on the health care program sponsored by President Obama (*National Federation of*

Independent Business v. Sebelius) showed similar findings. Christenson and Glick, "Chief Justice Roberts's Health Care Decision Disrobed."

94. James L. Gibson and Gregory A. Caldeira, "Blacks and the United States Supreme Court: Models of Diffuse Support," *Journal of Politics* 54 (November 1992): 1120–1145.
95. The frequency of references to the Court's legitimacy in the Justices' opinions since the 1950s is discussed in Dion Farganis, "Do Reasons Matter? The Impact of Opinion Content on Supreme Court Legitimacy," *Political Research Quarterly* 65 (March 2012): 207. One well-known discussion of legitimacy considerations is in the joint opinion of Justices O'Connor, Kennedy, and Souter in *Planned Parenthood v. Casey*, 505 U.S. 833, 865–869 (1992). During the time between his two periods of service on the Court, Charles Evans Hughes wrote a book in which he cited three "self-inflicted wounds," decisions that he thought had weakened the Court's legitimacy. Charles Evans Hughes, *The Supreme Court of the United States: Its Foundation, Methods, and Achievements: An Interpretation* (New York: Columbia University Press, 1928), 50–54.
96. James A. Stimson, *Public Opinion in America: Moods, Cycles, and Swings*, 2nd ed. (Boulder, CO: Westview Press, 1999).
97. Thomas R. Marshall, *Public Opinion and the Supreme Court* (Boston: Unwin Hyman, 1989), 78–82; Thomas R. Marshall, *Public Opinion and the Rehnquist Court* (Albany: State University of New York Press, 2008), 35–39.
98. Marshall, *Public Opinion and the Supreme Court*, 104–130; Marshall, *Public Opinion and the Rehnquist Court*, 77–105.
99. This process is analogous to the linkage between the other branches and the Court that is posited in Robert A. Dahl's landmark article on the exercise of judicial review: Dahl, "Decision-Making in a Democracy."
100. Benjamin N. Cardozo, *The Nature of the Judicial Process* (New Haven, CT: Yale University Press, 1921), 168. See Micheal W. Giles, Bethany Blackstone, and Richard L. Vining Jr., "The Supreme Court in American Democracy: Unraveling the Linkages between Public Opinion and Judicial Decision Making," *Journal of Politics* 70 (April 2008): 295.
101. Although the Court's influence on public opinion should not be overstated, some studies have found evidence that the Court does have an impact on public attitudes. Examples include Valerie J. Hoekstra, *Public Reaction to Supreme Court Decisions* (New York: Cambridge University Press, 2003), 87–114; and Brandon L. Bartels and Diana C. Mutz, "Explaining Processes of Institutional Opinion Leadership," *Journal of Politics* 71 (January 2009): 255–259. The various reasons that Court and public majorities might agree are discussed in Marshall, *Public Opinion and the Supreme Court*, 16–26.
102. Rosen, *The Most Democratic Branch*, 185. See also Friedman, *The Will of the People*, 375–376.
103. Alison Gash and Angelo Gonzales, "School Prayer," in *Public Opinion and Constitutional Controversy*, ed. Nathaniel Persily, Jack Citrin, and Patrick J. Egan

(New York: Oxford University Press, 2008), 62, 69. The decisions were *Engel v. Vitale*, 370 U.S. 421 (1962), and *School District of Abington Township v. Schempp*, 374 U.S. 203 (1963).

104. Lucas A. Powe Jr., *The Warren Court and American Politics* (Cambridge, MA: Belknap Press, 2002), 394–395. For a somewhat competing perspective (arguing that Warren Court decision making was less countermajoritarian than it is often portrayed), see Corinna Barrett Lain, "Countermajoritarian Hero or Zero? Rethinking the Warren Court's Role in the Criminal Procedure Revolution," *University of Pennsylvania Law Review* 152 (April 2004): 1361–1452.

105. Donald Grier Stephenson Jr., *Campaigns and the Court: The U.S. Supreme Court in Presidential Elections* (New York: Columbia University Press, 1999), 180–181.

106. Bernard Schwartz, "Earl Warren as a Judge," *Hastings Constitutional Law Quarterly* 12 (Winter 1985): 179–200. These appointees became part of "the most cohesive [voting] bloc in modern Court history"—more willing to overturn constitutional precedent than any Court before it. Edward V. Heck, "Justice Brennan and the Heyday of Warren Court Liberalism," *Santa Clara Law Review* 20 (1980): 872. See also Powe, *The Warren Court and American Politics*, 290; Michal R. Belknap, *The Supreme Court under Earl Warren 1953–69* (Columbia: University of South Carolina Press, 2005), 308.

107. Rosen, *The Most Democratic Branch*, 59, 89–90, 169; Friedman, *The Will of the People*, 245, 269, 273.

108. Friedman, *The Will of the People*, 252–253, 264–265.

109. Peter Hanson, "Flag Burning," in *Public Opinion and Constitutional Controversy*, ed. Persily, Citrin, and Egan, 187. See also Robert Justin Goldstein, *Flag Burning and Free Speech: The Case of* Texas v. Johnson (Lawrence: University Press of Kansas, 2000), 112–113. The decision was *Texas v. Johnson*, 491 U.S. 397 (1989).

110. Janice Nadler, Shari Seidman Diamond, and Matthew M. Patton, "Government Takings of Private Property," in *Public Opinion and Constitutional Controversy*, ed. Persily, Citrin, and Egan, 286, 297. The decision was *Kelo v. City of New London*, 545 U.S. 469 (2005).

111. *Washington Post-ABC News Poll of February 4–8, 2010*, http://www.washingtonpost.com/wp-srv/politics/polls/postpoll_021010.html; Dan Eggen, "Poll: Large Majority Opposes Supreme Court's Decision on Campaign Financing," *Washington Post*, February 17, 2010, http://www.washingtonpost.com/wp-dyn/content/article/2010/02/17/AR2010021701151.html. However, while finding similar levels of opposition to the decision, a Gallup Poll also found that 55 percent think that corporate contributions deserve some speech protections. Lydia Saad, "Public Agrees with Court: Campaign Money Is 'Free Speech,'" *Gallup*, January 22, 2010, http://www.gallup.com/poll/125333/public-agrees-court-campaign-money-free-speech.aspx.

112. Goldstein, *Flag Burning and Free Speech*, 108–171; Ilya Somin, *The Grasping Hand:* Kelo v. City of New London *and the Limits of Eminent Domain*

(Chicago: University of Chicago Press, 2015), 135–164; Eggen, "Poll: Large Majority Opposes Supreme Court's Decision on Campaign Financing."

113. The preshift decisions include *A.L.A. Schechter Poultry Corp. v. United States*, 295 U.S. 495 (1935), and *Carter v. Carter Coal Co.*, 298 U.S. 238 (1936); the postshift decisions include *National Labor Relations Board v. Jones & Laughlin Steel Corp.*, 301 U.S. 1 (1937), and *Wickard v. Filburn*, 317 U.S. 111 (1942).
114. The preshift decisions included *Yates v. United States*, 354 U.S. 298 (1957), and *Watkins v. United States*, 354 U.S. 178 (1957); the postshift decisions included *Barenblatt v. United States*, 360 U.S. 109 (1959), and *Uphaus v. Wyman*, 360 U.S. 72 (1959).
115. Compare *Furman v. Georgia*, 408 U.S. 238 (1972), with *Gregg v. Georgia*, 428 U.S. 153 (1976).
116. The major Warren Court decisions included *Mapp v. Ohio*, 367 U.S. 643 (1961), and *Miranda v. Arizona*, 384 U.S. 436 (1966). Burger Court decisions that gave narrow interpretations to the rights established by the Warren Court include *Harris v. New York*, 401 U.S. 222 (1971), and *United States v. Calandra*, 414 U.S. 338 (1974).
117. The scholarly debate over the causes for the Court's 1937 "switch in time" is reviewed in "AHR Forum: The Debate over the Constitutional Revolution of 1937," *American Historical Review* 110 (October 2005): 1046–1115. The possible influence of public opinion is discussed in William G. Ross, *The Chief Justiceship of Charles Evans Hughes, 1930–1941* (Columbia: University of South Carolina Press, 2007), 135.
118. This episode is discussed in C. Herman Pritchett, *Congress versus the Supreme Court, 1957–1960* (Minneapolis: University of Minnesota Press, 1961) and Walter F. Murphy, *Congress and the Court: A Case Study in the American Political Process* (Chicago: University of Chicago Press, 1962).
119. Alternative explanations for the 1976 decisions are discussed in Lee Epstein and Joseph F. Kobylka, *The Supreme Court and Legal Change: Abortion and the Death Penalty* (Chapel Hill: University of North Carolina Press, 1992), 99–115. It is also possible that the pivotal Justices simply responded to the differences between the features of the earlier death penalty statutes and those that were enacted in response to the Court's 1972 decisions.
120. On abortion, see *Planned Parenthood v. Casey*, 505 U.S. 833 (1992). On school segregation, see *Board of Education v. Dowell*, 498 U.S. 237 (1991).
121. Neal Devins and Louis Fisher, *The Democratic Constitution*, 2nd ed. (New York: Oxford University Press, 2015), 172–185, 215–218.
122. Goldstein, *Flag Burning and Free Speech*.
123. *Lee v. Weisman*, 505 U.S. 577 (1992); *Wallace v. Jaffree*, 472 U.S. 38 (1985).
124. *Kennedy v. Louisiana*, 554 U.S. 407, 554 U.S. 945 (2008).
125. Eggen, "Poll: Large Majority Opposes Supreme Court's Decision on Campaign Financing."

126. *Am. Tradition Partnership, Inc. v Bullock*, 567 U.S. 516 (2012).
127. *McCutcheon v. Federal Election Commission*, 134 S. Ct. 1434 (2014).
128. Chris Good, "Citizens United Decision: Republicans Like It, Liberals Don't," *Atlantic*, January 21, 2010, https://www.theatlantic.com/politics/archive/2010/01/citizens-united-decision-republicans-like-it-liberals-dont/33935/.
129. *Roe v. Wade*, 410 U.S. 113 (1973); *Obergefell v. Hodges* (2015).
130. The Court literally did dismiss the argument for same-sex marriage in a two-word opinion in *Baker v. Nelson*, 409 U.S. 810 (1972).
131. Stimson, *Public Opinion in America*, 37–66.
132. Flemming and Wood, "The Public and the Supreme Court"; Giles, Blackstone, and Vining, "The Supreme Court in American Democracy," 293; Casillas, Enns, and Wohlfarth, "How Public Opinion Constrains the U.S. Supreme Court"; William Mishler and Reginald S. Sheehan, "The Supreme Court as a Countermajoritarian Institution? The Impact of Public Opinion on Supreme Court Decisions," *American Political Science Review* 87 (March 1993): 87–101; William Mishler and Reginald S. Sheehan, "Public Opinion, the Attitudinal Model, and Supreme Court Decision Making: A Micro-Analytic Perspective," *Journal of Politics* 58 (February 1996): 169–200; Michael W. Link, "Tracking Public Mood in the Supreme Court: Cross-Time Analyses of Criminal Procedure and Civil Rights Cases," *Political Research Quarterly* 48 (March 1995): 61–78; Kevin T. McGuire and James A. Stimson, "The Least Dangerous Branch Revisited: New Evidence on Supreme Court Responsiveness to Public Preferences," *Journal of Politics* 66 (November 2004): 1018–1035. Also relevant are Helmut Norpoth and Jeffrey A. Segal, "Popular Influence on Supreme Court Decisions: Comment," *American Political Science Review* 88 (September 1994): 711–716, a reanalysis of the data in the 1993 Mishler-Sheehan study; and Peter K. Enns and Patrick Wohlfarth, "The Swing Justice," *Journal of Politics* 75 (October 2013): 1089–1107, which analyzes the impact of public mood among other phenomena.
133. The clearest exception is the findings in Norpoth and Segal, "Popular Influence on Supreme Court Decisions." The findings of relevant studies are summarized in Lee Epstein and Andrew D. Martin, "Does Public Opinion Influence the Supreme Court? Possibly Yes (but We're Not Sure Why)," *University of Pennsylvania Journal of Constitutional Law* 13 (December 2010): 265–267.
134. Casillas, Enns, and Wohlfarth, "How Public Opinion Constrains the U.S. Supreme Court."
135. See also Schauer, "Incentives, Reputation, and the Inglorious Determinants of Judicial Behavior"; Epstein, Landes, and Posner, *The Behavior of Federal Judges*, 43.
136. Miceli and Cosgel, "Reputation and Judicial Decision-Making," 38.
137. See Benjamin J. Roesch, "Crowd Control and the Reflection of Public Opinion in Doctrine," *Suffolk University Law Review* 39 (2006): 396.
138. Lawrence Baum, "Recruitment and the Motivations of Supreme Court Justices," in *Supreme Court Decision-Making: New Institutionalist Approaches*, ed. Cornell

W. Clayton and Howard Gillman (Chicago: University of Chicago Press, 1999), 209–210; Lee Epstein, Jack Knight, and Andrew D. Martin, "The Norm of Prior Judicial Experience and Its Consequences for Career Diversity on the U.S. Supreme Court," *California Law Review* 91 (July 2003): 903–965.

139. Harriet Miers, nominated to the Court by President George W. Bush in 2005, also lacked judicial experience.

140. For the Justices appointed between 1937 and 1968, the median proportion of their careers spent in private practice, law school teaching, and the judiciary was 67 percent; the comparable figure for appointees between 1969 and 2017 was 87 percent. Lawrence Baum, *The Supreme Court*, 12th ed. (Washington, DC: CQ Press, 2016), 51; updated to include Justice Gorsuch.

141. John Paul Stevens (who served from 1975 to 2010) attended Northwestern Law School; Thurgood Marshall (who served from 1967 to 1991) attended Howard. Ruth Bader Ginsburg transferred from Harvard to Columbia for her last year in law school.

142. John Paul Stevens clerked for Wiley Rutledge; Stephen Breyer clerked for Arthur Goldberg; John Roberts clerked for William Rehnquist; Elena Kagan clerked for Thurgood Marshall; Neil Gorsuch clerked for Byron White and Anthony Kennedy; and Brett Kavanaugh clerked for Anthony Kennedy.

143. Antonin Scalia taught at Virginia and Chicago; Elena Kagan taught at Chicago and Harvard; Stephen Breyer taught at Harvard; Ruth Bader Ginsburg taught at Columbia.

144. These Justices were Ruth Bader Ginsburg, John Roberts, Samuel Alito, Elena Kagan, and Brett Kavanaugh.

145. In the 2013–2017 terms, during which all the Justices had attended Harvard or Yale Law School (although Justice Ginsburg transferred to Columbia for her third year), those two schools accounted for slightly more than half of all the Justices' law clerks. Most of the other clerks attended other elite schools such as Chicago, Columbia, Stanford, and Virginia.

146. See Allison Orr Larsen and Neal Devins, "The Amicus Machine," *Virginia Law Review* 102 (December 2016): 1933–1936. Indeed, a 2016 study of the Supreme Court's occasional practice of appointing lawyers to argue before the Court found that—since the 1950s—forty out of fifty-nine appointments were of former Supreme Court law clerks. Kate Shaw, "Friends of the Court: Evaluating the Supreme Court's Amicus Invitations," *Cornell Law Review* 101 (September 2016): 1556.

147. Joan Biskupic, Janet Roberts, and John Shiffman, *The Echo Chamber*, December 8, 2014, http://www.reuters.com/investigates/special-report/scotus/.

148. Richard L. Hasen, "Celebrity Justice: Supreme Court Edition," *Green Bag 2d* 19 (Winter 2016): 157–173.

149. Alan F. Westin, "Out-of-Court Commentary by United States Supreme Court Justices, 1790–1962: Of Free Speech and Judicial Lockjaw," in *An Autobiography of the Supreme Court*, ed. Alan F. Westin (New York: Macmillan, 1963), 1–47;

Christopher S. Schmidt, "Beyond the Opinion: Supreme Court Justices and Extrajudicial Speech," *Chicago-Kent Law Review* 88 (2013): 487–526; Robert A. (Sid) Whitaker, "Freedom of a Speech: The Speeches of the Warren Court Justices and the Legitimacy of the Supreme Court" (PhD diss., State University of New York at Albany, 2016), 311–353.

150. The time period covered is from the beginning of the Court's 2014 term in October 2014 through the 2017 summer recess. Justice Scalia served until February 2016, Justice Gorsuch from April 2017 on.

The numbers in the table are based on listings of appearances in scotusmap, http://www.scotusmap.com. These numbers undoubtedly are underestimates, because not all public appearances are reported. Appearances are classified on the basis of the sponsoring organization. Where an appearance was sponsored by organizations in different categories, they are classified on the basis of the category with the largest number of organizations; where the numbers are equal, precedence is given to law schools and then to the bench/bar category. Some appearances in the "other colleges" category probably were sponsored by law schools.

151. Data were taken from the Justices' annual Financial Disclosure Reporters. In general, under 5 U.S.C. §102(a)(2)(B), the Justices must report reimbursements of more than $250.

152. Justice Sotomayor is a partial exception to that pattern. See David Fontana, "The People's Justice?," *Yale Law Journal Forum* 123 (March 24, 2014): 466–478.

153. Schauer, "Incentives, Reputation, and the Inglorious Determinants of Judicial Behavior," 628.

154. Of the thirty-eight clerks who served the Court in its 1996 term, at least twelve became law professors in the next two decades, several of them at elite law schools such as Yale, Stanford, and Michigan.

155. See the biographical information in Baum, *The Supreme Court*, 52–53.

156. Steven M. Teles, *The Rise of the Conservative Legal Movement: The Battle for Control of the Law* (Princeton, NJ: Princeton University Press, 2008), 135–180; Michael Avery and Danielle Mclaughlin, *The Federalist Society: How Conservatives Took the Law Back from Liberals* (Nashville, TN: Vanderbilt University Press, 2013); Amanda Hollis-Brusky, *Ideas with Consequences: The Federalist Society and the Conservative Counterrevolution* (New York: Oxford University Press, 2015).

157. Hollis-Brusky, *Ideas with Consequences*, 166–167.

158. Fred Barbash, "Judge Bazelon's 'Network': The Salon of the Ultimate Liberal," *Washington Post*, March 1, 1981, A2; Francis X. Clines and Warren Weaver Jr., "Briefing," *New York Times*, May 18, 1982, A18.

159. Robert Barnes, "Federalists Relish Well-Placed Friends: President, Several Justices Help Celebrate Legal Society's 25 Years of Conservatism," *Washington Post*, November 16, 2007, A3.

160. Richard Davis, *Decisions and Images: The Supreme Court and the Press* (Englewood Cliffs, NJ: Prentice-Hall, 1994), 106.

161. Epstein and Knight, *The Choices Justices Make*, 145; Bernard Schwartz, *Super Chief: Earl Warren and His Supreme Court—a Judicial Biography* (New York: New York University Press, 1983), 251, 256; Ken Foskett, *Judging Thomas: The Life and Times of Clarence Thomas* (New York: William Morrow, 2004), 18.
162. Potter Stewart, "Justice Stewart Dissents," *Wall Street Journal*, July 3, 1968, 6; Antonin Scalia, "Scalia: Article Off Base," *Legal Times*, October 2, 2000, 85.
163. Examples include David P. Bryden, "Is the Rehnquist Court Conservative?," *Public Interest* 109 (1992): 83–84; Max Boot, *Out of Order: Arrogance, Corruption, and Incompetence on the Bench* (New York: Basic Books, 1998), 119–120; and Mark R. Levin, *Men in Black: How the Supreme Court Is Destroying America* (Washington, DC: Regnery, 2005), 60–61.
164. The informational function of amicus briefs is discussed in James F. Spriggs III and Paul J. Wahlbeck, "Amicus Curiae and the Role of Information at the Supreme Court," *Political Research Quarterly* 50 (June 1997): 365–386; Paul M. Collins Jr., *Friends of the Supreme Court: Interest Groups and Judicial Decision Making* (New York: Oxford University Press, 2008), 75–164; and Allison Orr Larsen, "The Trouble with Amicus Facts," *Virginia Law Review* 100 (December 2014): 1773–1783.
165. Kelly Lynch, "Best Friends?: Supreme Court Law Clerks on Effective Amicus Curiae Briefs," *Journal of Law & Politics* 20 (Winter 2004): 52–54.
166. This paragraph is drawn from Neal Devins, "Talk Loudly and Carry a Small Stick: The Supreme Court and Enemy Combatants," *University of Pennsylvania Journal of Constitutional Law* 12 (February 2010): 499–503.
167. Devins, "Talk Loudly and Carry a Small Stick," 500.
168. Devins, "Talk Loudly and Carry a Small Stick," 500–503. Fifteen top newspapers were surveyed. Most have a liberal bent, but others critical of the administration do not (*San Diego Union, Washington Times*).
169. Larsen and Devins, "The Amicus Machine," 1911–1912.
170. Joseph D. Kearney and Thomas W. Merrill, "The Influence of Amicus Briefs on the Supreme Court," *University of Pennsylvania Law Review* 148 (January 2000): 751–756. The average (more precisely, the mean) for the 2016 term was calculated from the docket sheets for orally argued cases in that term.
171. Lawrence Baum, *Ideology in the Supreme Court* (Princeton, NJ: Princeton University Press, 2017), 61–63, 158.
172. Neal Devins, "Measuring Party Polarization in Congress: Lessons from Congressional Participation as Amicus Curiae," *Case Western Reserve Law Review* 65 (Summer 2015): 942–946.
173. See Richard A. Lazarus, "Advocacy Matters before and within the Supreme Court: Transforming the Court by Transforming the Bar," *Georgetown Law Journal* 96 (June 2008): 1513, 1525, 1528; Larsen and Devins, "The Amicus Machine."
174. See Larsen and Devins, "The Amicus Machine," 1934.

175. *Grutter v. Bollinger*, 539 U.S. 306 (2003). See Neal Devins, "Explaining *Grutter v. Bollinger*," *University of Pennsylvania Law Review* 152 (November 2003): 366–369.
176. *Lawrence v. Texas*, 539 U.S. 558, 602 (2003).
177. Paul M. Smith, "The Sometimes Troubled Relationship between Courts and Their 'Friends,'" *Litigation* 24 (Summer 1998): 25.
178. Dale Carpenter, *Flagrant Conduct: The Story of Lawrence v Texas* (New York: W. W. Norton & Company, 2012), 198; Larsen and Devins, "The Amicus Machine," 1924 (quoting Pam Karlan).
179. Paul M. Collins Jr., "Lobbyists before the U.S. Supreme Court: Investigating the Influence of Amicus Curiae Briefs," *Political Research Quarterly* 60 (March 2007): 55–70; Janet M. Box-Steffensmeier, Dino P. Christenson, and Matthew P. Hitt, "Quality Over Quantity: Amici Influence and Judicial Decision Making," *American Political Science Review* 107 (August 2013): 446–460.
180. *Grutter v. Bollinger*, 309 U.S. 306, 330–331.
181. Baum, *Judges and Their Audiences*, 46–47.
182. *Gannett v. DePasquale*, 443 U.S. 368 (1979).
183. Anthony Lewis, "A Public Right to Know about Public Institutions: The First Amendment as Sword," *Supreme Court Review* (1980): 13 and notes 101–103.
184. *Richmond Newspapers, Inc. v. Virginia*, 448 U.S. 555 (1980).
185. Warren Weaver Jr., "Burger's View on Right to Attend Trial," *New York Times*, August 11, 1979, 43; Linda Greenhouse, "Stevens Says Closed Trials May Justify New Laws," *New York Times*, September 9, 1979, 41.
186. *Minersville School District v. Gobitis*, 310 U.S. 586 (1940).
187. *West Virginia State Board of Education v. Barnette*, 319 U.S. 624 (1943).
188. David R. Manwaring, *Render unto Caesar: The Flag-Salute Controversy* (Chicago: University of Chicago Press, 1962), 149.
189. Manwaring, *Render unto Caesar*, 153–159; Alpheus Thomas Mason, *Harlan Fiske Stone: Pillar of the Law* (New York: Viking Press, 1956), 532.
190. H. N. Hirsch, *The Enigma of Felix Frankfurter* (New York: Basic Books, 1981), 152. Justice Douglas later offered a different explanation for Black's (and his own) change in position. William O. Douglas, *The Court Years 1939–1975: The Autobiography of William O. Douglas* (New York: Random House, 1980), 44–45. Black, Douglas, and Murphy had indicated their change of mind in a joint dissenting opinion in *Jones v. City of Opelika*, 316 U.S. 584, 623–624 (1942).
191. See Shawn Francis Peters, *Judging Jehovah's Witnesses: Religious Persecution and the Dawn of the Rights Revolution* (Lawrence: University Press of Kansas, 2000), 79–95 (on violent attacks), and Neal Devins and Louis Fisher, *The Democratic Constitution* (New York: Oxford University Press, 2004), 199–200 (on these attacks and on responses by Congress and the Department of Justice).
192. *Furman v. Georgia*, 408 U.S. 238 (1972).

193. *Roe v. Wade*, 410 U.S. 113 (1973). Among the later decisions are *Planned Parenthood v. Casey*, 505 U.S. 833 (1992), and *Whole Woman's Health v. Hellerstedt*, 136 S. Ct. 2292 (2016).

194. *Romer v. Evans*, 517 U.S. 620 (1996); *United States v. Windsor*, 570 U.S. 744 (2013); *Obergefell v. Hodges*, 135 S. Ct. 2584 (2015).

195. Herbert McClosky, "Consensus and Ideology in American Politics," *American Political Science Review* 58 (June 1964): 361–382; Lawrence Bobo and Frederick C. Licari, "Education and Political Tolerance: Testing the Effects of Cognitive Sophistication and Target Group Affect," *Public Opinion Quarterly* 53 (Autumn 1989): 285–308; Jo Phelan, Bruce G. Link, Ann Steuve, and Robert E. Moore, "Education, Social Liberalism, and Economic Conservatism: Attitudes Toward Homeless People," *American Sociological Review* 60 (February 1995): 126–140.

196. Herbert McClosky and Alida Brill, *Dimensions of Tolerance: What Americans Believe about Civil Liberties* (New York: Russell Sage Foundation, 1983).

197. McClosky and Brill, *Dimensions of Tolerance*, 66 (reporters' privilege not to testify), 109 (flag burning), 133 (school prayer), 160 (right of suspects to remain silent), 164 (exclusion of illegally obtained evidence).

198. Mark A. Graber, "The Coming Constitutional Yo-Yo? Elite Opinion, Polarization, and the Direction of Judicial Decision Making," *Howard Law Journal* 56 (2013): 684–692.

199. The book is Nathaniel Persily, Jack Citrin, and Patrick J. Egan, eds., *Public Opinion and Constitutional Controversy* (New York: Oxford University Press, 2008). The findings are in Michael Murakami, "Desegregation," 32; Alison Gash and Angelo Gonzales, "School Prayer," 71, 73; Samantha Luks and Michael Salamone, "Abortion," 97; Serena Mayeri, Ryan Brown, Nathaniel Persily, and Son Ho Kim, "Gender Equality," 148, 156, 159; Peter Hanson, "Flag Burning," 189, 191, 194; and Patrick J. Egan, Nathaniel Persily, and Kevin Wallsten, "Gay Rights," 238, 246, 257, 259. Education had little impact on attitudes toward capital punishment: John Hanley, "The Death Penalty," 116, 121. For some other issues analyzed in the book, survey results were not broken down in a way that allowed comparison of highly educated people with other respondents.

200. The percentages in the table were derived from public opinion poll data that were analyzed using the SPSS statistical package, to disaggregate the data by party and education level. Percentages are of respondents who took a position on one side of the issue. In the surveys on school prayer, flag burning, and same-sex marriage, "postgraduate" refers to a degree beyond an undergraduate degree. In the other surveys, "postgraduate" refers to education beyond the undergraduate degree.

The decisions were *Engel v. Vitale*, 370 U.S. 421 (1962); *Abington School District v. Schempp*, 374 U.S. 203 (1963); *Texas v. Johnson*, 491 U.S. 397 (1989); *Reno v. American Civil Liberties Union*, 521 U.S. 844 (1997); *Lawrence v. Texas*, 539 U.S. 558 (2003); *Grutter v. Bollinger*, 539 U.S. 306 (2003); *Roper v. Simmons*, 543 U.S. 551 (2005); *Boumediene v. Bush*, 553 U.S. 723 (2008); *District of Columbia v. Heller*,

554 U.S. 570 (2008); *Citizens United v. Federal Election Commission*, 558 U.S. 310 (2010); and *Obergefell v. Hodges*, 135 S. Ct. 2584 (2015).

The sources for the survey results and question wording are as follows:

School prayer: University of Michigan, Survey Research Center, Pre-election Study 13 (September–November 1964), http://www.electionstudies.org/studypages/1964prepost/1964prepost_qnaire_pre.pdf. The question was worded as follows: "Some people think it is all right for the public schools to start each day with a prayer. Others feel that religion does not belong in the public schools but should be taken care of by the family and the church. Have you been interested enough in this to favor one side over the other?" Respondents who answered in the affirmative were then asked: "Which do you think: 1. Schools be allowed to start each day with a prayer or 5. Religion does not belong in the schools?" The data file is available at http://www.electionstudies.org/ studypages/data/1964prepost/anes1964por.zip.

Flag burning: University of Michigan, Survey Research Center, Post-election Survey, 1990 National Election Studies 59 (November 1990–January 1991), http://www.electionstudies.org/studypages/1990post/1990post_qnaire.pdf. The question was worded as follows: "Should burning or destroying the American flag as a form of political protest be legal or should it be against the law?" The data file is available at http://www.electionstudies.org/studypages/data/1990post/anes1990por.zip.

Homosexual relations: Gallup Organization, Gallup News Service Poll # 2003–37: Terrorism/Homosexual Civil Unions/Iraq/Children/College/Dangerous Drivers 10 (July 18–20, 2003) (version distributed by the Roper Center, Cornell University), https://ropercenter.cornell.edu/CFIDE/cf/action/catalog/abstract.cfm?type=&start=&id= &archno=USAIPOGNS2003-37&abstract=. The question was worded as follows: "Do you think homosexual relations between consenting adults should or should not be legal?"

Affirmative action: NBC News & The Wall Street Journal, Hart-Teeter/NBC/WSJ Poll # 6030: 2004 Presidential Election/Bush/Economic Policy/The Economy/Iraq/North Korea 20 (January 19–21, 2003) (version distributed by the Roper Center, Cornell University), https://ropercenter.cornell.edu/CFIDE/cf/action/catalog/abstract.cfm?type=&start=&id=&archno=USNBCWSJ2003-6030&abstract=. The question was worded as follows: "As you may know, the U.S. Supreme Court will be deciding whether public universities can use race as one of the factors in admissions to increase diversity in the student body. Do you favor or oppose this practice?"

Juvenile death penalty: Pew Research Center for the People & the Press, Pew/PSRAI Poll # 2005-RELIG: Religion and Public Life 2005, at 12 (July 7–17, 2005) (version distributed by the Roper Center, Cornell University), https://ropercenter.cornell.edu/CFIDE/ cf/action/catalog/abstract.cfm?type=&s

tart=&id=&archno=USPEW2005-RELIG&abstract=. The question was worded as follows: "All in all, do you strongly favor, favor, oppose, or strongly oppose . . . [t]he death penalty for persons convicted of murder when they were under the age of 18?"

Enemy combatants: ABC News & The Washington Post, ABC News/Washington Post Poll # 2008-1065: June Monthly—2008 Presidential Election/Iraq/Race Relations 9 (June 12–15, 2008) (version distributed by the Roper Center, Cornell University), https://ropercenter.cornell.edu/CFIDE/cf/action/catalog/abstract.cfm?type=&start=&id=&archno=USABCWASH2008-1065&abstract=. The question was worded as follows: "The U.S. Supreme Court has ruled that non-citizens suspected of terrorism who are being held in Guantanamo Bay, Cuba, should be allowed to challenge their detentions in the U.S. civilian court system. . . . What's your view—do you think these detainees should or should not be able to challenge their detentions in the civilian court system?"

Internet speech: Freedom Forum, Poll # 1999-1STAMEND: The First Amendment Q28 (February 26–March 24, 1999) (version distributed by the Roper Center, Cornell University), https://ropercenter.cornell.edu/CFIDE/cf/action/catalog/ abstract.cfm?type=&start=&id=&archno=USCSRA1999-1STAMEND&abstract=. The question was worded as follows: "As you may know, courts have traditionally given broad First Amendment protections to books and newspapers that contain material that may be offensive to some people. Recently the U.S. (United States) Supreme Court ruled that material on the Internet has the same First Amendment protections as printed material such as books and newspapers. Do you agree or disagree with this ruling . . . strongly or mildly?" (In the dataset for this poll, postgraduate education is coded as 5, not 7 as stated in the documentation.)

Second Amendment: Cable News Network, CNN/ORC Poll #2008-007: 2008 Presidential Election/Price of Gasoline/Gun Control 13 (June 4–5, 2008) (version distributed by the Roper Center, Cornell University), https://ropercenter.cornell.edu/CFIDE/ cf/action/catalog/abstract.cfm?type=&start=&id=&archno=USORCCNN2008-007&abstract=. The question was worded as follows: "Part of the debate about gun ownership hinges on how we interpret the U.S. constitution. The exact words of the constitution are as follows: 'A well regulated militia, being necessary to the security of a free state, the right of the people to keep and bear arms shall not be infringed upon.' Do you think these words guarantee each person the right to own a gun, or do they protect the right of citizens to form a militia without implying that each individual has the right to own a gun?"

Campaign finance: CBS News and New York Times, CBS News/New York Times Poll: 2010 Elections/Government 36 (October 21–26, 2010) (version distributed by the Roper Center, Cornell University), https://ropercenter.

cornell.edu/CFIDE/cf/ action/catalog/abstract.cfm?type=&start=&id=&archno=USCBSNYT2010-10E&abstract=. The question was worded as follows: "Currently, groups not affiliated with a candidate are able to spend unlimited amounts of money on advertisements during a political campaign. Do you think this kind of spending should be limited by law, or should it remain unlimited?"

Same-sex marriage: Cable News Network, CNN/ORC Poll: New Congress/Foreign Policy/2016 Presidential Election 13 (December 18–21, 2014) (version distributed by the Roper Center, Cornell University), http://www.ropercenter.uconn.edu/CFIDE/cf/action/ipoll/abstract.cfm?keyword=marry%20or%20marriage&keywordoptions=1&exclude=&excludeOptions=1&topic=Any&organization=Any&label=&fromdate=1/1/1935&toDate=&&archno=USORCCNN2014-012&start=summary. The question was worded as follows: "Do you think gays and lesbians do or do not have a constitutional right to get married and have their marriage recognized by law as valid?"

201. *Romer v. Evans*, 517 U.S. 620, 636 (1966). See also *Lawrence v. Texas*, 539 U.S. 558, 602 (2003) ("Today's opinion is the product of a Court, which is the product of a law-profession culture, that has largely signed on to the so-called homosexual agenda . . . "); *United States v. Virginia*, 518 U.S. 515, 567 (1996) (The Court "has embarked on a course of inscribing one after another of the current preferences of the society (and in some cases only the countermajoritarian preferences of the society's law-trained elite) into our Basic Law").
202. On school religious observances, the original decision was *Engel v. Vitale*, 307 U.S. 421 (1962); the follow-up was *School District of Abington Township v. Schempp*, 374 U.S. 203 (1963). On flag burning, the original decision was *Texas v. Johnson*, 491 U.S. 397 (1989), the follow-up *United States v. Eichman* 491 U.S. 397 (1990).
203. Friedman, *The Will of the People*, 378.
204. On property rights and elite opinion, see Michael J. Klarman, "What's So Great about Constitutionalism?," *Northwestern University Law Review* 93 (1998): 190.
205. Neal Devins and Will Federspiel, "The Supreme Court, Social Psychology, and Group Formation," in *The Psychology of Judicial Decision Making*, ed. Klein and Mitchell, 85–100.
206. Wendy L. Martinek, "Judges as Members of Small Groups," in *The Psychology of Judicial Decision Making*, ed. Klein and Mitchell, 74–75.
207. The quotations are from (in order) J. Woodford Howard, *Courts of Appeals in the Federal Judicial System: A Study of the Second, Fifth, and District of Columbia Circuits* (Princeton, NJ: Princeton University Press, 1981), 193; Steven A. Peterson, "Dissent in American Courts," *Journal of Politics* 43 (May 1981): 417; and Frank B. Cross, "Collegial Ideology in the Courts," *Northwestern University Law Review* 103 (Summer 2009): 1416.

208. In past eras, many Justices have come from careers primarily in politics rather than law, but that is not true of the current era. Baum, *The Supreme Court*, 51–54.
209. See Lewis A. Kornhauser and Lawrence G. Sager, "The One and the Many: Adjudication in Collegial Courts," *California Law Review* 81 (January 1993): 1–10; and Harry T. Edwards, "Collegiality and Decision Making on the D.C. Circuit," *Virginia Law Review* 84 (October 1998): 1358–1362.
210. Between 1975 and 2017, eleven of the thirteen Justices who joined the Court (all but O'Connor and Kagan) first served on federal courts of appeals.
211. Linda Greenhouse, "The Court: Same Time Next Year. And Next Year," *New York Times*, October 6, 2002, C3.
212. John Paul Stevens, Samuel Alito, and Neil Gorsuch have not participated in the cert pool. Adam Liptak, "A Sign of Independence from the Newest Justice," *New York Times*, May 2, 2017, A22.
213. William H. Rehnquist, *The Supreme Court*, new ed. (New York: Alfred A. Knopf, 2001), 252–254.
214. Martinek, "Judges as Members of Small Groups," 74.
215. Rehnquist, *The Supreme Court*, 254.
216. Forrest Maltzman and Paul J. Wahlbeck, "Strategic Policy Considerations and Voting Fluidity on the Burger Court," *American Political Science Review* 90 (September 1996): 587; Lawrence Baum, *The Puzzle of Judicial Behavior* (Ann Arbor: University of Michigan Press, 1997), 107–108; Lawrence S. Wrightsman, *The Psychology of the Supreme Court* (New York: Oxford University Press, 2006), 152.
217. Thomas G. Walker, Lee Epstein, and William J. Dixon, "On the Mysterious Demise of Consensual Norms in the United States Supreme Court," *Journal of Politics* 50 (May 1988): 362.
218. Lee Epstein, Jeffrey A. Segal, and Harold J. Spaeth, "The Norm of Consensus on the U.S. Supreme Court," *American Journal of Political Science* 45 (April 2001): 376.
219. Barry Cushman, "Vote Fluidity on the Hughes Court: The Critical Terms, 1934–1936," *University of Illinois Law Review* (2017): 279–283.
220. Epstein, Segal, and Spaeth, "The Norm of Consensus"; Stacia L. Haynie, "Leadership and Consensus on the U.S. Supreme Court," *Journal of Politics* 54 (November 1992): 1158–1169; Gregory A. Caldeira and Christopher J. W. Zorn, "Of Time and Consensual Norms in the Supreme Court," *American Journal of Political Science* 42 (July 1998): 874–902; and Marcus E. Hendershot, Mark S. Hurwitz, Drew Noble Lanier, and Richard L. Pacelle, "Dissensual Decision Making: Revisiting the Demise of Consensual Norms within the U.S. Supreme Court," *Political Research Quarterly* 66 (June 2013): 467–481.
221. Cass R. Sunstein, "Unanimity and Disagreement on the Supreme Court," *Cornell Law Review* 100 (2015): 780–781.

222. These statistics were calculated from data in Table I(C) of the "The Statistics" articles in the November issues of the *Harvard Law Review*. The level of consensus was somewhat lower in the 2017 term.
223. Jeffrey Rosen, "Roberts's Rules," *The Atlantic*, January/February 2007, https://www.theatlantic.com/magazine/archive/2007/01/robertss-rules/305559/.
224. David A. Yalof, Joseph Mello, and Patrick Schmidt, "Collegiality among U.S. Supreme Court Justices? An Early Assessment of the Roberts Court," *Judicature* 95 (July–August 2011): 17.
225. Adam Liptak, "Rulings and Remarks Tell Divided Story of an 8-Member Supreme Court," *New York Times*, May 30, 2016, https://www.nytimes.com/2016/05/31/us/politics/rulings-and-remarks-tell-divided-story-of-an-8-member-supreme-court.html.
226. This proportion of unanimous decisions is from SCOTUSblog, whose criteria for inclusion of cases appear to differ a little from those in the *Harvard Law Review*, the source of the figures for the 2010–2016 terms cited earlier. Kedar S. Bhatia, "Final October Term 2017 Stat Pack and Key Takeaways," *SCOTUSblog* (June 29, 2018), 15. The decisions were, respectively, *Gill v. Whitford*, 138 S. Ct. 1204 (2018); and *Masterpiece Cakeshop v. Colorado Civil Rights Commission*, 138 S. Ct. 1719 (2018).
227. There were fourteen such decisions in the 2017 term, about one-fifth of all decisions. Kedar S. Bhatia, "Final October Term 2017 Stat Pack and Key Takeaways," *SCOTUSblog* (June 29, 2018), 18.
228. Leary, *Self-Presentation*, 2.
229. Leary, *Self-Presentation*, 67.
230. Martinek, "Judges as Members of Small Groups," 77.
231. Dan Kahan et al., " 'Ideology' or 'Situation Sense'? An Experimental Investigation of Motivated Reasoning and Professional Judgment," *University of Pennsylvania Law Review* 164 (January 2016): 349–439.
232. Rehnquist, *The Supreme Court*, 222.
233. Charles Lane, "A Defeat for Users of Medical Marijuana," *Washington Post*, June 7, 2005, http://www.washingtonpost.com/wp-dyn/content/article/2005/06/06/AR2005060600564.html.
234. Jerry de Jaager, "Justice Scalia Comes Home to the Law School," *News*, University of Chicago Law School, 2012, https://www.law.uchicago.edu/news/justice-scalia-comes-home-law-school; Rory Little, "The Court after Scalia: A Mixed Bag on Criminal Law and Procedure Issues," *SCOTUSblog*, September 9, 2016, http://www.scotusblog.com/2016/09/the-court-after-scalia-a-mixed-bag-on-criminal-law-and-procedure-issues/.
235. *Cooper v. Harris*, 137 S. Ct. 837 (2017).
236. *Sessions v. Dimaya*, 138 S. Ct 1204 (2018). Justice Gorsuch agreed with the opinion joined by the four liberal Justices only in part.

237. Devins and Federspiel, "The Supreme Court, Social Psychology, and Group Formation," 90–92.
238. Paul H. Edelman, David E. Klein, and Stefanie A. Lindquist, "Measuring Deviations from Expected Voting Patterns on Collegial Courts," *Journal of Empirical Legal Studies* 5 (December 2008): 819–852; Adam Feldman, "When Opposites Attract Ideology Falls to the Wayside," *Empirical SCOTUS*, March 7, 2018, https://empiricalscotus.com/2018/03/07/when-opposites-attract/.
239. Fischman and Jacobi, "The Second Dimension of the Supreme Court," 1676–1677 ("Although it is common now . . . to depict the Justices as occupying only a left-right, one-dimensional spectrum, . . . such a characterization does not come close to capturing the [judges'] full considerations. . . . It is well understood that legal considerations are also significant determinants. . . . More specifically, the division between legalism and pragmatism is a well-established distinction"). See also Paul H. Edelman, David E. Klein, and Stefanie A. Lindquist, "Consensus, Disorder, and Ideology on the Supreme Court," *Journal of Empirical Legal Studies* 9 (2012): 129–148.
240. Swing or median Justices are discussed in Lee Epstein and Tonja Jacobi, "Super Medians," *Stanford Law Review* 61 (October 2008): 37–99.

CHAPTER 3

1. Morris P. Fiorina with Samuel J. Abrams and Jeffrey C. Pope, *Culture War?: The Myth of a Polarized America*, 3rd ed. (Boston: Longman, 2011). Fiorina and his collaborators argue that ideological extremism, which we discuss shortly, has not developed at the mass level. See also Donald R. Kinder and Nathan P. Malmoe, *Neither Liberal nor Conservative: Ideological Innocence in the American Public* (Chicago: University of Chicago Press, 2017). However, the mass public has become considerably more polarized in other respects as similar changes have occurred among elites. See Lilliana Mason, *Uncivil Agreement: How Politics Became Our Identity* (Chicago: University of Chicago Press, 2018).
2. These characteristics are discussed and contrasted, though under somewhat different terminology, in Lilliana Mason, "The Rise of Uncivil Agreement: Issue versus Behavioral Polarization in the American Electorate," *American Behavioral Scientist* 57 (2013): 140–159.
3. Extremism in positions on specific issues, when accompanied by other aspects of polarization, is likely to be manifested in a stronger tendency for people to take the positions that that are considered to be conservative or the positions considered to be liberal across the full set of issues on which they have opinions or act as policymakers. To use a term widely employed by students of public opinion, extremism could lead to higher levels of constraint, so that knowing how a person stands ideologically on one issue allows us to predict more confidently that person's positions on other issues. The concept of constraint is described in Philip E. Converse, "The

Nature of Belief Systems in Mass Publics," in *Ideology and Discontent*, ed. David E. Apter (New York: Free Press, 1964), 206–261.

4. Shanto Iyengar, Gaurav Sood, and Yphtach Lelkes, "Affect, Not Ideology: A Social Identity Perspective on Polarization," *Public Opinion Quarterly* 76 (Fall 2012): 406.
5. On partisan sorting, see Sean M. Theriault, *Party Polarization in Congress* (New York: Cambridge University Press, 2008), 16–38; Kevin Arcenaux and Martin Johnson, "More a Symptom Than a Cause," in *American Gridlock: The Sources, Character, and Impact of Political Polarization*, ed. James A. Thurber and Antoine Yoshinaka (New York: Cambridge University Press, 2015), 311–314; and Nolan McCarty, Keith T. Poole, and Howard Rosenthal, *Polarized America: The Dance of Ideology and Unequal Resources*, 2nd ed. (Cambridge, MA: MIT Press, 2016), 28–32.
6. Mason, "The Rise of Uncivil Agreement"; Lilliana Mason, "'I Disrepectfully Agree': The Differential Effects of Partisan Sorting on Social and Issue Polarization," *American Journal of Political Science* 59 (January 2015): 128–145.
7. See Richard L. Hasen, "Polarization and the Judiciary," *Annual Review of Political Science* (2019), forthcoming.
8. Tonja Jacobi and Matthew Sage, "The New Oral Argument: Justices as Advocates," *Notre Dame Law Review* 94 (2019), forthcoming.
9. Several studies have analyzed polarization on the Court in terms of phenomena that are related to extremism to varying degrees. Tom S. Clark, "Measuring Ideological Polarization on the United States Supreme Court," *Political Research Quarterly* 62 (March 2009): 146–157; Brandon L. Bartels, "The Sources and Consequences of Polarization in the U.S. Supreme Court," in *American Gridlock*, ed. Thurber and Yoshinaka, 171–200; Donald Michael Gooch, "Ideological Polarization on the Supreme Court: Trends in the Court's Institutional Environment and across Regimes, 1937–2008," *American Politics Research* 43 (November 2015): 999–1040.
10. Alexander Bickel, *The Unpublished Opinions of Mr. Justice Brandeis: The Supreme Court at Work* (Cambridge, MA: Harvard University Press, 1957); Robert Post, "The Supreme Court as Institutional Practice: Dissent, Legal Scholarship, and Decisionmaking in the Taft Court," *Minnesota Law Review* 85 (May 2001): 1331–1355; Lee Epstein, Jeffrey A. Segal, and Harold J. Spaeth, "The Norm of Consensus on the U.S. Supreme Court," *American Journal of Political Science* 45 (April 2001): 362–377; Barry Cushman, "Vote Fluidity on the Hughes Court: The Critical Terms, 1934–1936," *University of Illinois Law Review* 2017 (2017): 269–306.
11. Those terms were 1836, 1845, 1852, and 1854. Lee Epstein, Jeffrey A. Segal, Harold J. Spaeth, and Thomas G. Walker, *The Supreme Court Compendium: Data, Decisions, and Developments*, 6th ed. (Washington, DC: CQ Press, 2015), 252–255.
12. Tara Leigh Grove, "The Exceptions Clause as a Structural Safeguard," *Columbia Law Review* 113 (May 2013): 952–959, 962–968.
13. See Robert G. McCloskey, rev. Sanford Levinson, *The American Supreme Court*, 6th ed. (Chicago: University of Chicago Press, 2016), chaps. 3–6.

14. The database (actually separate databases for the 1791–1945 terms and for the 1946 term through the present) is archived at http://scdb.wustl.edu/.
15. Carolyn Shapiro, "The Context of Ideology: Law, Politics, and Empirical Legal Scholarship," *Missouri Law Review* 75 (Winter 2010): 81–142; Anna Harvey and Michael J. Woodruff, "Confirmation Bias in the United States Supreme Court Judicial Database," *Journal of Law, Economics, and Organization* 29 (April 2013): 414–459. The rules for ideological coding of decisions and votes in the database are described at http://scdb.wustl.edu/documentation.php?var=decisionDirection.
16. This problem is reduced somewhat by the cautious coding of the ideological direction of decisions and Justices' votes for nineteenth-century cases in the Supreme Court Database: a substantial minority of cases were not coded for direction because the issues in those cases could not be fit within the definitions of conservative and liberal positions used in the database. The proportion of "nonideological" cases was 36.7 percent in the Marshall Court (1801–1835) and steadily declined to 18.0 percent in the Fuller Court (1888–1910), then fell below 10 percent (9.7 percent) in the White Court (1910–1921) and declined further in later Courts.
17. Analysis of one important subset of decisions in the Fuller Court (1888–1910), those in which the Court struck down state or local economic regulations, found that the Justices' varying support for regulatory policies did not fall along party lines at all. Sheldon Goldman, *Constitutional Law and Supreme Court Decision-Making: Cases and Essays* (New York: Harper & Row, 1982), 176. A comprehensive history of the Fuller Court found that there was no ideological divide between Republicans and Democrats in that period. Owen M. Fiss, *Oliver Wendell Holmes Devise History of the United States Supreme Court: Troubled Beginnings of the Modern States, 1888–1910* (New York: Cambridge University Press, 1993), 35.
18. These analyses begin with agreements and disagreements of the Justices in individual cases and use statistical techniques to place each Justice on a scale for particular time periods. Although the votes used in these analyses are not labeled ideologically, the scales can be interpreted in ideological terms because patterns of agreement and disagreement tend to reflect a dominant ideological dimension. See Bernard Grofman and Timothy J. Brazill, "Identifying the Median Justice on the Supreme Court through Multidimensional Scaling: Analysis of 'Natural Courts' 1953–1991," *Public Choice* 112 (July 2002): 55–79.
19. Donald Carl Leavitt, "Attitudes and Ideology on the White Supreme Court 1910–1920" (PhD diss., Michigan State University, 1970), 186. Leavitt undertook several dimensional analyses of the Justices' votes. We used the first principal axis loading in Q-analyses of votes.
20. For the 1916–1920 terms, another analysis of the Justices' voting patterns found a similar pattern. Roger Handberg, "Decision-Making in a Natural Court, 1916–1921," *American Politics Quarterly* 4 (July 1976): 365. Chief Justice Edward White

might be classified as a Democratic appointee because of his initial appointment by President Grover Cleveland or as a Republican because of his elevation to Chief Justice by President William Howard Taft. In Leavitt's analysis, White stood somewhat to the left among his colleagues in the 1910–1915 terms and somewhat to the right in the 1916–1921 terms.

21. Eloise C. Snyder, "The Supreme Court as a Small Group," *Social Forces* 36 (March 1958): 235. Snyder analyzed cases "involving one or more of the Amendments to the Constitution of the United States" (p. 233). That choice probably reflected the importance of those cases and the relatively high rates of disagreement among the Justices in that subset. The Snyder study extended to 1953, but we will use the Martin-Quinn ideological scores (discussed in the next section) for the Court terms from 1937 on.
22. This alignment of the Justices is also documented in C. Herman Pritchett, *The Roosevelt Court: A Study in Judicial Politics and Values 1937–1947* (New York: Macmillan, 1948), 32, 34, 242.
23. Isaac Unah and Ange-Marie Hancock, "U.S. Supreme Court Decision Making, Case Salience, and the Attitudinal Model," *Law & Policy* 28 (July 2006): 295–320; Brandon L. Bartels, "Choices in Context: How Case-Level Factors Influence the Magnitude of Ideological Voting on the U.S. Supreme Court," *American Politics Research* 39 (January 2011): 142–175; David A. Lewis and Roger P. Rose, "Case Salience and the Attitudinal Model: An Analysis of Ordered and Unanimous Votes on the Rehnquist Court," *Justice System Journal* 35 (2014): 27–44.
24. David G. Savage, *Guide to the U.S. Supreme Court*, 5th ed. (Washington, DC: CQ Press, 2010), 1276–1294.
25. For evaluations of the list, see Saul Brenner, "Majority Opinion Assignment in Salient Cases on the U.S. Supreme Court: Are New Associate Justices Assigned Fewer Opinions?," *Justice System Journal* 22 (2001): 212 note 4; Beverly Blair Cook, "Measuring the Significance of U.S. Supreme Court Decisions," *Journal of Politics* 55 (November 1993): 1132, 1136; and Lee Epstein and Jeffrey A. Segal, "Measuring Issue Salience," *American Journal of Political Science* 44 (January 2000): 68–71.
26. That decision was *United States v. Texas*, 143 U.S. 621 (1892). The dissenters were Melville Fuller and Lucius Q. C. Lamar, appointed by Democratic President Grover Cleveland.
27. *Dred Scott v. Sandford*, 19 Howard 393 (1857); *Lochner v. New York*, 198 U.S. 45 (1905).
28. Examples include *Railroad Retirement Board v. Alton Railroad Co.*, 295 U.S. 330 (1935); *United States v. Butler*, 297 U.S. 1 (1936); and *National Labor Relations Board v. Jones & Laughlin Steel Co.*, 301 U.S. 1 (1937).
29. John Gerring, *Party Ideologies in America, 1828–1996* (New York: Cambridge University Press, 1998), 15–18, 57–124. Disagreements between the platforms of the two parties are analyzed in Benjamin Ginsberg, "Critical Elections and the Substance of Party Conflict: 1844–1968," *Midwest Journal of Political Science* 16 (November 1972): 603–625.

30. The decisions were *Hepburn v. Griswold*, 75 U.S. 603 (1870), and *Knox v. Lee*, 79 U.S. 457 (1871).
31. Lawrence Baum, *The Supreme Court*, 12th ed. (Washington, DC: CQ Press, 2015), 35–40.
32. Henry J. Abraham, *Justices, Presidents, and Senators: A History of the U.S. Supreme Court Appointments from Washington to Bush II* (Lanham, MD: Rowan & Littlefield, 2008); David Alistair Yalof, *Pursuit of Justices: Presidential Politics and the Selection of Supreme Court Nominees* (Chicago: University of Chicago Press, 1999); Christine L. Nemacheck, *Strategic Selection: Presidential Nomination of Supreme Court Justices from Herbert Hoover through George W. Bush* (Charlottesville: University of Virginia Press, 2007).
33. Abraham, *Justices, Presidents, and Senators*, 159–161.
34. James E. Bond, *I Dissent: The Legacy of Chief Justice* [sic] *James Clark McReynolds* (Fairfax, VA: George Mason University Press, 1992), 49–51; Lucas A. Powe Jr., *The Supreme Court and the American Elite, 1789–2008* (Cambridge, MA: Harvard University Press, 2009), 179. If he misunderstood McReynolds's views, Wilson may not have been as perceptive as the Progressive Republicans who cast five of the six votes against McReynolds's confirmation. Abraham, *Justices, Presidents, and Senators*, 139. An alternative view is that Wilson simply wanted to get the troublesome McReynolds out of his cabinet and appointed him without regard to his policy views. In this view, "Wilson got exactly what he deserved in the nomination." John E. Semonche, *Charting the Future: The Supreme Court Responds to a Changing Society, 1890–1920* (Westport, CT: Greenwood Press, 1978), 295.
35. Keith E. Whittington, "Presidents, Senates, and Failed Supreme Court Nominations," *Supreme Court Review* 2007 (2008): 401–438; Henry B. Hogue, "Supreme Court Nominations Not Confirmed, 1789–August 2010," Congressional Research Service Report RL31171 (2010). In the version of senatorial courtesy that prevailed in that era, senators of the president's party had a quasi-veto power not only over appointments of people to serve in their state but also over Supreme Court nominations of people from their state. Hogue, "Supreme Court Nominations Not Confirmed," 10–11.
36. President Cleveland's positions are discussed in Richard E. Welch Jr., *The Presidencies of Grover Cleveland* (Lawrence: University Press of Kansas, 1988), 9–17. His interest in choosing conservative Justices is discussed in Henry J. Abraham, *Justices, Presidents, and Senators: A History of U.S. Supreme Court Appointments from Washington to Bush II* (Lanham, MD: Rowman & Littlefield, 2008), 111–116.
37. James L. Sundquist, *Dynamics of the Party System: Alignment and Realignment of Political Parties in the United States* (Washington, DC: Brookings Institution, 1973), 163.
38. Abraham, *Justices, Presidents, and Senators*, 124.
39. Epstein et al., *Supreme Court Compendium*, 300–306.

40. John R. Schmidhauser, "The Justices of the Supreme Court: A Collective Portrait," *Midwest Journal of Political Science* 3 (February 1959): 6–13; John R. Schmidhauser, *Judges and Justices: The Federal Appellate Judiciary* (Boston: Little, Brown, 1979), 49–53.
41. Schmidhauser, "Justices of the Supreme Court," 12.
42. Schmidhauser, "Justices of the Supreme Court," 29–31; Schmidhauser, *Judges and Justices*, 72–79.
43. Paul Kerns, *Judicial Power and Reform Politics: The Anatomy of Lochner v. New York* (Lawrence: University Press of Kansas, 1990), 69.
44. Barry Friedman, *The Will of the People: How Public Opinion Has Influenced the Supreme Court and Shaped the Meaning of the Constitution* (New York: Farrar, Straus and Giroux, 2010), 171.
45. Alpheus Thomas Mason, *Brandeis: A Free Man's Life* (New York: Viking, 1946), 472–473, 489; Powe, *Supreme Court and the American Elite*, 180.
46. Philip H. Burch Jr., *Elites in American History: The Civil War to the New Deal* (New York: Holmes & Meier, 1981), 465–481.
47. Charles Fairman, *Mr. Justice Miller and the Supreme Court, 1862–1890* (Cambridge, MA: Harvard University Press, 1939), 374.
48. Wallace Mendelson, "Mr. Justice Field and Laissez-Faire," *Virginia Law Review* 36 (1950): 55.
49. Benjamin R. Twiss, *Lawyers and the Constitution: How Laissez Faire Came to the Supreme Court* (Princeton, NJ: Princeton University Press, 1942), 3.
50. Robert G. McCloskey, *American Conservatism in the Age of Enterprise* (Cambridge, MA: Harvard University Press, 1951), 84; Archibald Cox, *The Court and the Constitution* (Boston: Houghton Mifflin Harcourt, 1987), 135.
51. William G. Ross, *A Muted Fury: Populists, Progressives, and Labor Unions Confront the Courts, 1890–1937* (Princeton, NJ: Princeton University Press, 1994), 1.
52. See Michael J. Phillips, *The Lochner Court, Myth and Reality* (Westport, CT: Praeger Publishers, 2001); David E. Bernstein, *Rehabilitating Lochner: Defending Individual Rights against Progressive Reform* (Chicago: University of Chicago Press, 2011); Barry Cushman, *Rethinking the New Deal Court* (New York: Oxford University Press, 1998); and Ross, *A Muted Fury*.
53. These decisions included *West Coast Hotel v. Parrish*, 300 U.S. 379 (1937), which upheld a state minimum wage for women; *National Labor Relations Board v. Jones & Laughlin Steel Corp.*, 301 U.S. 1 (1937), which upheld federal regulation of labor relations under the Wagner Act; and *Helvering v. Davis*, 310 U.S. 619 (1937), which upheld the Social Security Act. On this confrontation and related events, see Jeff Shesol, *Supreme Power: Franklin Roosevelt vs. the Supreme Court* (New York: W. W. Norton, 2011).
54. Robert McCloskey referred to the era that began in 1937 as "The Modern Court." Robert G. McCloskey, *The American Supreme Court* (Chicago: University of Chicago Press, 1960), 180. Other sources on the Court that refer to the New Deal

as the beginning of the modern era are Bruce Ackerman, *We the People: Foundations* (Cambridge, MA: Belknap Press, 1993), 105; and Thomas M. Keck, *The Most Activist Supreme Court in History* (Chicago: University of Chicago, 2004), 17.

55. Alan F. Westin and C. Herman Pritchett, "The Supreme Court since 1937," in *The Third Branch of Government: 8 Cases in Constitutional Politics*, ed. C. Herman Pritchett and Alan F. Westin (New York: Harcourt, Brace & World, 1963), 1.

56. Robert C. Post, "The Supreme Court Opinion as Institutionalized Practice: Dissent, Legal Scholarship, and Decisionmaking in the Taft Court," *Minnesota Law Review* 85 (May 2001): 1267–1389; Grove, "The Exceptions Clause," 962–968.

57. See Edward A. Hartnett, "Questioning Certiorari: Some Reflections Seventy-Five Years after the Judges' Bill," *Columbia Law Review* 100 (November 2000): 1643–1738.

58. Amanda Frost, "The Limits of Advocacy," *Duke Law Journal* 59 (December 2009): 447, 452, 493; Robert Bone, "Lon Fuller's Theory of Adjudication and the False Dichotomy between Dispute Resolution and Public Models of Litigation," *Boston University Law Review* 75 (November 1995): 1275.

59. The timing and sources of the increased rates of dissents, dissenting opinions, and concurring opinions are analyzed in Thomas G. Walker, Lee Epstein, and William M. Dixon, "On the Mysterious Demise of Consensual Norms in the United States Supreme Court," *Journal of Politics* 50 (May 1988): 361–389; Stacia L. Haynie, "Leadership and Consensus on the U.S. Supreme Court," *Journal of Politics* 54 (November 1992): 1158–1169; Gregory A. Caldeira and Christopher J. W. Zorn, "Of Time and Consensual Norms in the Supreme Court," *American Journal of Political Science* 42 (July 1998): 874–902; and Marcus E. Hendershot, Mark S. Hurwitz, Drew Noble Lanier, and Richard L. Pacelle, "Dissensual Decision Making: Revisiting the Demise of Consensual Norms within the U.S. Supreme Court," *Political Research Quarterly* 66 (June 2013): 467–481.

60. The procedure was first set out in a 2002 article, Andrew D. Martin and Kevin M. Quinn, "Dynamic Ideal Point Estimation via Markov Chain Monte Carlo for the U.S. Supreme Court 1953–1999," *Political Analysis* 10 (2002): 134–153. The scores, now available for Court terms since 1937, have been widely used in research on the Court by political scientists and legal scholars. Because of the way they are computed, they have some limitations, which are discussed in Daniel E. Ho and Kevin M. Quinn, "How Not to Lie with Judicial Votes: Misconceptions, Measurement, and Models," *California Law Review* 98 (June 2010): 844–848. Most relevant to our purposes, the scores are not fully linear, so that the differences in scores between pairs of Justices are not necessarily comparable with each other. However, the scores work well (although imperfectly) for putting Justices in ideological order for any given term, and like the Leavitt and Snyder scores they have the positive quality that they do not rest on any assumptions about how to code votes as conservative or liberal.

61. The scores shown in the table are the mean estimates of the Justices' scores. Because the calculation procedure for the scores takes other Court terms into account,

the ordering of Justices sometimes changes even for terms in the distant past; the ordering shown is based on the estimates after the Court's 2017 term. When the Court's membership changed during a term, scores are shown only for the nine Justices who participated in the largest number of decisions during that term. The calculation procedure sometimes produces scores for Justices who participated in very few decisions (or even no decisions) during a term; those Justices are not shown.

Where multiple terms are shown on the same line, the ordering of the Justices was the same for each of the included terms.

Abbreviations for Justices' names are as follows: Blmn = Blackmun, Bren = Brennan, Brey = Breyer, Butl = Butler; Burg = Burger, Burt = Burton, Card = Cardozo, Doug = Douglas, Fort = Fortas, Fran = Frankfurter, Gins = Ginsburg, Gold = Goldberg, Gors = Gorsuch, Harl = Harlan, Hugh = Hughes, Jack = Jackson, JRob = John Roberts, Kenn = Kennedy, Mint = Minton, Murp = Murphy, O'Con = O'Connor, ORob = Owen Roberts, Powe = Powell, Rehn = Rehnquist, Rutl = Rutledge, Scal = Scalia, Soto = Sotomayor, Sout = Souter, Stev = Stevens, Stew = Stewart, Thom = Thomas, Warr = Warren, Whit = Whittaker.

62. The same was true for the actual proportions of liberal and conservative votes as coded in the Supreme Court Database. By that measure, as with the Martin-Quinn scores, Roberts had the most conservative voting record in the 1941–1944 terms and Stone had a more conservative record than any of the Roosevelt appointees in 1941, 1942, and 1944—though not in the 1945 term.
63. *Wickard v. Filburn*, 317 U.S. 111 (1942).
64. See Barry Cushman, "Formalism and Realism in Commerce Clause Jurisprudence," *University of Chicago Law Review* 67 (Fall 2000): 1143–1146.
65. *Jones v. Opelika*, 316 U.S. 584 (1942); *Murdoch v. Pennsylvania*, 319 U.S. 105 (1943); *West Virginia State Board of Education v. Barnette*, 319 U.S. 624 (1943).
66. See Noah Feldman, *Scorpions: The Battles and Triumphs of FDR's Great Supreme Court Justices* (New York: Grand Central, 2010); and H. N. Hirsch, *The Enigma of Felix Frankfurter* (New York: Basic Books, 1981), 127–200.
67. *Miranda v. Arizona*, 384 U.S. 436 (1966). Clark wrote a concurring and dissenting opinion, but like the full dissenters he rejected the Court's *Miranda* rules.
68. *Roe v. Wade*, 410 U.S. 113 (1973).
69. *Planned Parenthood v. Casey*, 505 U.S. 833 (1992).
70. Savage, *Guide to the U.S. Supreme Court*, 1294–1310. Savage's list of important cases terminated in the middle of the 2009 term.
71. The case was *Federal Election Commission v. National Conservative Political Action Committee*, 470 U.S. 480 (1985). Four Justices (two Democrats and two Republicans) wrote or joined dissenting opinions. Of these four, the Court's two Democrats (White and Marshall) dissented most fully from the Court's decision, and the *Guide to the U.S. Supreme Court* (p. 1240) treats the Court's vote as 7–2.

72. The original quotation is a little different, reflecting Mr. Dooley's Irish brogue. Finley Peter Dunne, selected by Robert Hutchinson, *Mr. Dooley on Ivrything and Ivrybody* (New York: Dover Publications, 1963), 160.
73. Fred Rodell, *Nine Men* (New York: Random House, 1955), 9.
74. Justin Crowe and Christopher F. Karpowitz, "Where Have You Gone, Sherman Minton? The Decline of the Short-Term Supreme Court Justice," *Perspectives on Politics* 5 (September 2007): 425–445.
75. Jeffrey A. Segal, Richard J. Timpone, and Robert M. Howard, "Buyer Beware? Presidential Success through Supreme Court Appointments," *Political Research Quarterly* 53 (September 2000): 562.
76. Abraham, *Justices, Presidents, and Senators*, 166; William E. Leuchtenburg, *The Supreme Court Reborn* (New York: Oxford University Press, 1995), 154.
77. Abraham, *Justices, Presidents, and Senators*, 181.
78. Leuchtenburg, *The Supreme Court Reborn*, 233.
79. Leuchtenburg, *The Supreme Court Reborn*, 235.
80. Louis Fisher and Neal Devins, *Political Dynamics of Constitutional Law* (St. Paul, MN: Thompson Reuters, 2011), 63, 66–67; Leuchtenburg, *The Supreme Court Reborn*.
81. Fowler V. Harper, *Justice Rutledge and the Bright Constellation* (Indianapolis, IN: Bobbs-Merrill, 1965), 23–26, 38–42; John M. Ferren, *Salt of the Earth, Conscience of the Court: The Story of Justice Wiley Rutledge* (Chapel Hill: University of North Carolina Press, 2004), 208–219.
82. Robert Scigliano, *The Supreme Court and the Presidency* (New York: Free Press, 1971), 95.
83. Yalof, *Pursuit of Justices*, 20.
84. William O. Douglas, *The Court Years 1939–1975: The Autobiography of William O. Douglas* (New York: Random House, 1980), 247; Clark's version of the story was related by retired Justice John Paul Stevens in *Five Chiefs: A Supreme Court Memoir* (New York: Little, Brown, 2011), 60–61.
85. Based on the coding of votes in the Supreme Court Database, all four Truman appointees ranked above the median among Justices serving in the 1937–2006 terms for their proportions of conservative votes. With the exception of Clark, all were well above the median. William M. Landes and Richard A. Posner, "Rational Judicial Behavior: A Statistical Study," *Journal of Legal Analysis* 1 (Summer 2009): 782–783. Among Justices who served in the 1946–1985 terms, the Truman appointees have similar rankings in civil liberties cases, based on voting scores that were modified in an effort to take into account change in the composition of the Court's agenda over time. Lawrence Baum, "Comparing the Policy Positions of Supreme Court Justices from Different Periods," *Western Political Quarterly* 42 (December 1989): 511.
86. Merle Miller, *Plain Speaking: An Oral Biography of Harry S. Truman* (New York: Berkley, 1973), 225.

87. This discussion of the Kennedy nominations is based primarily on Yalof, *Pursuit of Justices*, 71–81.
88. Yalof, *Pursuit of Justices*, 236 note 44; Sheldon Goldman, *Picking Federal Judges: Lower Court Selection from Roosevelt Through Reagan* (New Haven, CT: Yale University Press, 1999), 166.
89. Yalof, *Pursuit of Justices*, 79–80.
90. Laura Kalman, *The Long Reach of the Sixties: LBJ, Nixon, and the Making of the Contemporary Supreme Court* (New York: Oxford University Press, 2017), 48.
91. This discussion of the Johnson nominations draws from Yalof, *Pursuit of Justices*, 81–94; and Kalman, *Long Reach of the Sixties*, 53–65, 85–96, 126–137.
92. Yalof, *Pursuit of Justices*, 89.
93. Yalof, *Pursuit of Justices*, 44–45; G. Edward White, *Earl Warren: A Public Life* (New York: Oxford University Press, 1982), 143–152; Ed Cray, *Chief Justice: A Biography of Earl Warren* (New York: Simon & Schuster, 1997), 246–253. Warren received a recess appointment in 1953 and was nominated and confirmed in 1954.
94. White, *Earl Warren*, 152.
95. Cray, *Chief Justice*, 255.
96. Like Warren, Brennan received a recess appointment and was nominated and confirmed in the following year.
97. Yalof, *Pursuit of Justices*, 55–61; Seth Stern and Stephen Wermiel, *Justice Brennan: Liberal Champion* (Boston: Houghton Mifflin Harcourt, 2010), 72–82.
98. Stern and Wermiel, *Justice Brennan*, 81.
99. J. L. Bernstein, "The Philosophy of Mr. Justice Brennan," *The Reporter: An Antidote to Law Reviews* 6 (1984): 30–33. The article was originally published in *The Reporter* in November 1956 and January 1957.
100. Yalof, *Pursuit of Justices*, 81–82. In his first term, Eisenhower had appointed John Harlan along with Warren and Brennan, and Harlan's record on the Court was close to the president's preferences. But Harlan, who had the strong support of Attorney General Herbert Brownell, was not scrutinized carefully; in any event, he had less than one year's judicial experience to scrutinize. Yalof, *Pursuit of Justices*, 52–55.
101. Donald Grier Stephenson Jr., *Campaigns and the Court: The U.S. Supreme Court in Presidential Elections* (New York: Columbia University Press, 1999), 179–182.
102. An analysis based on information about nominees' policy positions in newspaper editorials about nominees after their nominations found that all six nominees were perceived to be near the conservative end of a liberal-conservative continuum. "Perceived Qualifications and Ideology of Supreme Court Nominees, 1937–2012," http://www.stonybrook.edu/polsci/jsegal/. The methodology on which this analysis is based is described in Jeffrey A. Segal and Albert D. Cover, "Ideological Values and the Votes of U.S. Supreme Court Justices," *American Political Science Review* 83 (June 1989): 559.
103. Kevin J. McMahon, *Nixon's Court: His Challenge to Judicial Liberalism and Its Political Consequences* (Chicago: University of Chicago Press, 2011).

104. Kalman, *Long Reach of the Sixties*, 257.
105. Eric A. Posner, "Casual with the Court," *New Republic*, October 24, 2011, https://newrepublic.com/article/94516/nixons-court-kevin-mcmahon.
106. John W. Dean, *The Rehnquist Choice: The Untold Story of the Nixon Appointment that Redefined the Supreme Court* (New York: Free Press, 2002).
107. Kalman, *Long Reach of the Sixties*, 307.
108. McMahon, *Nixon's Court*, 6.
109. Yalof, *Pursuit of Justices*, 107, 110–112.
110. Vincent Blasi, ed., *The Burger Court: The Counter-Revolution That Wasn't* (New Haven, CT: Yale University Press, 1983). For a contrary assessment of the Burger Court, see Michael J. Graetz and Linda Greenhouse, *The Burger Court and the Rise of the Judicial Right* (New York: Simon and Schuster, 2016).
111. In civil liberties, the raw voting records of Warren Burger, Lewis Powell, and Blackmun (before his move to the left) were strongly conservative compared with other Justices who served in the modern era. But those records are partly a product of the composition of the Burger Court's agenda. With an adjustment for agenda change, these Justices move to more moderate positions relative to Justices from other periods. Baum, "Comparing the Policy Positions," 517.
112. Yalof, *Pursuit of Justices*, 125–131.
113. George L. Priest and William Ranney Levi, "Justice Stevens, Edward Levi, and the Chicago School of Antitrust," *National Law Review*, May 24, 2010, http://www.law.uchicago.edu/news/justice-stevens-edward-levi-and-chicago-school-antitrust.
114. Douglas E. Kneeland, "Reagan Pledges Woman on Court; Carter Challenges Foe on Economy," *New York Times*, October 15, 1980, A1.
115. Nemacheck, *Strategic Selection*, 9–13; Yalof, *Pursuit of Justices*, 135–141.
116. References to O'Connor's ideological positions in newspaper editorials at the time put her only somewhat on the conservative side of the continuum. Segal and Cover, "Ideological Values," 560.
117. M. Louise Rutherford, "The Influence of the American Bar Association on Public Opinion and Legislation" (PhD diss., University of Pennsylvania, 1937), 129–130, 249–250; Steven M. Teles, *The Rise of the Conservative Legal Movement* (Princeton, NJ: Princeton University Press, 2008), 28–29.
118. Joel B. Grossman, *Lawyers and Judges: The ABA and the Politics of Judicial Selection* (New York: John Wiley and Sons, 1965), 52–58.
119. Teles, *Rise of the Conservative Legal Movement*, 29.
120. Teles, *Rise of the Conservative Legal Movement*, 24–30.
121. Peter Irons, *The New Deal Lawyers* (Princeton, NJ: Princeton University Press, 1982).
122. The ABA is now perceived by conservatives in the legal community as a strongly liberal organization, and that perception has led to an unwillingness by recent Republican presidents to give the ABA a role in the screening of candidates for federal judgeships. Adam Liptak, "White House Cuts A.B.A. Out of Judge Evaluations," *New York Times*, April 1, 2017, A16.

123. Seymour Martin Lipset, "The Academic Mind at the Top: The Political Behavior and Values of Faculty Elites," *Public Opinion Quarterly* 46 (Summer 1982): 143–168; Neil Gross and Solon Simmons, "The Social and Political Views of American College and University Professors," in *Professors and Their Publics*, ed. Neil Gross and Solon Simmons (Baltimore, MD: Johns Hopkins University Press, 2014), 19–49.
124. Everett Carll Ladd Jr. and Seymour Martin Lipset, *The Divided Academy: Professors and Politics* (New York: McGraw-Hill, 1975), 80.
125. Teles, *Rise of the Conservative Legal Movement*, 41–46.
126. Deborah Jones Merritt, "Research and Teaching on Law Faculties: An Empirical Exploration," *Chicago-Kent Law Review* 73 (1998): 780 note 54; John O. McGinnis, Matthew A. Schwartz, and Benjamin Tisdell, "The Patterns and Implications of Political Contributions by Elite Law School Faculty," *Georgetown Law Journal* 93 (April 2005): 1167–1212.
127. McGinnis, Schwartz, and Tisdell, "Patterns and Implications of Political Contributions," 1177.
128. This pattern is discussed and criticized in William D. Bader and Roy M. Mersky, *The First One Hundred Eight Justices* (Buffalo, NY: William S. Hein & Co., 2004), 57–64. Ratings of Justices through the Lyndon Johnson appointees by Supreme Court scholars are presented in Albert P. Blaustein and Roy M. Mersky, *The First One Hundred Justices: Statistical Studies on the Supreme Court of the United States* (Hamden, CT: Archon Books, 1978), 37–40.
129. William E. Nelson, Harvey Rishikof, I. Scott Messinger, and Michael Jo, "The Liberal Tradition of the Supreme Court Clerkship: Its Rise, Fall, and Reincarnation?," *Vanderbilt Law Review* 62 (November 2009): 1747–1814.
130. Todd C. Peppers, *Courtiers of the Marble Palace: The Rise and Influence of the Supreme Court Law Clerk* (Stanford, CA: Stanford University Press, 2006), 35, 37; Artemus Ward and David L. Weiden, *Sorcerers' Apprentices: 100 Years of Law Clerks at the United States Supreme Court* (New York: New York University Press, 2006), 104.
131. David H. Weaver and G. Cleveland Wilhoit, *The American Journalist: A Portrait of U.S. News People and Their Work*, 2nd ed. (Bloomington: Indiana University Press, 1991), 28, 31.
132. Stanley Rothman and S. Robert Lichter, "Personality, Ideology, and World View: A Comparison of Media and Business Elites," *British Journal of Political Science* 15 (January 1985): 36.
133. That difficulty is illustrated by the disagreement about the findings of one research project on ideological bias in the news media. See Tim Groseclose and Jeffrey Milyo, "A Measure of Media Bias," *Quarterly Journal of Economics* 120 (November 2005): 1991–1237; Timothy Groseclose, *Left Turn: How Liberal Media Bias Distorts the American Mind* (New York: St. Martin's Press, 2011); Brendan Nyhan, "The Problems with the Groseclose/Milyo Study of Media Bias," Brendan Nyhan blog, December 22, 2005, http://www.brendan-nyhan.com/blog/2005/12/the_problems_wi.html; and Andrew Gelman, "Thought on Groseclose Book on

Media Bias," *Monkey Cage*, July 29, 2011, http://themonkeycage.org/2011/07/thoughts-on-groseclose-book-on-media-bias/.

134. Because of limited availability of the *Boston Globe* and *Dallas Morning News* for the early part of that time period, we omitted six decisions that were less important than the others for those two newspapers. The *Chicago Tribune* published some editorials from other newspapers on decisions on which the *Tribune* did not have its own editorial; those editorials were treated as reflecting the *Tribune*'s position. Some newspapers had editorials on nearly all of the thirty-two decisions; others responded to smaller numbers of the decisions.
135. The *Post, New York Times*, and *Globe* can best be characterized as liberal in their orientation, the *Wall Street Journal* and *Tribune* as conservative; the *Los Angeles Times* and *Dallas Morning News* were strongly conservative in the 1950s but became more liberal with changes in ownership; this change came earlier for the *Times* than for the *Morning News*.
136. *Brown v. Board of Education*, 347 U.S. 483 (1954); *Burwell v. Hobby Lobby Stores*, 134 L. Ed. 2d 2751 (2014); *Riley v. California*, 134 L. Ed. 2d 2473 (2014). In addition to these decisions and those discussed in the notes that follow, our sample included *Baker v. Carr*, 369 U.S. 186 (1962); *Gideon v. Wainwright*, 372 U.S. 335 (1963); *Loving v. Virginia*, 388 U.S. 1 (1967); *Swann v. Charlotte-Mecklenburg Board of Education*, 402 U.S. 1 (1971); *Roe v. Wade*, 410 U.S. 113 (1973); *San Antonio Independent School District v. Rodriguez*, 411 U.S. 1 (1973); *Regents v. Bakke*, 438 U.S. 265 (1978); *Bob Jones University v. United States*, 461 U.S. 574 (1983); *Texas v. Johnson*, 491 U.S. 397 (1989); *Webster v. Reproductive Health Services*, 492 U..S. 490 (1989); *Planned Parenthood v. Casey*, 505 U.S. 833 (1992); *Reno v. American Civil Liberties Union*, 521 U.S. 844 (1997); *Lawrence v. Texas*, 539 U.S. 558 (2003); *Grutter v. Bollinger*, 539 U.S. 306 (2003); *McConnell v. Federal Election Commission*, 540 U.S. 93 (2003); *Roper v.* Simmons, 543 U.S. 551 (2005); *District of Columbia v. Heller*, 554 U.S. 570 (2008); *Citizens United v. Federal Election Commission*, 558 U.S. 310 (2010); *Jones v. United States*, 565 U.S. 400 (2012); *National Federation of Independent Business v. Sebelius*, 567 U.S. 519 (2012); and *Shelby County v. Holder*, 570 U.S. 529 (2013).
137. *Mapp v. Ohio*, 367 U.S. 643 (1961) (establishing the exclusionary rule for illegal searches and seizures); *Miranda v. Arizona*, 384 U.S. 436 (1966) (requiring that certain rights be provided to suspects questioned in police custody); *Furman v. Georgia*, 408 U.S. 238 (1972) (striking down existing death penalty laws); *Engel v. Vitale*, 370 U.S. 431 (1962) (prohibiting the requirement that a state-composed prayer be recited in public schools); *Abington School District v. Schempp*, 374 U.S. 203 (1963) (prohibiting the requirement that public schools have Bible reading or recitations of the Lord's Prayer at the beginning of the school day).
138. Examples include a pro-*Mapp* editorial in the *Wall Street Journal*, an editorial mostly favorable to *Roe v. Wade* in the *Journal*, and editorials favorable to *Engel*

v. Vitale and *Texas v. Johnson* in the *Chicago Tribune.* As we discussed in chapter 2, newspaper editorials overwhelmingly backed Supreme Court limitations on initiatives concerning enemy combatants in the George W. Bush administration, and that was true of the newspapers in our sample. The decisions were *Hamdi v. Rumsfeld*, 542 U.S. 207 (2004); *Hamdan v. Rumsfeld*, 548 U.S. 557 (2006); and *Boumediene v. Bush*, 553 U.S. 723 (2008).

139. Richard Reeves, *President Nixon: Alone in the White House* (New York: Simon & Schuster, 2001), 338.
140. Judges and Justices who presented Madison Lectures were identified from the published versions of their talks in the *NYU Law Review* and from "Read the Madison Lectures," NYU Law, http://www.law.nyu.edu/academics/fellowships/haysprogram/LitigationandLectures/JamesMadisonLectures/ReadPastMadisonLectures/.
141. On changes in the composition of the Court's agenda over time, see Richard L. Pacelle Jr., *The Transformation of the Supreme Court's Agenda from the New Deal to the Reagan Administration* (Boulder, CO: Westview Press, 1991).
142. Edwin Meese III, "The Law of the Constitution," *Tulane Law Review* 61 (1987): 979–990.
143. "Transcript of the Republican Presidential Debate in Houston," *New York Times*, February 26, 2016.
144. Reeves, *President Nixon*, 338.
145. Dean, *The Rehnquist Choice*, 171.
146. Linda Greenhouse, *Becoming Justice Blackmun: Harry Blackmun's Supreme Court Journey* (New York: Times Books, 2005), 48.
147. Joan Biskupic, *Sandra Day O'Connor: How the First Woman on the Supreme Court Became Its Most Influential Justice* (New York: HarperCollins, 2005), 42.
148. Yalof, *Pursuit of Justices*, 139.
149. Thomas Sowell, "Blackmun Plays to the Crowd," *St. Louis Post-Dispatch*, March 4, 1994, 7B.
150. "Attacking Activism, Judge Names Names," *Legal Times*, June 22, 1992, 14; Martin Tolchin, "Press Is Condemned by a Federal Judge for Court Coverage," *New York Times*, June 15, 1992, A13. Silberman credited Sowell for the term.
151. David P. Bryden, "Is the Rehnquist Court Conservative?," *Public Interest* 109 (Fall 1992): 83–84; Andrew J. Kleinfeld, "Politicization: From the Law Schools to the Courts," *Academic Questions* 6 (Winter 1993–1994): 18; Mary Ann Glendon, *A Nation under Lawyers: How the Crisis in the Legal Profession Is Transforming American Society* (New York: Farrar, Straus and Giroux, 1994), 150–151; Max Boot, *Out of Order: Arrogance, Corruption and Incompetence on the Bench* (New York: Basic Books, 1998), 119–120; Robert H. Bork, *Coercing Virtue: The Worldwide Rule of Judges* (Washington, DC: AEI Press, 2003), 9–10; Mark R. Levin, *Men in Black: How the Supreme Court Is Destroying America* (Washington, DC: Regnery Publishing, 2005), 60–61; Michael Barone, "Why America's House of Lords Seems to Tilt to the Left," *Chicago Sun-Times*, July 13,

2005, 55. Proponents of the view that Justices respond to left-leaning elites are discussed in Mark Kozlowski, *The Myth of the Imperial Judiciary: Why the Right Is Wrong about the Courts* (New York: New York University Press, 2003), 18–28.

152. Thomas Sowell, "Justice Kennedy Goes Soft on Crime," *Columbus Dispatch*, August 13, 2003, A11.
153. *Romer v. Evans*, 517 U.S. 620, 636 (1996); *United States v. Virginia*, 518 U.S. 515, 567 (1996); *Lawrence v. Texas*, 539 U.S. 558, 602 (2003); *Obergefell v. Hodges*, 135 S. Ct. 2584, 2629 (2015).
154. Sowell, "Blackmun Plays to the Crowd"; Terry Eastland, "The Tempting of Justice Kennedy: Is It the Greenhouse Effect That Has Turned Anthony Kennedy into the Harry Blackmun of Our Time—That Is, a Justice Who 'Grew'?," *American Spectator* 26 (February 1993): 32–37; Dana Milbank, "And the Verdict on Justice Kennedy Is: Guilty," *Washington Post*, April 9, 2005, A3. One lawyer for a conservative public interest group, later appointed to a federal judgeship by President Trump, described Kennedy in a 2007 blog posting as "a judicial prostitute, 'selling' his vote as it were to four other Justices in exchange for the high that comes from aggrandizement of power and influence, and the blandishments of the fawning media and legal academy." "Kennedy as the Most Powerful Justice?," *Omnia omnibus*, June 29, 2007, quoted in Dahlia Lithwick, "Will He or Won't He?," *Slate*, May 26, 2017, http://www.slate.com/articles/news_and_politics/jurisprudence/2017/05/how_anthony_kennedy_s_retirement_decision_became_a_battle_over_the_trump.html.
155. See Frederick Schauer, "Incentives, Reputation, and the Inglorious Determinants of Judicial Behavior," *University of Cincinnati Law Review* 68 (Spring 2000): 617–620.
156. *National Federation of Independent Business v. Sebelius*, 567 U.S. 519 (2012).
157. *Romer v. Evans; United States v. Windsor*, 570 U.S. 744 (2013), and *Obergefell v. Hodges*.
158. That movement is discussed later in this section.
159. Lawrence Baum, *Ideology in the Supreme Court* (Princeton, NJ: Princeton University Press, 2017).
160. Jonathan P. Kastellec and Jeffrey R. Lax, "Case Selection and the Study of Judicial Politics," *Journal of Empirical Legal Studies* 5 (September 2008): 407–446; Kevin T. McGuire, George Vanberg, Charles E. Smith Jr., and Gregory A. Caldeira, "Measuring Policy Content on the U.S. Supreme Court," *Journal of Politics* 71 (October 2009): 1305–1320; Jeff Yates, Damon M. Cann, and Brent D. Boyea, "Judicial Ideology and the Selection of Disputes for U.S. Supreme Court Adjudication," *Journal of Empirical Legal Studies* 10 (December 2013): 847–865.
161. Ho and Quinn, "How Not to Lie with Judicial Votes," 844–846.
162. Michael A. Bailey, "Is Today's Court the Most Conservative in Sixty Years? Challenges and Opportunities in Measuring Judicial Preferences," *Journal of Politics* 75 (July 2013): 821–834.

163. Bailey, "Is Today's Court the Most Conservative," 826.
164. Bailey, "Is Today's Court the Most Conservative," 828.
165. "1st Year" is the first calendar year in which a Justice participated in a substantial number of decisions.
166. Lee Epstein and Jeffrey A. Segal, "Measuring Issue Salience," *American Journal of Political Science* 44 (January 2000): 66–83.
167. This is especially true because the numbers of salient decisions in a Justice's first two terms can be relatively small. There were only ten such cases for Justice Harlan and fourteen for Chief Justice Warren.
168. If the Democratic appointees are included, the correlation is .594, almost identical.
169. Terry Eastland, "The Tempting of Justice Kennedy," *American Spectator*, February 1993, 34 note 3. A similar view is expressed in David M. Wagner, "Beyond 'Strange New Respect,'" *Weekly Standard*, March 14, 2005, 21. One legal scholar has pointed to experience in the federal executive branch as the key factor, because that experience allows ideological prescreening of prospective nominees. Michael C. Dorf, "Does Federal Executive Branch Experience Explain Why Some Republican Supreme Court Justices 'Evolve' and Others Don't?," *Harvard Law & Policy Review* 1 (Summer 2007): 457–476.
170. That tendency is discussed as it applies to political phenomena in Carol Mock and Herbert F. Weisberg, "Political Innumeracy: Encounters with Coincidence, Improbability, and Chance," *American Journal of Political Science* 36 (November 1992): 1023–1046.
171. See generally Tinsley E. Yarbrough, *David Hackett Souter: Traditional Republican on the Rehnquist Court* (New York: Oxford University Press, 2005). On the Court, Souter made fewer appearances outside the Court than did any of his colleagues. Lawrence Baum, *Judges and Their Audiences: A Perspective on Judicial Behavior* (Princeton, NJ: Princeton University Press, 2006), 166.
172. The data on agreement rates are taken from the annual statistics presented in the November issues of the *Harvard Law Review*.
173. Linda Greenhouse, *Becoming Justice Blackmun: Harry Blackmun's Supreme Court Journey* (New York: Times Books, 2005). Other discussions of Blackmun's shift include "Note: The Changing Social Vision of Justice Blackmun," *Harvard Law Review* 96 (January 1983): 717–736, and Joseph F. Kobylka, "The Judicial Odyssey of Harry Blackmun: The Dynamics of Individual-Level Change on the U.S. Supreme Court," paper presented at the annual conference of the Midwest Political Science Association, Chicago, April 9–11, 1992.
174. Several explanations are discussed in Baum, *Judges and Their Audiences*, 152–155.
175. Sowell, "Blackmun Plays to the Crowd."
176. "The Justice Harry A. Blackmun Oral History Project," interviews conducted by Harold Hongju Koh (Washington, DC: Supreme Court Historical Society and Federal Judicial Center), 204–205, 305, 453–454; Chai Feldblum, "Former Law Clerk Recalls Blackmun's Humility," *National Law Journal*, March 15, 1999, A24.

177. Richard Davis, *Decisions and Images: The Supreme Court and the Press* (Englewood Cliffs, NJ: Prentice-Hall, 1994), 106.
178. John A. Jenkins, "A Candid Talk with Justice Blackmun," *New York Times Magazine*, February 20, 1983, 20–29, 57–66; Fred Barbash and Al Kamen, "Third Justice Speaks Out," *Washington Post*, September 20, 1984, A1, A42; "Transcript of Broadcast," *ABC Nightline*, November 18, 1993 (#3259).
179. Radhika Rao, "The Author of Roe," *Hastings Constitutional Law Quarterly* 26 (Fall 1998): 22. Blackmun's concern about the vitality of *Roe* was reflected in his opinions in *Webster v. Reproductive Health Services*, 492 U.S. 490, 557 (1989), and *Planned Parenthood v. Casey*, at 922–923.
180. "Blackmun Oral History Project," 207–208.
181. "Blackmun Oral History Project," 469; Greenhouse, *Becoming Justice Blackmun*, 223–224.
182. Neil A. Lewis, "Blackmun on Search for the Center," *New York Times*, March 8, 1986, A7; Reynolds Holding, "Blackmun Says Court Direction Disappointing," *San Francisco Chronicle*, June 10, 1991, A12.
183. Based on the coding of cases in the Supreme Court Database, Blackmun's proportion of conservative votes in civil liberties cases moved 26 percentage points closer to Brennan's proportion between the 1971–1976 and 1984–1989 terms while moving 28 percentage points further from Rehnquist's proportion. In economic cases, Blackmun moved 6 percentage points closer to both Brennan and Rehnquist. The cases analyzed were those decided after oral argument. Civil liberties cases were those in issue areas 1 through 6 in the database, economic cases those in issue areas 7 and 8.
184. "Justice Harry Blackmun," *Washington Post*, March 6, 1999, A20; "Justice Blackmun's Journey," *New York Times*, March 5, 1999, A20.
185. *National Federation of Independent Business v. Sebelius; King v. Burwell*, 135 S. Ct. 2480 (2015); *Zubik v. Burwell*, 136 S. Ct. 1557 (2016).
186. Based on the coding of cases in the Supreme Court Database, during the natural Court of the 2010–2014 terms, Kennedy had the most conservative record of any Justice in economic cases (issue areas 7 and 8), in contrast with his position between the Court's other conservatives and its liberals in civil liberties cases (issues areas 1 through 6).
187. *Webster v. Reproductive Health Services*, 492 U.S. 490 (1989).
188. *Atkins v. Virginia*, 536 U.S. 304 (2002); *Roper v. Simmons*, 543 U.S. 551 (2005). The earlier decisions were *Penry v. Lynaugh*, 492 U.S. 302 (1989) (intellectual disability), and *Stanford v. Kentucky*, 492 U.S. 361 (1989) (juveniles).
189. The three earlier decisions were *Romer v. Evans* (1996), *Lawrence v. Texas* (2003), and *United States v. Windsor* (2013).
190. *Fisher v. Texas*, 136 S. Ct. 2198 (2016). His skepticism is exemplified by his dissenting opinion in another university admissions case, *Grutter v. Bollinger*, 539 U.S. 306, 387–395 (2003).

191. Jason DeParle, "In Battle to Pick Next Justice, Right Says Avoid a Kennedy," *New York Times*, June 27, 2005, A12. The critic was James C. Dobson, founder of the group Focus on the Family.
192. These quotations are from, respectively, "High Court Performs Arrogant Act of Judicial Tyranny," *Human Events* 52 (May 31, 1996): 485, and "Justice Anthony Kennedy: Surely Reagan's Biggest Disappointment," *Human Events* 52 (May 31, 1996): 488.
193. Sowell, "Justice Kennedy Goes Soft on Crime"; David M. Wagner, "Beyond 'Strange New Respect,'" *Weekly Standard*, March 14, 2005, 20–21; John Yoo, "SCOTUS' *Fisher* Ruling a Blow to the Constitution," *National Review Online*, June 23, 2016, http://www.nationalreview.com/corner/437033/supreme-court-fisher-v-university-texas-affirmative-action-case.
194. Jeffrey Rosen, "The Agonizer," *New Yorker*, November 11, 1996, 86. That concern may be reflected in Kennedy's dissenting opinion in *Young v. United Parcel Service*, 135 S. Ct. 1338, 1366–1367 (2015), in which he took pains to emphasize his sensitivity to the difficulties faced by pregnant employees even though he was voting against the pregnant woman who had brought a case under the Pregnancy Discrimination Act.
195. Rosen, "The Agonizer," 82–90; Terry Carter, "Crossing the Rubicon," *California Lawyer*, October 1992, 39–40, 103–104.
196. Rosen, "The Agonizer," 85.
197. Adam Liptak, "Surprising Friend of Gay Rights in a High Place," *New York Times*, September 2, 2013, A1, A10.
198. Whether Eisenhower actually referred to Warren and Brennan as his two biggest mistakes as president is uncertain and disputed. Alyssa Sepinwall, "The Making of a Presidential Myth," *Wall Street Journal*, September, 4, 1990, A11; Tony Mauro, "Leak of Souter Keeps McGuigan in Plan," *Legal Times*, September 10, 1990, 11.

CHAPTER 4

1. See the sources cited in note 9 in chapter 3.
2. The parties' ideological positions over time, shown in Figure 3.1, are charted at https://voteview.com/parties/all. See also Sean M. Theriault, *Party Polarization in Congress* (New York: Cambridge University Press, 2008), 13–42; and Steven S. Smith and Gerald Gamm, "The Dynamics of Party Government in Congress," in *Congress Reconsidered*, 10th ed., ed. Lawrence C. Dodd and Bruce L. Oppenheimer (Washington, DC: CQ Press, 2013), 173.
3. Richard Pearson, "Former Alabama Governor George C. Wallace Dies," *Washington Post*, September 14, 1998, A1.
4. See Theriault, *Party Polarization in Congress*; Michael Barber and Nolan McCarty, "Causes and Consequences of Polarization," in *Negotiating Agreement in Politics: Report of the Task Force on Negotiating Agreement in Politics*, ed. Jane

Mansbridge and Cathie Jo Martin (Washington, DC: American Political Science Association, 2013), 19–53; and Jason M. Roberts and Steven S. Smith, "Procedural Contexts, Party Strategy, and Conditional Party Voting in the U.S. House of Representatives, 1971–2000," *American Journal of Political Science* 47 (April 2003): 305–317.

5. See Richard H. Pildes, "Why the Center Does Not Hold: The Causes of Hyperpolarized Democracy in America," *California Law Review* 99 (April 2011): 278–297; and Jason M. Roberts and Steven S. Smith, "Procedural Contexts, Party Strategy, and Conditional Party Voting in the U.S. House of Representatives, 1971–2000," *American Journal of Political Science* 47 (April 2003): 305–317 (tracking the rapid growth of Southern Republicans).
6. Nolan McCarty, Keith T. Poole, and Howard Rosenthal, "Does Gerrymandering Cause Polarization?," *American Journal of Political Science* 53 (July 2009): 666–680.
7. See Samuel Issacharoff, "Collateral Damage: The Endangered Center in American Politics," *William & Mary Law Review* 46 (November 2004): 428–431; and Nolan McCarty, "The Policy Effects of Political Polarization," in *The Transformation of American Politics: Activist Government and the Rise of Conservatism*, ed. Paul Pierson and Theda Skocpol (Princeton, NJ: Princeton University Press, 2007).
8. The rank orderings of House members and senators through the 113th Congress (2013–2014) are presented at https://legacy.voteview.com/HOUSE_SORT109.HTM. Plots of congressional voting along two dimensions show that, with the exception of the House in the 111th Congress (2009–2011), there has been a clear separation between all Republicans and all Democrats in each Congress since 2005. See https://voteview.com/congress/house and https://voteview.com/congress/senate.
9. See *Party Polarization: 1879–2010* (2013), https://web.archive.org/web/20131116022958/http://polarizedamerica.com/political_polarization.asp.
10. See *"Common Space" DW-NOMINATE Scores with Bootstrapped Standard Errors (Joint House and Senate Scaling)* (2015), https://legacy.voteview.com/dwnomin_joint_house_and_senate.htm.
11. See Richard L. Hasen, "End of the Dialogue? Political Polarization, the Supreme Court, and Congress," *Southern California Law Review* 86 (January 2013): 235–237.
12. See Hasen, "End of the Dialogue?," 235–237; and *The Polarization of the Congressional Parties* (2016), https://legacy.voteview.com/political_polarization_2015.htm.
13. See Roberts and Smith, "Procedural Contexts, Party Strategy, and Conditional Party Voting in the U.S. House of Representatives, 1971–2000," 313.
14. See "Tracking Congress in the Age of Trump," *Five Thirty Eight*, April 26, 2018, https://projects.fivethirtyeight.com/congress-trump-score/.
15. See Susan Webb Hammond, *Congressional Caucuses in National Policy Making* (Baltimore, MD: Johns Hopkins University Press, 1998), 87–92.
16. See C. Lawrence Evans, "Committees, Leaders, and Message Politics," in *Congress Reconsidered,* 7th ed., ed. Lawrence C. Dodd and Bruce I. Oppenheimer (Washington, DC: Congressional Quarterly Press, 2001), 217–219.

17. Richard L. Hasen, "Polarization and the Judiciary," *Annual Review of Political Science* (2019), forthcoming.
18. See Amy Steigerwalt, *Battle over the Bench: Senators, Interest Groups, and Lower Court Confirmations* (Charlottesville: University of Virginia Press, 2010).
19. See Sarah A. Binder and Forrest Maltzman, "Advice and Consent: The Politics of Confirming Federal Judges," in *Congress Reconsidered,* 10th ed., ed. Dodd and Oppenheimer, 265–285; Roger H. Davidson, Walter J. Oleszek, and Frances E. Lee, *Congress and Its Members* (Washington, DC: CQ Press, 2008), 379–387.
20. See Binder and Maltzman, "Advice and Consent: The Politics of Confirming Federal Judges," 269–271; Elliot Slotnick, Sara Schiavoni, and Sheldon Goldman, "Obama's Judicial Legacy: The Final Chapter," *Journal of Law and Courts* 5 (Fall 2017): 376–380.
21. See Humberto Sanchez, "A Landmark Change to the Filibuster," *C.Q. Weekly Report*, December 2, 2013, 1992. For tables detailing a dramatic rise in filibusters tied to judicial and other executive branch nominations, see U.S. Senate, *Senate Action on Cloture Motions*, http://www.senate.gov/pagelayout/reference/cloture_motions/clotureCounts.htm (last visited December 9, 2013); Sahi Kapur, "Charts: Why the Filibuster May Soon Be Dead," *Talking Points Memo*, November 25, 2013, http://talkingpointsmemo.com/dc/chart-senate-democrats-filibuster-nuclear-option.
22. U.S. Senate, *Congressional Record* 151 (September 22, 2005): 21032 (statement of Senator Barack Obama).
23. Hasen, "End of the Dialogue?," 246–248.
24. Audrey Carlsen and Wilson Andrews, "How Senators Voted on the Gorsuch Confirmation," *New York Times*, April 7, 2017; Sheryl Gay Stolberg, "Senate Votes 50–48 to Put Kavanaugh on Supreme Court," *New York Times*, October 7, 2018, A1. We count two independents who caucus with Democrats as Democrats—Bernie Sanders of Vermont and Angus King of Maine.
25. Nina Totenberg and Carrie Johnson, "Merrick Garland Has a Reputation of Collegiality, Record of Republican Support," *National Public Radio*, March 16, 2016, https://www.npr.org/2016/03/16/126614141/merrick-garland-has-a-reputation-of-collegiality-record-of-republican-support.
26. Mitch McConnell and Chuck Grassley, "The American People Should Not Be Robbed of Their Say," *Washington Post*, February 19, 2016, A21.
27. Astead W. Herndon, "Filibuster Broken, Gorsuch Vote Is Set," *Boston Globe*, April 7, 2017, A-1.
28. Herndon, "Filibuster Broken, Gorsuch Vote Is Set," A-1; Matt Flegenheimer, "Republicans Gut Filibuster Rule to Lift Gorsuch," *New York Times*, April 7, 2017, A1. The first quotation is from Durbin, the second from Schumer.
29. Boris Shor and Nolan McCarty, "The Ideological Mapping of American Legislatures," *American Political Science Review* 105 (August 2011): 546–549; Boris Shor, "Polarization in American State Legislatures," in *American Gridlock: The Sources, Character, and Impact of Political Polarization*, ed. James A. Thurber and Antoine Yoshinaka (New York: Cambridge University Press, 2015), 205–211.

30. Thomas B. Edsall, "The State-by-State Revival of the Right," *New York Times*, October 8, 2014, http://www.nytimes.com/2014/10/08/opinion/the-state-by-state-revival-of-the-right.html?_r=0.
31. See Neal Devins, "Rethinking Judicial Minimalism: Abortion Politics, Party Polarization, and the Consequences of Returning the Constitution to Elected Government," *Vanderbilt Law Review* 69 (May 2016): 953–962.
32. Elizabeth Nash, Rachel Benson Gold, Lizamarie Mohammed, Zohra Ansari-Thomas, and Olivia Cappello, "Policy Trends in the States, 2017," Guttmacher Institute, January 2, 2018, https://www.guttmacher.org/article/2018/01/policy-trends-states-2017.
33. See Neal Devins and Saikrishna Bangalore Prakash, "Fifty States, Fifty Attorneys General, and Fifty Approaches to the Duty to Defend," *Yale Law Journal* 124 (April 2015): 2100.
34. Niraj Chokshi, "Seven Attorneys General Won't Defend Their Own State's Gay-Marriage Bans," *Washington Post*, February 20, 2014.
35. For an inventory of nondefenses, see Devins and Prakash, "Fifty States, Fifty Attorneys General, and Fifty Approaches to the Duty to Defend," 2177–2187.
36. Dan Levine, "Republican Attorneys General Target Obama 'Dreamer' Program," *Reuters*, June 29, 2017, https://www.reuters.com/article/us-usa-immigration-daca-idUSKBN19K334; Dylan Scott, "Why GOP Attorneys General Are Suing Obama over Any and Everything," *Talking Points Memo*, February 19, 2015, http://talkingpointsmemo.com/dc/republican-attorneys-general-obama-white-house-lawsuits.
37. Alexander Burns, "Democrats Appear to Find a Bulwark against Trump: Attorneys General," *New York Times*, February 7, 2017, A9; Marilyn Geewax, "Attorneys General of Maryland and D.C. Sue Trump over His Businesses," *National Public Radio*, June 12, 2017, http://www.npr.org/sections/thetwo-way/2017/06/12/532635888/attorneys-general-of-maryland-and-d-c-sue-trump-over-his-hotel.
38. Email by Democratic Attorneys General Association, Subject: "We're still suing Trump. A lot." Sent Monday July 9, 2018 at 4:35 pm.
39. Marc J. Hetherington, "Resurgent Mass Partisanship: The Role of Elite Polarization," *American Political Science Review* 95 (September 2001): 619.
40. Pew Research Center, *The Partisan Divide on Political Values Grows Even Wider,* October 5, 2017, 13, http://www.people-press.org/2017/10/05/the-partisan-divide-on-political-values-grows-even-wider/.
41. Pew Research Center, *The Partisan Divide*, 12.
42. Pew Research Center, *The Partisan Divide*, 3.
43. See Alan Abramowitz, *The Great Alignment: Race, Party Transformation, and the Rise of Donald Trump* (New Haven, CT: Yale University Press, 2018); and Patrick R. Miller and Pamela Johnston Conover, "Red and Blue States of Mind: Partisan Hostility and Voting in the United States," *Political Research Quarterly* 68 (June 2015): 225–239.

44. See Ilya Somin, "Knowledge about Ignorance: New Directions in the Study of Political Information," *Critical Review* 18 (2006): 260–262; Neal Devins, "The D'Oh! of Popular Constitutionalism," *Michigan Law Review* 105 (April 2007): 1340–1346.
45. See Matthew S. Levendusky and Neil Malhotra, "(Mis)perceptions of Partisan Polarization in the American Public," *Public Opinion Quarterly* 80 (2016): 378–391; Lilliana Mason, " 'I Disrespectfully Agree': The Differential Effects of Partisan Sorting on Social and Issue Polarization," *American Journal of Political Science* 59 (January 2015): 128–145.
46. Shanto Iyengar, Gaurav Sood, and Yphtach Lelkes, "Affect, Not Ideology: A Social Identity Perspective on Polarization," *Public Opinion Quarterly* 76 (2012): 405.
47. Pew Research Center, *Political Polarization in the American Public: How Increasing Ideological Uniformity and Partisan Antipathy Affects Politics, Compromise and Everyday Life,* June 12, 2014, 48, http://www.people-press.org/files/2014/06/6-12-2014-Political-Polarization-Release.pdf.
48. Iyengar, Sood, and Lelkes, "Affect, Not Ideology," 416.
49. Emily Badger and Niraj Chokshi, "Partisan Relations Sink from Cold to Deep Freeze," *New York Times*, June 16, 2017, A1.
50. Lee Rainie and Aaron Smith, "Social Networking Sites and Politics," *Pew Research Center,* March 12, 2012, 7.
51. Ezra Klein and Alvin Chang, " 'Political Identity Is Fair Game for Hatred': How Republicans and Democrats Discriminate," *Vox*, December 7, 2015, https://www.vox.com/2015/12/7/9790764/partisan-discrimination.
52. Klein and Chang, " 'Political Identity Is Fair Game for Hatred.' "
53. Yphtach Lelkes, "Mass Polarization: Manifestations and Measurements," *Public Opinion Quarterly* 80 (2016): 392–410.
54. Lelkes, "Mass Polarization: Manifestations and Measurements," 392.
55. See Herbert McClosky, "Consensus and Ideology in American Politics," *American Political Science Review* 58 (June 1964): 361–382; Peter Skerry, "The Class Conflict Over Abortion," *Public Interest* 52 (Summer 1978): 69–84.
56. Morris P. Fiorina et al., *Culture War? The Myth of a Polarized America,* 3rd ed. (New York: Pearson Longman, 2011), 200.
57. See Morris P. Fiorina and Matthew S. Levendusky, "Disconnected: The Political Class versus the People," in *Red and Blue Nation?: Characteristics and Causes of America's Polarized Politics,* ed. Pietro S. Nivola and David W. Brady (Baltimore: Brookings Institution Press, 2006), 49–71; Mark A. Graber, "The Coming Constitutional Yo-Yo? Elite Opinion, Polarization, and the Direction of Judicial Decision Making," *Howard Law Journal* 56 (Spring 2013): 693–712; Geoffrey C. Layman and Thomas M. Carsey, "Party Polarization and 'Conflict Extension' in the American Electorate," *American Journal of Political Science* 46 (October 2002): 789.
58. Pew Research Center for the People and the Press, *The 2005 Political Typology*, May 10, 2005, http://www.people-press.org/files/legacy-pdf/242.pdf (hereinafter Pew,

2005 Political Topology); Pew Research Center for the People and the Press, *Beyond Red vs. Blue: Political Typology*, May 4, 2011, http://www.people-press.org/files/legacy-pdf/Beyond-Red-vs-Blue-The-Political-Typology.pdf (hereinafter Pew, *2011 Political Topology*); Pew Research Center, *Beyond Red vs. Blue: The Political Typology*, June 26, 2014, http://www.people-press.org/files/2014/06/6-26-14-Political-Typology-release1.pdf (hereinafter Pew, *2014 Political Typology*).

59. Pew, *2005 Political Topology*, 64–65; Pew, *2011 Political Topology*, 105, 109, 111.
60. Graber, "The Coming Constitutional Yo-Yo?," 697. The findings cited in the Graber article in this passage are from the 2005 and 2011 Pew *Political Typology* studies.
61. Pew, *2011 Political Topology*, 20, 109, 111. The quotation is from p. 20.
62. Graber, "The Coming Constitutional Yo-Yo?," 698.
63. Graber, "The Coming Constitutional Yo-Yo?," 698.
64. Differences by education and partisanship in attitudes toward issues relating to discrimination and equality in 2017 are shown in Pew Research Center, *The Partisan Divide*, 31–37, 41–45.
65. Except for the Affordable Care Act, information on the decisions and surveys is provided in the notes accompanying Table 2.2. The survey on the Affordable Care Act was conducted in 2012, and "postgraduate" referred to a degree beyond an undergraduate degree. The Court's decision was *National Federation of Independent Business v. Sebelius*, 567 U.S. 512 (2012). The survey data are at USA Today, USA Today/Gallup Poll: Supreme Court Healthcare Law Ruling Reaction 5 (June 28, 2012) (version distributed by the Roper Center, Cornell University), https://ropercenter.cornell.edu/CFIDE/cf/action/catalog/ abstract.cfm?type=&start=&id=&archno=USAIPOUSA2012-TR0628&abstract=. The question was worded as follows: "As you may know, the U.S. Supreme Court has upheld the entire 2010 healthcare law, declaring it constitutional. Do you agree or disagree with this decision?"
66. The American National Election Study is an election-year survey conducted by the Inter-university Consortium for Political and Social Research; the 2016 study is ICPSR 36853. Study materials are at https://electionstudies.org/project/2016-time-series-study/. The analyses reported here were conducted with the dataset constructed by Charles Prysby and Carmine Scavo; the codebook is Prysby and Scavo, *SETUPS: Voting Behavior: The 2016 Election* (Ann Arbor: Inter-university Consortium for Political and Social Research, n.d.). The marriage question was V161231; the abortion question was V161232.
67. The response options referred to "gay and lesbian couples."
68. This survey, "1976 Time Series Study," is archived at https://electionstudies.org/data-center/. The question item was VAR763796. The question wording was the same as in the 2016 study, but the descriptions of alternative policies was somewhat different.
69. The same is true of attitudes toward the death penalty, another issue related to Supreme Court decisions that was included in the 2016 ANES survey.

70. Gallup News, *GOP Approval of Supreme Court Surges, Democrats' Slides,* September 28, 2017, http://news.gallup.com/poll/219974/gop-approval-supreme-court-surges-democrats-slides.aspx.
71. Ariel Edwards-Levy, "Republicans and Democrats Flip Support on the Supreme Court," *HuffPost*, July 6, 2018, https://www.huffingtonpost.com/entry/republicans-democrats-supreme-court_us_5b3bf493e4b09e4a8b285dfo.
72. Justices undoubtedly differ in the strength of this interest in reputation. For instance, "swing" Justices in the Court's ideological center may have less intense legal policy preferences than their colleagues and thus a stronger interest in maintaining their reputation among media and other elites. See Neal Devins and Will Federspiel, "The Supreme Court, Social Psychology, and Group Formation," in *The Psychology of Judicial Decision Making*, ed. David Klein and Gregory Mitchell (New York: Oxford University Press, 2010), 90–94.
73. David H. Weaver and G. Cleveland Wilhoit, *The American Journalist: A Portrait of U.S. News People and Their Work* (Bloomington: Indiana University Press, 1991), 28, 31; Stanley Rothman and S. Robert Lichter, "Personality, Ideology, and World View: A Comparison of Media and Business Elites," *British Journal of Political Science* 15 (1985): 36.
74. Kathleen Hall Jamieson and Joseph N. Cappella, *Echo Chamber: Rush Limbaugh and the Conservative Media Establishment* (New York: Oxford University Press, 2008), 216.
75. Seth Flaxman, Sharad Goel, and Justin M. Rao, "Filter Bubbles, Echo Chambers, and Online News Consumption," *Public Opinion Quarterly* 80 (January 2016): 298–299.
76. Thomas W. Hazlett and David W. Sosa, "Was the Fairness Doctrine a 'Chilling Effect'? Evidence from the Postderegulation Radio Market," *Journal of Legal Studies* 26 (January 1997): 279–301.
77. Cass R. Sunstein, "Deliberative Trouble? Why Groups Go to Extremes," *Yale Law Journal* 110 (October 2000): 101.
78. Eli Pariser, *The Filter Bubble: How the New Personalized Web Is Changing What We Read and How We Think* (New York: Penguin Press, 2011).
79. Matthew A. Baum and Tim Groeling, "New Media and the Polarization of American Political Discourse," *Political Communication* 25 (2008): 356.
80. Cass R. Sunstein, *Republic.com 2.0* (Princeton, NJ: Princeton University Press), 65.
81. See Pew Research Center, *Americans Spending More Time Following the News,* September 12, 2010, http://www.people-press.org/2010/09/12/americans-spending-more-time-following-the-news/ (hereinafter Pew, *Americans Following the News*); Pew Research Center, "Political Polarization & Media Habits: From Fox New to Facebook, How Liberals and Conservatives Keep Up with Politics," Pew Research Center, October 21, 2014, 2, http://assets.pewresearch.org/wp-content/uploads/sites/13/2014/10/Political-Polarization-and-Media-Habits-FINAL-REPORT-7-27-15.pdf (hereinafter Pew, *Political Polarization & Media Habits*). See also Dan

Bernhardt, Stefan Krasa, and Mattias Polborn, "Political Polarization and the Electoral Effects of Media Bias," *Journal of Public Economics* 92 (June 2008): 1092–1104.

82. Pew, *Americans Following the News*, 60.
83. Pew, *Americans Following the News*, 60.
84. Pew, *Political Polarization & Media Habits*, 2, 4, 5.
85. Pew, *Political Polarization & Media Habits*, 2, 4, 5.
86. See Ann Southworth, *Lawyers of the Right: Professionalizing the Conservative Coalition* (Chicago: University Chicago Press, 2008), 8–40.
87. Mark Tushnet, *A Court Divided: The Rehnquist Court and the Future of Constitutional Law* (New York: W. W. Norton & Company, 2005), 38–39.
88. Southworth, *Lawyers of the Right*, 13.
89. Southworth, *Lawyers of the Right*, 38.
90. Steven M. Teles, *The Rise of the Conservative Legal Movement: The Battle for Control of the Law* (Princeton, NJ: Princeton University Press, 2008), 90.
91. Teles, *The Rise of the Conservative Legal Movement*, 183–219; Erin Cady, "The John M. Olin Fellowships and the Advancement of Conservatism in Legal Academia," *Harvard Journal of Law & Public Policy* 39 (Summer 2016): 917–961.
92. Michael Avery and Danielle McLaughlin, *The Federalist Society: How Conservatives Took the Law Back from Liberals* (Nashville, TN: Vanderbilt University Press, 2013); Amanda Hollis-Brusky, *Ideas with Consequences: The Federalist Society and the Conservative Counterrevolution* (New York: Oxford University Press, 2015), 1.
93. Hollis-Brusky, *Ideas with Consequences*, 1–2; Teles, *The Rise of the Conservative Legal Movement*, 137–142.
94. Hollis-Brusky, *Ideas with Consequences*, 13–15. For a general description, see http://www.fed-soc.org.
95. See William E. Nelson et al., "The Liberal Tradition of the Supreme Court Clerkship: Its Rise, Fall, and Reincarnation?," *Vanderbilt Law Review* 62 (November 2009): 1775–1791; Mike Sacks, "Former Supreme Court Clerks Find Conservative Home on Hill," *National Law Journal*, August 17, 2015, http://www.nationallawjournal.com/id=1202734837405/Former-Supreme-Court-Clerks-Find-Conservative-Home-on-Hill?slreturn=20170824140146.
96. See Hollis-Brusky, *Ideas with Consequences*, 166–167.
97. David H. Weaver, Randal A. Beam, Bonnie J. Brownlee, Paul S. Voakes, and G. Cleveland Wilhoit, *The American Journalist in the 21st Century: U.S. News People at the Dawn of a New Millennium* (Mahweh, NJ: Lawrence Erlbaum Associates, 2007), 16–23; Adam Bonica, Adam S. Chilton, and Maya Sen, "The Political Ideologies of American Lawyers," *Journal of Legal Analysis* 8 (Winter 2016): 294.
98. Bonica et al., "Political Ideologies of American Lawyers"; Adam Bonica, Adam Chilton, Kyle Rozema, and Maya Sen, "The Legal Academy's Ideological Uniformity," *Journal of Legal Studies* 47 (January 2018): 1–43.

99. There were no standard deviations for the 1991–1993 terms because there was only one Democrat on the Court; Marshall retired before the 1991 term and White before the 1993 term.
100. When Stevens retired, it fell from 16.2 to 9.1 percent; when Souter retired, it fell to 4 percent.
101. Evidence about differences between Kennedy's and Kavanaugh's positions is discussed in Adam Feldman, "Expect Kavanaugh to Shift the Court Rightward—How Far No One Knows," *SCOTUSblog*, July 10, 2018, http://www.scotusblog.com/2018/07/empirical-scotus-expect-kavanaugh-to-shift-the-court-rightward-how-far-no-one-knows/.
102. See Lee Epstein, William M. Landes, and Richard A. Posner, "Revisiting the Ideology Rankings of Supreme Court Justices," *Journal of Legal Studies* 44 (January 2015): S313–314 and Table 3.2 (ranking—based on percentage of conservative votes cast—Roberts, Thomas, Alito, and Scalia as among the ten most conservative since 1937); Sai Prakash and John Yoo, "Gorsuch Makes a Mark on the Court," *Wall Street Journal*, June 29, 2017; and Adam Liptak, "Moderating Force as a Lawyer, a Conservative Stalwart as Judge," *New York Times*, July 10, 2018, A1 (on Kavanaugh).
103. Those decisions are *Burwell v. Hobby Lobby Stores*, 134 S. Ct. 2751 (2014) (interpreting the Religious Freedom Restoration Act to protect closely held corporations from a mandate to include certain contraceptives in employee health plans); *McCutcheon v. FEC*, 134 S. Ct. 1434 (2014) (striking down a federal statutory provision that put limits on an individual's total contributions to election candidates and candidate committees); *Shelby County v. Holder*, 570 U.S. 529 (2013) (striking down Title IV of the Voting Rights Act); *Florence v. Board of Chosen Freeholders*, 566 U.S. 318 (2012) (allowing routine strip searches of arrestees at jails); *AT&T Mobility LLC v. Concepcion*, 563 U.S. 333 (2011) (disallowing state restrictions on contract provisions prohibiting class actions in arbitration); *Arizona Free Enterprise Club's Freedom Club PAC v. Bennett*, 564 U.S. 721 (2011) (striking down a state system of public funding for candidates for state offices); and *Chamber of Commerce v Whiting*, 563 U.S. 582 (2011) (allowing sanctions on employers for hiring of undocumented aliens). In preparing this inventory of cases, we consulted with David Savage, author of the *Guide*.
104. Those cases are *Friedrichs v. California Teachers Association*, 136 S. Ct. 1083 (2016) (dividing four to four on whether mandatory fees to public sector unions violate free speech rights), and *United States v. Texas*, 136 S. Ct. 2271 (2016) (dividing four to four on legality of 2014 Obama immigration directive). For news stories speculating that these four-to-four splits were a Democratic-Republican split, see Adam Liptak, "Justices' 4-4 Tie Gives Unions Win in Labor Lawsuit," *New York Times*, March 30, 2016, A1; Robert Barnes, "Plan to Shield Illegal Immigrants Suffers Loss," *Washington Post*, June 24, 2016, A1. In other high-profile cases (involving a religious liberty challenge to the Affordable Care Act and article

III standing limits on class action lawsuits), the Justices may well have masked partisan divisions by issuing ambiguous, inconclusive opinions. See Mark Joseph Stern, "SCOTUS Misses an Opportunity to Gut Class Actions and Consumer Privacy Laws," *Slate,* May 16, 2016, http://www.slate.com/blogs/the_slatest/2016/05/16/spokeo_v_robins_spares_class_actions_and_consumer_privacy.html; Garrett Epps, "The U.S. Supreme Court's Nonsense Ruling in *Zubik*," *The Atlantic,* May 16, 2016, http://www.theatlantic.com/politics/archive/2016/05/the-supreme-courts-non-sensical-ruling-in-zubik/482967/.

105. The two decisions that clearly qualify as important are *Trump v. Hawaii*, 138 S. Ct. 2392 (2018) (upholding a presidential proclamation restricting entrance to the U.S. by nationals of certain nations); and *Janus v. American Federation of State, County, and Municipal Employees*, 138 S. Ct. 2448 (2018) (prohibiting requirements that non-union members among public employees contribute fees to unions for collecting bargaining). The two other decisions that might qualify as important are *National Institute of Family and Life Advocates v. Becerra*, 138 S. Ct. 2361 (2018) (striking down one provision of a state law that requires certain notices by pro-life pregnancy centers and questioning a second provision); and *Epic Systems Corp. v. Lewis*, 138 S. Ct. 1612 (2018) (holding that agreements prohibiting employees from bringing class actions against employers in arbitration are enforceable).
106. Thomas M. Keck, *Judicial Politics in Polarized Times* (Chicago: University of Chicago Press, 2014), 149.
107. Lawrence Baum, *The Supreme Court*, 12th ed. (Washington, DC: CQ Press, 2016), 35–40.
108. C. Herman Pritchett, *The Roosevelt Court: A Study in Judicial Politics and Values, 1937–1947* (New York: Macmillan Company, 1948); Eric A. Posner, "Casual with the Court," *New Republic*, October 24, 2011.
109. See Adam Liptak, "Why Newer Appointees Offer Fewer Surprises from Bench," *New York Times*, April 18, 2010, Y1.
110. David Alistair Yalof, *Pursuit of Justices* (Chicago: University of Chicago Press, 1999), 134.
111. See Keith E. Whittington, *Political Foundations of Judicial Supremacy: The Presidency, the Supreme Court, and Constitutional Leadership in U.S. History* (Princeton, NJ: Princeton University Press, 2007), 274–279.
112. Teles, *The Rise of the Conservative Legal Movement*, 141–142.
113. See Yalof, *Pursuit of Justices*, 142–165.
114. Reflecting perceptions of those records, the four nominees all had Segal-Cover scores below .100. Jeffrey Segal, "Perceived Qualifications and Ideology of Supreme Court Nominees, 1937–2012," https://www.stonybrook.edu/commcms/polisci/jsegal/QualTable.pdf.
115. Douglas E. Kneeland, "Reagan Pledges Woman on Court; Carter Challenges Foe on Economy," *New York Times*, October 15, 1980, A1. On the array of

considerations that may have affected the choice of O'Connor, see Christine L. Nemacheck, *Strategic Selection: Presidential Nomination of Supreme Court Justices from Herbert Hoover through George W. Bush* (Charlottesville: University of Virginia Press, 2008), 9–13.

116. Yalof, *Pursuit of Justices*, 145–146. Kennedy's Segal-Cover score put him decidedly to the left of Bork and Ginsburg. Bork's score was .095, Ginsburg's .000, and Kennedy's .365. Segal, "Perceived Qualifications and Ideology of Supreme Court Nominees, 1937–2012."
117. The Senate confirmed Kennedy unanimously.
118. See Jan Crawford Greenburg, *Supreme Conflict: The Inside Story of the Struggle for Control of the United States Supreme Court* (New York: Penguin Group, 2007), 87–110.
119. See Yalof, *Pursuit of Justices*, 191; Greenburg, *Supreme Conflict*, 100–101.
120. Greenburg, *Supreme Conflict*, 110.
121. Jeremy Rabkin, "The Sorry Tale of David Souter, Stealth Justice," *Weekly Standard*, November 6, 1995, 30; James MacGregor Burns, *Packing the Court: The Rise of Judicial Power and the Coming Crisis of the Supreme Court* (New York: Penguin Group, 2009), 217.
122. Yalof, *Pursuit of Justices*, 194.
123. E.g., Robert Novak, "No More Souters," *Townhall*, February 12, 2001, http://townhall.com/columnists/robertnovak/2001/02/12/no_more_souters. See also Jason DeParle, "In Battle to Pick Next Justice, Right Says Avoid a Kennedy," *New York Times*, June 27, 2005, A1.
124. Jeffrey Toobin, *The Nine* (New York: Anchor Books, 2008), 266–270.
125. Toobin, *The Nine*, 297.
126. See Toobin, *The Nine*, 286–287.
127. Erwin Chemerinsky, "Senators Must Tell Miers: No Answers, No Confirmation," *Baltimore Sun*, October 6, 2005, http://articles.baltimoresun.com/2005-10-06/news/0510060065_1_miers-chief-justice-justice-rehnquist. On stealth candidates, see Fred Barnes, "Souter-Phobia," *Weekly Standard*, August 1, 2005, 11–12.
128. Alan Rappeport and Charlie Savage, "Trump Offers a List of Possible Supreme Court Nominees Who Reflect His Principles," *New York Times*, May 19, 2016, A16; Megan Carpenter, "Trump's Supreme Court Picks: From Tea Party Senator to Anti-Abortion Crusader," *The Guardian*, September 24, 2016; Michael D. Shear, "Trump Names Supreme Court Candidates for a Nonexistent Vacancy," *New York Times*, November 17, 2017, https://www.nytimes.com/2017/11/17/us/politics/trump-supreme-court.html; Jeffrey Toobin, "Full-Court Press: The Impresario behind Neil Gorsuch's Confirmation," *New Yorker*, April 17, 2017, 24–28.
129. Steven M. Teles, "Transformative Bureaucracy: Reagan's Lawyers and the Dynamics of Political Investment," *Studies in American Political Development* 23 (April 2009): 61.

130. Teles, "Transformative Bureaucracy," 76 (quoting Kenneth Cribb, who served as counselor to the attorney general).
131. Edwin Meese, III, "The Supreme Court of the United States: Bulwark of a Limited Constitution," *South Texas Law Review* 27 (Fall 1986): 464. This article was originally presented as a speech in July 1985. See also Teles, "Transformative Bureaucracy," 80–81.
132. Teles, "Transformative Bureaucracy," 75–82.
133. Teles, *The Rise of the Conservative Legal Movement*, 136.
134. Teles, "Transformative Bureaucracy," 76 (citing Meese and quoting Department of Justice official Kenneth Cribb).
135. Teles, "Transformative Bureaucracy," 74.
136. Teles, "Transformative Bureaucracy," 68, 74.
137. Teles, "Transformative Bureaucracy," 74 (quoting Kenneth Cribb).
138. Teles, "Transformative Bureaucracy," 73.
139. Amanda L. Hollis-Brusky, *The Reagan Administration and the Rehnquist Court's New Federalism: Understanding the Role of the Federalist Society* (Berkeley, CA: bepress, 2008), 16.
140. Hollis-Brusky, *The Reagan Administration and the Rehnquist Court's New Federalism*, 16.
141. Michael Avery and Danielle McLaughlin, "How Conservatives Captured the Law," *Chronicle of Higher Education*, April 15, 2013.
142. Avery and McLaughlin, "How Conservatives Captured the Law."
143. Stephen Markman, "Judicial Selection: The Reagan Years," in *Judicial Selection: Merit, Ideology, and Politics*, ed. Henry J. Abraham et al. (Washington, DC: National Legal Center for the Public Interest, 1990), 33.
144. Nancy Scherer and Banks Miller, "The Federalist Society's Influence on the Federal Judiciary," *Political Research Quarterly* 62 (June 2009): 367.
145. Scherer and Miller, "The Federalist Society's Influence on the Federal Judiciary," 367; Charles Lane, "Roberts Listed in Federalist Society '97–98 Directory; Court Nominee Said He Has No Memory of Membership," *Washington Post,* July 25, 2005, A1.
146. Avery and McLaughlin, "How Conservatives Captured the Law"; Scherer and Miller, "The Federalist Society's Influence on the Federal Judiciary," 368 (noting that around two-thirds of Bush's first-term judicial nominees were Federalist Society members).
147. Tessa Berenson, "Here's What to Know about President Trump's 3 Supreme Court Finalists," *Time*, January 31, 2017, http://time.com/4650544/supreme-court-nominees-donald-trump/.
148. Teles, "Transformative Bureaucracy," 70–71.
149. *The Meese Department of Justice: Its Accomplishments and Its Relevance Today*, http://www.fed-soc.org/multimedia/detail/the-meese-department-of-justice-its-accomplishments-and-its-relevance-today-event-audio (remarks of T. Kenneth Cribb, Jr., Counselor to Attorney General Meese in 1985–1987).

150. Greenburg, *Supreme Conflict*, 95–101.
151. Hollis-Brusky, *Ideas with Consequences*, 154.
152. See Hollis-Brusky, *Ideas with Consequences*, 153 (quoting Federalist Society member Tony Cotto as saying, "No Fed Society credentials, that's going to hurt you. It hurt Harriet [Miers] a lot. . . . We want credentials. We want to see you've spoken at Federalist Society conferences, we want to know you've been to dinners, gripping and grinning").
153. See "Miers v. The Federalist Society," *Daily Kos*, October 7, 2005.
154. Todd J. Zywicki, "A Great Mind?," *Legal Times*, October 10, 2005, 2.
155. David D. Kirkpatrick, "In Alito, G.O.P. Reaps Harvest Planted in '82," *New York Times*, January 30, 2006, A1. See also Greenburg, *Supreme Conflict*, 269–270.
156. The Heritage Foundation, another leading conservative organization, also played a key role in the process of identifying potential Trump nominees. Edward-Isaac Dovere, "The Man Who Picked the Next Supreme Court Justice," *Politico*, January 30, 2017, https://www.politico.com/story/2017/01/trump-supreme-court-justice-mcdonald-234352/.
157. Lawrence Baum and Neal Devins, "Federalist Court: How the Federalist Society Became the De Facto Selector of Republican Supreme Court Justices," *Slate*, January 31, 2017; see also Toobin, "Full-Court Press," *New Yorker*, 27–28.
158. See Baum and Devins, "Federalist Court."
159. Eric Lipton and Jeremy W. Peters, "Conservatives Press Overhaul in the Judiciary," *New York Times*, March 19, 2017, A1.
160. Zoe Tillman, "After Eight Years on the Sidelines, This Conservative Group Is Primed to Reshape the Courts under Trump," *Buzzfeed News*, November 20, 2017, https://www.buzzfeed.com/zoetillman/after-eight-years-on-the-sidelines-this-conservative-group?utm_term=.kpVKKQ4v4#.nsEllW282.
161. Joel Achenbach, "The List Helping Trump Reshape Supreme Court," *Washington Post*, July 9, 2018, A1; Mark Landler and Maggie Haberman, "Former Bush Aide is Trump Pick for Court," *New York Times*, July 10, 2018, A1; and Ashley Parker and Robert Costa, "President Wavered Late on Nominee Decision," *Washington Post*, July 11, 2018, A1.
162. Southworth, *Lawyers of the Right*, 135–141.
163. Anthony Paik, Ann Southworth, and John P. Heinz, "Lawyers of the Right: Networks and Organizations," *Law & Social Inquiry* 32 (Fall 2007): 906–909.
164. Quoted in Hollis-Brusky, *Ideas with Consequences*, 152.
165. Yalof, *Pursuit of Justices*, 196; Toobin, *The Nine*, 70–71. The quotation is from Yalof.
166. See Elizabeth Drew, *On the Edge: The Clinton Presidency* (New York: Simon & Schuster, 1994), 217–218; Toobin, *The Nine*, 70.
167. Drew, *On the Edge*, 219.
168. On the unhappiness of some liberals about Breyer's appointment, see Greenburg, *Supreme Conflict*, 182; Drew, *On the Edge*, 214. On Obama's appointments, see Peter Baker, "Favorites of Left Don't Make Obama's Court List," *New York Times*, May 26,

2009, A12, and Jeffrey Toobin, "Bench Press: Are Obama's Judges Really Liberals?," *New Yorker*, September 21, 2009, 42. The Segal-Cover scores (Segal, "Perceived Qualifications and Ideology of Supreme Court Nominees, 1937–2012") for these four nominees underline the difference: .680 for Ginsburg, .475 for Breyer, .780 for Sotomayor, and .730 for Kagan. In contrast, Roberts's score was .120 and Alito's .100.

169. Jeffrey Toobin, "Obama's Unfinished Judicial Legacy," *New Yorker*, July 31, 2012, https://www.newyorker.com/news/daily-comment/obamas-unfinished-judicial- legacy.
170. Elliot Slotnick, Sara Schiavoni, and Sheldon Goldman, "Obama's Judicial Legacy: The Final Chapter," *Journal of Law and Courts* 5 (2017): 413. For a discussion of Clinton, see Sheldon Goldman and Matthew D. Saronson, "Clinton's Nontraditional Judges: Creating a More Representative Branch," *Judicature* 78 (September–October 1994): 68–73. In its first eighteen months, the Trump administration's appointees were overwhelmingly white males. Trump's two Supreme Court picks were white men; overall, 90 percent were white and 77 percent were male. Rorie Solberg and Eric N. Waltenburg. "Trump's Choice to Replace Justice Kennedy Will Likely Be a White Man, Like His Other Court Nominees," *The Conversation*, June 29, 2018, http://theconversation.com/trumps-choice-to-replace-justice-kennedy-will-likely-be-a-white-man-like-his-other-court-nominees-99129.
171. Mark Tushnet, *In the Balance: Law and Politics on the Roberts Court* (New York: W. W. Norton & Company, 2013), 74.
172. Matt Grossman and David A. Hopkins, *Asymmetric Politics: Ideological Republicans and Group Interest Democrats* (New York: Oxford University Press, 2016); Matt Grossman and David A. Hopkins, "Ideological Republicans and Group Interest Democrats: The Asymmetry of American Party Politics," *Perspectives on Politics* 13 (March 2015): 119–139.
173. See Teles, *The Rise of the Conservative Legal Movement*, 22–57.
174. The scores are compiled at http://faculty.georgetown.edu/baileyma/JOPIdealPointsJan2013.htm. The method for creating them is discussed in Michael A. Bailey, "Is Today's Court the Most Conservative in Sixty Years? Challenges and Opportunities in Measuring Judicial Preferences," *Journal of Politics* 75 (July 2013): 821–834. Because these scores were compiled only through calendar year 2011, only two terms are available for Justice Sotomayor and one term for Justice Kagan, but the stability of their voting records relative to their colleagues since that time indicates that their scores over a more extended period would be similar.
175. The Bailey scores are for calendar years rather than Court terms. Calculations in this paragraph were prepared by the authors based on scores compiled by Bailey.
176. See Adam Liptak and Alicia Parlapiano, "How Clinton's or Trump's Nominees Could Affect the Balance of the Supreme Court," *New York Times*, September 25, 2016, https://www.nytimes.com/interactive/2016/09/25/us/politics/

how-clintons-or-trumps-nominees-could-affect-the-balance-of-the-supreme-court.html.

177. Each entry in the table refers to a pair of terms. Thus, "2005–2006," for instance, includes the 2005 and 2006 terms of the Court.

   Percentages in the table were calculated from data in the Supreme Court Database, archived at http://scdb.wustl.edu/. Cases were included if they were decided after oral argument. Civil liberties cases are those under issue areas 1 through 6 in the Database. Criteria for coding of votes as conservative or liberal are described in the documentation for the database. Justice Alito participated in only 72 percent of the civil liberties cases in the 2005–2006 terms, so his proportion of conservative votes for those terms is not fully comparable with the proportions for the other Justices. Before his death in February 2016, Justice Scalia participated in only six civil liberties cases in the 2015 term.

178. See Brendan Nyhan, "Supreme Court: Liberal Drift v. Conservative Overreach," *New York Times*, June 25, 2015, http://www.nytimes.com/2015/06/26/upshot/supreme-court-liberal-drift-v-conservative-overreach.html; Kevin T. McGuire, George Vanberg, Charles E. Smith Jr., and Gregory A. Caldeira, "Measuring Policy Content on the U.S. Supreme Court," *Journal of Politics* 71 (October 2009): 1305–1321; and Richard Primus, "Senator Flake Isn't a Liberal, and Neither Is Chief Justice Roberts," *Balkinization*, December 1, 2017, https://balkin.blogspot.com/2017/12/senator-flake-isnt-liberal-and-neither.html.

179. As discussed in chapter 3, conservatives who were disappointed with the relative liberalism of some Republican appointees to the Court ascribed their movement to the left as the result of their desire to win favorable coverage by national news media, including the *New York Times*, for which Linda Greenhouse was the long-time Supreme Court reporter.

180. *National Federation of Independent Business v. Sebelius*, 567 U.S. 519 (2012). See John C. Yoo, "Chief Justice Roberts and His Apologists," *Wall Street Journal*, June 29, 2012, https://www.law.berkeley.edu/article/john-yoo-chief-justice-roberts-and-his-apologists/.

181. *CNN Reagan Library Debate: Later Debate Full Transcript,* September 16, 2015, http://cnnpressroom.blogs.cnn.com/2015/09/16/cnn-reagan-library-debate-later-debate-full-transcript; Bob Egelko, "Trump, Rubio Weigh in on Supreme Court Ahead of Debate," *San Francisco Chronicle*, December 14, 2015.

182. Adam Liptak, "Chief Justice John Roberts Amasses a Conservative Record, and Wrath from the Right," *New York Times*, September 29, 2015, A16.

183. Roberts's Martin-Quinn scores also highlight his relative conservatism, as does a competing ideological ranking devised by William Landes and Judge Richard Posner. William M. Landes and Richard A. Posner, "Rational Judicial Behavior: A Statistical Study," *Journal of Legal Analysis* 1 (Summer 2009): 782–783.

184. See Adam Liptak, "Angering Conservatives and Liberals, Chief Justice Roberts Defends Steady Restraint," *New York Times*, June 27, 2015, A13; Richard J. Lazarus,

"Back to 'Business' at the Supreme Court: The 'Administrative Side' of Chief Justice Roberts," *Harvard Law Review Forum* 129 (2015), http://harvardlawreview.org/2015/11/back-to-business-at-the-supreme-court-the-administrative-side-of-chief-justice-roberts; Chris Geidner, "Chief Justice John Roberts Has Changed a Little Bit, and That Could Be a Big Deal," *BuzzFeed News*, January 21, 2018, https://www.buzzfeed.com/chrisgeidner/chief-justice-john-roberts-has-changed-a-little-bit-and?utm_term=.fxWV1jZBpO#.ldEXWybOg7; and Primus, "Senator Flake Isn't a Liberal, and Neither Is Chief Justice Roberts."

185. Voting trends in economic cases (those that fall in issue areas 7 and 8 in the Supreme Court Database) are more difficult to track than those in civil liberties because of the smaller numbers of economic cases and the greater difficulty of defining conservative and liberal positions in that field. But Roberts's voting record in economic cases relative to the Court's other conservatives shows no movement to the left over time. His position is symbolized by his joining the conservative majority in what are probably the two most important economic decisions of the 2017 term, *Janus v. AFSCME* (2018) and *Epic Systems Corp. v. Lewis* (2018). Both decisions involved employer-employee relations.
186. Simon van Zuylen-Wood, "Little Scalia," *New York Magazine*, May 28, 2018, http://nymag.com/daily/intelligencer/2018/05/how-gorsuch-became-the-second-most-polarizing-man-in-d-c.html.
187. Hollis-Brusky, *Ideas with Consequences*, 21.
188. This paragraph draws from Lawrence Baum, *Judges and Their Audiences: A Perspective on Judicial Behavior* (Princeton, NJ: Princeton University Press, 2006), 132–135.
189. Marc Fisher, "The Private World of Justice Thomas," *Washington Post*, September 11, 1995, B1.
190. Lee Roderick, *Leading the Charge: Orrin Hatch and 20 Years of America* (Carson City, NV: Gold Leaf Press, 1994), 369–370.
191. Baum, *Judges and Their Audiences*, 133–134.
192. Clarence Thomas, *Address before the Federalist Society at the 1999 National Lawyers Convention,* November 12, 1999, http://www.fed-soc.org/publications/detail/clarence-thomas-address-before-the-federalist-society-at-the-1999-national-lawyers-convention.
193. Yale Law School, *Justice Clarence Thomas '74 Visits the Law School; Meets with Student Groups, Teaches Class,* December 14, 2011, https://www.law.yale.edu/yls-today/news/justice-clarence-thomas-74-visits-law-school-meets-student-groups-teaches-class.
194. The source is "scotusmap," http://www.scotusmap.com/, which compiles information on public appearances by the Justices.
195. Alex Swoyer, "Justice Thomas Warns of a 'Cynical' Society: 'It's Got to Be More Positive,'" *Washington Times*, March 11, 2018, https://www.washingtontimes.com/news/2018/mar/11/clarence-thomas-supreme-court-justice-warns-cynica/.

196. The conversation is at "Conversation with Bill Kristol," http://conversationswithbillkristol.org/video/clarence-thomas/.
197. Ariane de Vogue, "In Rare Interview, Clarence Thomas Calls Gorsuch 'Outstanding,'" *CNN*, November 2, 2017, https://www.cnn.com/2017/11/02/politics/clarence-thomas-neil-gorsuch/index.html.
198. Neil A. Lewis, "2 Years after His Bruising Hearing, Justice Thomas Can Rarely Be Heard," *New York Times*, November 27, 1993, A7. See also Jeffrey Toobin, "The Burden of Clarence Thomas," *New Yorker*, September 27, 1993, 39; Joan Biskupic, "Thomas Is Bolder, Confident—Outside Court," *USA Today*, January 31, 2001, 6A.
199. Teles, *The Rise of the Conservative Legal Movement*, 141–142; Joan Biskupic, *American Original: The Life and Constitution of Supreme Court Justice Antonin Scalia* (New York: Sarah Crichton Books, 2009), 5.
200. Joan Biskupic, *American Original*, 7.
201. Antonin Scalia, *Financial Disclosure Report for Calendar Year 2012*, May 15, 2013, 3, http://pfds.opensecrets.org/N99999921_2012.pdf. The financial disclosure reports indicate reimbursed travel, so they do not include appearances in Washington, DC.
202. Laura Lundquist, "Supreme Court Justice Is Draw for Conservative Luncheon," *Bozeman Chronicle*, August 19, 2013, http://www.bozemandailychronicle.com/news/politics/%20article_4659375c-0957-11e3-8ea5-0019bb2963f4.html.
203. Antonin Scalia, *Financial Disclosure Report for Calendar Year 2014*, May 15, 2015, 3, http://www.documentcloud.org/documents/2157458-scalia-antonin-2014.html.
204. Antonin Scalia, *Financial Disclosure Report for Calendar Year 2012*, May 15, 2013, 3, https://www.judicialwatch.org/document-archive/antonin-scalia-2012/. On the Friends of Abe, see Amy Fagan, "Hollywood's Conservative Underground," *Washington Times*, July 23, 2008, A1.
205. Bill Mears, "Justice Scalia Set to Address Tea Party Caucus on Capitol Hill," *CNN*, January 21, 2011, http://www.cnn.com/2011/POLITICS/01/21/scotus.scalia.tea.party.
206. "Clarence Thomas: Honor Scalia by Reining in Government," *Chicago Tribune*, November 17, 2016.
207. Tushnet, *A Court Divided: The Rehnquist Court and the Future of Constitutional Law*, 49.
208. Samuel A. Alito, *Financial Disclosure Report for Calendar Year 2010*, May 12, 2010, 3, http://pfds.opensecrets.org/N99999926_2010.pdf; Samuel A. Alito, *Financial Disclosure Report for Calendar Year 2011*, August 13, 2012, 2–3 http://pfds.opensecrets.org/N99999926_2011.pdf. The Manhattan Institute for Public Policy describes its mission and activities at https://www.manhattan-institute.org/about.
209. Jeff Shesol, "Should Justices Keep Their Opinions to Themselves?," *New York Times*, June 29, 2011, A23. The 2010 appearance featured a confrontation with a

liberal blogger who challenged Alito's involvement in a fundraising dinner. Debra Cassens Weiss, "Blogger Loudly Questions Alito's Dinner Attendance, Tapes Irate Security Guard," *American Bar Association Journal*, November 11, 2010, http://www.abajournal.com/news/article/blogger_loudly_questions_alitos_dinner_attendance_tapes_irate_security_guar.

210. See Mark Sherman, "Supreme Court Justice Samuel Alito Takes on Critics, Defends Citizens United," *Christian Science Monitor*, November 17, 2012, https://www.csmonitor.com/USA/Latest-News-Wires/2012/1117/Supreme-Court-Justice-Samuel-Alito-takes-on-critics-defends-Citizens-United.
211. Linda Greenhouse, "It's All Right with Sam," *New York Times*, January 7, 2015, http://www.nytimes.com/2015/01/08/opinion/its-all-right-with-samuel-alito.html?rref=collection%2Fcolumn%2Flinda.
212. These events are reported in the compilation of the Justices' appearances at scotusmap, http://www.scotusmap.com/.
213. Calvin TerBeek, "Is Justice Alito a Crit (or Just a Movement Conservative)?," *Faculty Lounge*, May 4, 2017, http://www.thefacultylounge.org/2017/05/is-justice-alito-a-crit.html.
214. Adam Liptak et al., "For Court Pick, Painful Lesson from Boyhood," *New York Times*, February 5, 2017, A1.
215. Neil Gorsuch, "Liberals & Lawsuits," *National Review*, February 7, 2005.
216. Toobin, "Full-Court Press," 28.
217. A few months after his appointment, Gorsuch also traveled with Senate Majority Leader Mitch McConnell of Kentucky for appearances at the McConnell Center at the University of Louisville and the University of Kentucky. McConnell had been instrumental in preventing Senate consideration of President Obama's Supreme Court nominee Merrick Garland and thus leaving the vacancy that Gorsuch filled. Gorsuch received some criticism for making the trip with McConnell. Charles Pierce, "So, What's Neil Gorsuch Up to These Days?," *Esquire*, September 25, 2017, http://www.esquire.com/news-politics/politics/a12465124/neil-gorsuch-mitch-mcconnell/.
218. Adam Liptak, "Gorsuch Talk at Trump Site Generates Ethical Issues," *New York Times*, August 18, 2017, A12.
219. Josh Gerstein, "Gorsuch Takes Victory Lap at Federalist Dinner," *Politico*, November 16, 2017, https://www.politico.com/story/2017/11/16/neil-gorsuch-federalist-society-speech-scotus-246538.
220. Paul M. Barrett, "Thomas Is Emerging as Strong Conservative Out to Prove Himself," *Wall Street Journal*, April 27, 1993, A6; and van Zuylen-Wood, "Little Scalia."
221. Information on Kavanaugh's participation in activities of the Federalist Society and other conservative groups is taken from the Society website, https://fedsoc.org/, and from his responses to the questionnaire of the Senate Judiciary

Committee in 2018, https://www.judiciary.senate.gov/press/rep/releases/judge-kavanaugh-returns-senate-judiciary-questionnaire.

222. Peter Baker, "A 3-Decade Dream for Conservatives Is within Reach," *New York Times*, July 10, 2018, A1.
223. Robert Barnes, "Federalists Relish Well-Placed Friends: President, Several Justices Help Celebrate Legal Society's 25 Years of Conservatism," *Washington Post*, November 16, 2007, A3.
224. *7th Annual Barbara K. Olson Memorial Lecture*, November 16, 2007, http://www.fed-soc.org/multimedia/detail/7th-annual-barbara-k-olson-memorial-lecture-event-audiovideo.
225. Toobin, "Full-Court Press," 28.
226. Artemus Ward and David L. Weiden, *Sorcerers' Apprentices: 100 Years of Law Clerks at the United States Supreme Court* (New York: New York University Press, 2006).
227. Todd C. Peppers, *Courtiers of the Marble Palace: The Rise and Influence of the Supreme Court Law Clerk* (Stanford, CA: Stanford University Press, 2006), 34–37.
228. Amy Bach, "Movin' on Up with the Federalist Society: How the Right Rears Its Young Lawyers," *Nation*, September 13, 2001.
229. Adam Bonica, Adam S. Chilton, Jacob Goldin, Kyle Rozema, and Maya Sen, "Measuring Judicial Ideology Using Law Clerk Hiring," *American Law and Economics Review* 19 (April 2017): 156. By another calculation with the same measure, the sets of clerks hired by those five Justices were among the seven most conservative sets (p. 143).
230. Corey Ditslear and Lawrence Baum, "Selection of Law Clerks and Polarization in the U.S. Supreme Court," *Journal of Politics* 63 (August 2001): 869–885; Lawrence Baum, "Hiring Supreme Court Law Clerks: Probing the Ideological Linkage between Judges and Justices," *Marquette Law Review* 98 (Fall 2014): 333–360; Adam Liptak, "A Sign of Court's Polarization: Choice of Clerks," *New York Times*, September 7, 2010, A1; Geoffrey R. Stone, "The Difference between Conservative and Liberal Justices," *Huffington Post*, November 2, 2013, http://www.huffingtonpost.com/geoffrey-r-stone/the-difference-between-co_b_4205674.html.
231. The percentages in the table were calculated from the information sheets compiled by the Court each term, *Law Clerks—October Term [various years]: Law Schools and Prior Clerkships*, and from reports in the *Above the Law* blog, http://abovethelaw.com. Clerks who served only in state courts and those who served in a court of appeals with the hiring Justice are excluded. For clerks who served multiple lower-court judges, the most recent clerkship is counted.

    Justice Gorsuch is not included in the table because all eight of his clerks in the 2016 and 2017 terms had served with him in the Tenth Circuit. Of those eight clerks, one also served with the conservative Fifth Circuit judge Edith Jones, three with Justice Scalia, one with Justice Alito, and one with Justice Sotomayor. David Lat, "Supreme Court Clerk Hiring Watch: Meet Justice Neil Gorsuch's Clerks," *Above the Law*, April 7, 2017, http://abovethelaw.com/2017/04/supreme-court-clerk-hiring-watch-meet-justice-neil-gorsuchs-clerks/.

232. Ditslear and Baum, "Selection of Law Clerks and Polarization in the U.S. Supreme Court."

233. Christopher D. Kromphardt, "Fielding an Excellent Team: Law Clerk Selection and Chambers Structure at the U.S. Supreme Court," *Marquette Law Review* 98 (Fall 2014): 289–311.

234. Jon O. Newman, *Benched: Abortion, Terrorists, Drones, Crooks, Supreme Court, Kennedy, Nixon, Demi Moore, and Other Tales from the Life of a Federal Judge* (Getzville, NY: William S. Hein & Co., 2017), 40.

235. Dahlia Lithwick and Mark Joseph Stern, "The Clarence Thomas Takeover," *Slate*, August 2, 2017.

236. See Richard H. Pildes, "Why the Center Does Not Hold: The Causes of Hyperpolarized Democracy in America," *California Law Review* 99 (April 2011): 290.

237. Teles, *The Rise of the Conservative Legal Movement*, 28–29.

238. Crystal Nix Hines, "Young Liberal Law Group Is Expanding," *New York Times*, June 1, 2001, A17.

239. Alexander Wohl, "Liberalizing the Law," *Nation*, June 16, 2003, 6; Carol D. Leonnig, "Dancing? It's Good for the Constitution: Janet Reno and Friends Try an Unconservative Approach," *Washington Post*, August 4, 2003, C1; Tresa Baldas, "Law School Turf War Ignites," *National Law Journal*, April 26, 2004, 1, 12.

240. The most recent keynote speakers were Ginsburg in 2015 and Sotomayor in 2014. See Adam Liptak, "Justices Get Out More, but Calendars Aren't Open to Just Anyone," *New York Times*, June 1, 2015, http://www.nytimes.com/2015/06/02/us/politics/Justices-get-out-more-but-calendars-arent-open-to-just-anyone.html. Breyer's 2017 speech was noted by the society at https://www.acslaw.org/convention/2017. Breyer was also the keynote speaker at the banquet of the ACS national conference in 2004; see *Justice Stephen Breyer at the 2004 Annual Convention*, http://www.acslaw.org/news/video/justice-stephen-breyer-at-the-2004-annual-convention. And Ginsburg spoke at the first national conference in 2003, "because the Society's mission is important to the health and welfare of our Nation." Ruth Bader Ginsburg, "Looking beyond Our Borders: The Value of a Comparative Perspective in Constitutional Adjudication," *Yale Law & Policy Review* 22 (Spring 2004): 329.

241. Tushnet, *A Court Divided: The Rehnquist Court and the Future of Constitutional Law*, 90.

242. Richard L. Hasen, "Celebrity Justice: Supreme Court Edition," *Green Bag 2d* 19 (2016): 171 note 33. The study also found no record of a sitting conservative Justice speaking to the ACS annual meeting.

243. See Table 4.3.
244. Among the books are Irin Carmon and Shana Knizhnik, *Notorious RBG: The Life and Times of Ruth Bader Ginsburg* (New York: Simon & Schuster, 2016), and Debbie Levy, *I Dissent: Ruth Bader Ginsburg Makes Her Mark* (New York: Simon & Schuster, 2016). The movies were *RBG*, an admiring documentary that was released in 2018, and *On the Basis of Sex*, a Hollywood feature about Ginsburg's work as a litigator, scheduled for release later in 2018.
245. Richard L. Hasen, "Celebrity Justice: R.B.G. Edition," *Los Angeles Times*, February 15, 2018, A11.
246. The procedures for Table 4.2 were followed in the creation of Table 4.4. Justice Kagan participated in only about one-third of the civil liberties cases that the Court decided in the 2009–2010 terms.
247. See John O. McGinnis, Matthew A. Schwartz, and Benjamin Tisdell, "The Patterns and Implications of Political Contributions by Elite Law School Faculty," *Georgetown Law Journal* 93 (April 2005): 1167–1212; Bonica, Chilton, Rozema, and Sen, "The Legal Academy's Ideological Uniformity."; Bonica, Chilton, and Sen, "Political Ideologies of American Lawyers."
248. Lars Willnat and David H. Weaver, *The American Journalist in the Digital Age: Key Findings* (Bloomington: School of Journalism, Indiana University, 2014), 9.
249. Keck, *Judicial Politics in Polarized Times*, 147–162.
250. Tony Mauro, "Sotomayor: Don't Blame the Justices for Politicization of Supreme Court," *Legal Times*, April 10, 2015; Ryan Lovelace, "Sonia Sotomayor Saddened by Perception of Judges as Political," *Washington Examiner*, March 10, 2017.
251. Catherine Lutz, "Justice Elena Kagan Talks Power on the Supreme Court," *Aspen Institute*, July 18, 2017: Jamie Ehrlich, "Kagan: Confirmation Gridlock Makes Supreme Court Look Like 'Junior Varsity Politicians,'" *CNN Politics*, July 25, 2018, https://www.cnn.com/2018/07/25/politics/kagan-kavanaugh-junior-varsity-politicians/index.html.
252. Lincoln Caplan, "A Workable Democracy," *Harvard Magazine*, March–April 2017; Ellen Powell, "Does the Supreme Court Need a Ninth Justice? Not by November, Says Breyer," *Christian Science Monitor*, October 25, 2016. The quotation is from the Caplan article.
253. Joan Biskupic, "Justice Ruth Bader Ginsburg Calls Trump a 'Faker,' He Says She Should Resign," *CNN*, July 13, 2016, https://www.cnn.com/2016/07/12/politics/justice-ruth-bader-ginsburg-donald-trump-faker/index.html; Max Greenwood, "Ginsburg: Trump Supreme Court Nominee Neil Gorsuch Is 'Very Easy to Get Along With,'" *The Hill*, February 23, 2017, https://thehill.com/blogs/blog-briefing-room/news/320950-ruth-bader-ginsburg-neil-gorsuch-is-very-easy-to-get-along-with.
254. Ariane de Vogue, "#MeToo Will Have Staying Power, Ruth Bader Ginsburg Insists," *CNN Politics*, February 12, 2018, https://www.cnn.com/2018/02/11/politics/ruth-bader-ginsburg-me-too-poppy-harlow/index.html.

255. Joan Biskupic, "Supreme Court Still Feeling the Impact of Antonin Scalia's Death," *CNN*, February 13, 2018, https://www.cnn.com/2018/02/13/politics/scalia-gorsuch-supreme-court/index.html.
256. *Obergefell v. Hodges*, 135 S. Ct. 2584, 2630 note 22 (2015).
257. Adam Liptak, "A Supreme Court Not So Much Deadlocked as Diminished," *New York Times*, May 18, 2016, A1.
258. Adam Liptak, "A Cautious Supreme Court Sets a Modern Record for Consensus," *New York Times*, June 27, 2017, A16.
259. Liptak, "A Cautious Supreme Court Sets a Modern Record for Consensus."
260. Cass R. Sunstein, "Unanimity and Disagreement on the Supreme Court," *Cornell Law Review* 100 (2015): 783–784.
261. Adam Feldman, "Crunching Data from This Past Term," *Empirical SCOTUS*, August 20, 2017.
262. The exception was Alito and Sotomayor, who agreed 49 percent of the time. Data on the 2017 term were obtained from Kedar S. Bhatia, "Final October Term 2017 Stat Pack and Key Takeaways," *SCOTUSblog* (June 29, 2018), 5, 23.
263. The percentages in the table were calculated from data in the "Justice Agreement—All Cases" tables in SCOTUSblog, Stat Pack for each term, archived at http://www.scotusblog.com/statistics/.
264. The comparable proportion for agreement between pairs of Democrats was 89 percent, and for pairs of Republicans 84 percent. These proportions are the means of the term-level rates of agreement between all pairs of Justices within the three categories. Justice Scalia was excluded for the 2015 term and Justice Gorsuch for the 2016 term because of their limited participation in those terms. These figures were calculated from data in "Stat Pack Archive," SCOTUSblog, http://www.scotusblog.com/reference/stat-pack/.
265. Greg Stohr, "As Washington Splits over Trump, Four Justices Seek Consensus," *Bloomberg Politics*, February 13, 2018, https://www.bloomberg.com/news/articles/2018-02-13/as-washington-divides-over-trump-four-Justices-seek-consensus.
266. Jeffrey Rosen, "Roberts's Rules," *The Atlantic*, January–February 2007, 105.
267. Rosen, "Roberts's Rules," 105.
268. This conclusion is based on data in the Supreme Court Database, http://scdb.wustl.edu/, supplemented for the 2017 term with data from Kedar Bhatia, "Final October Term 2017 Stat Pack and Key Takeaways," *SCOTUSblog*, June 29, 2018, http://www.scotusblog.com/2018/06/final-october-term-2017-stat-pack-and-key-takeaways/.
269. See Richard Wolf, "From Chief Justice Roberts, A Liberal Dose of Independence," *USA Today*, May 6, 2015, https://www.usatoday.com/story/news/politics/2015/05/06/supreme-court-john-roberts/26935809/.
270. Robert Barnes, "Chief Justice Wary of Partisan Battles," *Washington Post*, April 12, 2017, A15.

271. Hasen, "Celebrity Justice: Supreme Court Edition," 164–165. As Hasen notes (pp. 167–168), it is likely that a higher proportion of all public appearances are reported and thus available for counting in the current era than in past eras. One close study of the Warren Court found about 40 percent more appearances in the 1960s than Hasen did. (This figure was calculated from listings of appearances in Robert A. [Sid] Whitaker, "Freedom of a Speech: The Speeches of the Warren Court Justices and the Legitimacy of the Supreme Court" [PhD diss., State University of New York at Albany, 2016], 311–353.) Even so, it appears that the number of appearances is considerably higher than it was in the 1960s and other periods prior to the current era. On recent Justices as celebrities, see also Richard A. Posner, "The Supreme Court and Celebrity Culture," *Chicago-Kent Law Review* 88 (2013): 299–305.
272. Richard J. Lazarus, "Advocacy Matters before and within the Supreme Court: Transforming the Court by Transforming the Bar," *Georgetown Law Journal* 96 (June 2008): 1487–1564; Allison Orr Larsen and Neal Devins, "The Amicus Machine," *Virginia Law Review* 102 (December 2016): 1901–1968.
273. Joan Biskupic, Janet Roberts, and John Shiffman, "The Echo Chamber," *Reuters*, December 8, 2014, http://www.reuters.com/investigates/special-report/scotus/.
274. Margaret Meriwether Cordray and Richard Cordray, "The Solicitor General's Changing Role in Supreme Court Litigation," *Boston College Law Review* 51 (November 2010): 1356.
275. Biskupic et al., "The Echo Chamber"; Katherine Shaw, "Friends of the Court: Evaluating the Supreme Court's Amicus Invitations," *Cornell Law Review* 101 (September 2016): 1533–1595.
276. See Tonja Jacobi, "Obamacare as a Window on Judicial Strategy," *Tennessee Law Review* 80 (Summer 2013): 763–845.

CHAPTER 5

1. John R. Schmidhauser, "The Justices of the Supreme Court: A Collective Portrait," *Midwest Journal of Political Science* 3 (February 1959): 1–57.
2. After spending her first two years at Harvard, Ruth Bader Ginsburg transferred to Columbia for family reasons and graduated from there.
3. *Romer v. Evans*, 517 U.S. 620, 636 (1996).
4. That expression was from President Richard Nixon. See Joan Biskupic, *Sandra Day O'Connor: How the First Woman on the Supreme Court Became Its Most Influential Justice* (New York: HarperCollins, 2005), 42
5. Thomas Sowell, "Blackmun Plays to the Crowd," *St. Louis Post-Dispatch*, March 4, 1994, 7B. We discuss the hypothesis of a "Greenhouse effect" in chapter 3.
6. Truman nominee Harold Burton *was* a Republican. One sign of change in the appointment process is that cross-party nominations such as the selection of Burton,

once fairly common, have not occurred since Nixon's appointment of Lewis Powell in 1971.

7. https://www.washingtonpost.com/news/volokh-conspiracy/?utm_term=.495cod50cc1a.
8. See Richard L. Hasen, "Celebrity Justice: Supreme Court Edition," *Green Bag 2d* 19 (2016): 170–171. However, as we discussed in chapter 3, Justices differ in how frequently they participate in groups on their side of the ideological spectrum, and a few participate very little.
9. See Joan Biskupic Janet Roberts, and John Shiffman, *The Echo Chamber,* December 8, 2014, http://www.reuters.com/investigates/special-report/scotus/.
10. Thomas M. Keck, *Judicial Politics in Polarized Times* (Chicago: University of Chicago Press, 2014), 149.
11. One example is David G. Winter, "Motivation and Political Leadership," in *Political Leadership for the New Century: Personality and Behavior among American Leaders*, ed. Linda O. Valenty and Oter Feldman (Westport, CT: Praeger, 2002), 25–47.
12. Hasen, "Celebrity Justice."
13. Jimmy Carter, the only Democrat to win a presidential election between 1968 and 1988, not only failed to win re-election in 1980 but also was the victim of bad luck—the only president in US history to serve a full term but have no Court vacancies during his presidency.
14. In 2004, voters largely ignored Chief Justice Rehnquist's recent surgery and the possibility that the winner of the presidential race might well set the Court's direction for a generation to come. See Fox News/Opinion Dynamics, "The Bush Administration, Supreme Court Nominations," November 18, 2004, http://nationaljournal.com/members/polltrack/2004/todays/11/1119fox.htm
15. The question of whether 2016 was an outlier or harbinger of things to come remains to be seen. Chapter 2 explained why voters historically have downplayed the Court as a high-salience issue; that, however, may change for reasons detailed in this paragraph.
16. Mark A. Graber, "The Coming Constitutional Yo-Yo: Elite Opinion, Polarization, and the Direction of Judicial Decision Making," *Howard Law Journal* 56 (Spring 2013): 665.
17. We discussed Gorsuch's appointment and background in chapter 4.
18. Josh Gerstein, "Gorsuch Takes Victory Lap at Federalist Dinner," *Politico*, November 16, 2017, https://www.politico.com/story/2017/11/16/neil-gorsuch-federalist-society-speech-scotus-246538.

Index